Rashid Khatib-Shahidi holds a DPhil from the University of Oxford.

GERMAN FOREIGN POLICY TOWARDS IRAN BEFORE WORLD WAR II

Political Relations, Economic Influence and the National Bank of Persia

Rashid Armin Khatib-Shahidi

I.B. TAURIS
LONDON · NEW YORK

Published in 2013 by I.B.Tauris & Co Ltd
6 Salem Road, London W2 4BU
175 Fifth Avenue, New York NY 10010
www.ibtauris.com

Library of International Relations 66

ISBN 978 1 84885 324 9

A full CIP record for this book is available from the British Library
A full CIP record for this book is available from the Library of Congress

Library of Congress catalog card: available

Typeset by *editorial et cetera*, Stroud, Gloucestershire

However much science thou may acquire
Thou art ignorant when there is no practice in thee

The Gulistan [rose garden] of Sa'di
Chapter 8, on rules for conduct of life, maxim 2
Translated by Edward Rehatsek

To my parents, with gratitude
In memory of my grandmother Anna Doll

CONTENTS

ILLUSTRATIONS

Tables

Figures

Maps

ACKNOWLEDGEMENTS

This book is largely based on my university D.Phil. thesis research (1993–99), at the University of Oxford. It relies on German primary sources, of which approximately 120,000 document pages were evaluated. I have had the privilege to meet numerous people who provided me with both technical and moral support: family, friends and colleagues alike. My special gratitude goes to my peerless supervisors Dr Derek Hopwood and Dr Paul Luft.

For their invaluable services I give thanks to the archives and institutions I visited and their supportive staff. These include the Middle East Centre, St Antony's College, Oxford; the German Foreign Office Archives, Bonn; the German National Archive, Potsdam; the Public Record Office, London; the German–Iranian Chamber of Commerce, Hamburg; Harris Manchester College, Oxford; the German Orient Institute, Hamburg; the Bodleian Library, Oxford; the German National Archive, Koblenz; the Library of Congress, Washington, D.C.; and the Foreign Office of the Islamic Republic of Iran, Tehran.

I enjoyed invaluable meetings and discussions with a number of exceptional academics who inspired my work. In particular I would like to express my gratitude to Dr Ralf Waller, Professor Ali Reza Sheikholeslami, Dr John Gurney, Dr Houchang Chehabi, Professor Eric Hooglund, Dr Ali Gheissari, Dr Eugene Rogan, Dr Lothar Kettenacker, Mr Hebert Riedel, Mr Anthony Nicholls, Dr Rowena Archer, with special gratitude to Professor Ali Rahnema.

I would like to acknowledge Mrs Judith Nisbet, Mrs Elizabeth Anderson, Mr David Barton, Mrs Patricia Edwards, Mrs Ann Luke, and Mrs Anne Martin for their professional support and kindness. I also would like to highly commend my accomplished editor Matthew Brown, and Liz Fawcett, who prepared the index of the book.

I greatly value my fellow D. Phil. students who through their friendship made my time at Oxford fun and exciting, including Cliff Ohl, Peter Roberts, Julio Crespo-MacLennan, Marion Müller, John Freeh, Eric Eve, Sam Daws, Phillip Endicott, Philip Barton, Anastasia Economou, Danica Kilbarda, Aliza Samorly, Rouzbeh Pirouz and Felix Wichman. Many thanks also for their moral support and companionship to Reza Imani, Simon Roser, Marcus Gerhard, Stefan and Bastian Gries, Farhad and Farzad Mirzai, Amir Ebrahim Chahardehi, Memet Erdemgil, Uve Kupka, John Tate, Sussane Müller, Gabi Shwarz, Yoav Alon, Kevin Rosser, Bj Newal, Graham Gepson, Jussi Laurimaa, Deli Maleknia and my cousins Fereshteh and Hooman.

Finally, I thank my parents Anneliese and Mansour and my brothers Sassan and Ali, for instilling in me the confidence and drive to pursue my work and for their extraordinary support at all times – a debt I shall never be able to pay back.

Rashid A. Khatib-Shahidi

INTRODUCTION

The objective of this book is to examine German foreign policy and economic influence towards Iran between the two world wars. We shall depend on the analysis of documented events largely cited in German primary sources that have, partly because of their classification and partly owing to the reunification of Germany, only recently become accessible. This approach provides for the utilisation of the most up-to-date available primary sources and assures a clear-cut and verifiable insight into the background of German foreign policy and economic influence in Iran before World War II.

A main objective of this analysis is to show that after World War I the National Bank of Persia emerged as an ideal accessory to Germany's strategic desire to establish a foothold in Iran. It will be argued that the main motive behind Germany's involvement in the National Bank was to utilise the bank as a vehicle for extending German national interest into the country. It will become clear that Germany's main interest was to gain economic influence in Iran to facilitate commercially well-grounded and profitable trade relations. However, it will also emerge that the National Bank of Persia provided Germany with a tool that furthered its desire for political participation and the establishing of authority within the spheres of interest of the dominant powers of the region, Britain and Russia.

Even the most superficial look at these issues raises a number of inherent questions about German foreign relations with Iran. These include the character of German involvement, its policies towards Iran, and their consequences. The scope of this examination is confined to the inter-war period, and carries out a critical analysis of the evolution of German policy towards Iran while considering developments relating to the National Bank of Persia.

Before World War I Germany did not maintain significant relations with Iran. The desire to import raw materials from Iran in exchange for German manufactured goods appeared after World War I to be the foremost attraction for Germany to develop its trade and transport facilities with Iran.

Since German companies had been strongly involved in the construction of the Trans-Iranian Railway between 1927 and 1938, this monumental project in its magnitude would have rendered itself appropriate for the purposes of looking at German relations with Iran.

Nevertheless, the National Bank of Persia, and the German involvement in its establishment, proves itself more relevant for the purposes of analysing the development of German foreign policy towards and economic influence in Iran. One main reason for choosing the National Bank of Persia as the vehicle for this examination was that German nationals were key to its initial development. The first two directors of the bank were German nationals, and so were its first vice director and the managers of the majority of the bank's branches. The National Bank, established in 1927, contributed significantly to Germany's cause in Iran. During the period under investigation, not only did the bank undergo notable developments contributing to its maturity as a fully functioning national bank of the Iranian government, but these developments also reflected the stages of the evolution of Germany's foreign and economic policy towards Iran. The National Bank of Persia, which is today known by the name Bank Melli, continues to play a major role as a financial institution for the Islamic Republic of Iran and its international business interests.

This approach manifests itself almost exclusively through highlighting how German government agencies approached and dealt with issues and challenges regarding Iran. Therefore, it strongly relies on sources originating from the files of a number of key government agencies, including the German Foreign Office in Berlin and the German ministry of trade and industry. In order also to be able to analyse the effects of decisions made and actions taken by these agencies towards Iran, we shall rely on the opinions cited in the diplomatic communications of the successive German ambassadors to Iran vis-à-vis different government agencies in Germany.

The objective of this examination is not to establish a comprehensive and complete overview of the German political and economic strategy vis-à-vis Iran and its interactions with the National Bank of Persia, nor does its scope permit taking into account in depth the undoubtedly important role of British and Russian foreign policy. It aims rather at highlighting a number of events that are significant for an understanding of the evolution of the relations between both countries until the outset of World War II. Hence, we shall proceed by analysing a sequence of key developments associated with German foreign policy, economic influence and the National Bank of Persia.

In pursuit of this task, emphasis is given to the opinion expressed at the time, as largely reflected in German primary sources, rather than the historical reality behind those sources. Therefore, the picture given is, from a German point of view, reliant on the opinions and perceptions of the relevant government departments and principal figures associated with the events at the time. This approach provides a unique insight into Germany's assessment of Iran, its strategy towards the country, associated developments during the inter-war period and topics relevant to the period of Reza Shah, while also contributing to the understanding of issues relevant to current developments in the Middle East.

1

PERSIA, THE INTERNATIONAL ENVIRONMENT, AND THE GERMAN ECONOMIC APPROACH

Before 1921, two factors operated to encourage German involvement in Persia. The first was Germany's desire to become a major player on the world stage, partly to distract attention from its domestic difficulties. The second was Persia's realisation of being squeezed between the rival interests of Britain and Russia. Russia wished to extend its influence in Persia, primarily to gain access to the Persian Gulf and Indian resources;[1] Britain, on the other hand, was anxious about forestalling what it saw as a potential Russian threat to India.

As a result, from the turn of the twentieth century both powers became more heavily involved in the region to the detriment of Persia's autonomy. Persia therefore looked to a third power to counterbalance these two. Ideally, it needed a major power that had no direct interests in the region and would therefore pose no threat to Persia's desire for independence, while contributing to its economic development. From a Persian point of view, Germany appeared to fit the bill perfectly. However, Germany's defeat in 1918 in the interim limited its potential to exercise any real influence in the Middle East.

In the formation of Germany's relations with late Qajar Persia, German foreign policy was motivated by economic objectives. This chapter will cover the political background of German foreign policy towards Persia and conclude by mapping out Reza Khan's motives for involving Germany.

British and Russian National Interests in Qajar Persia

How Persia came to find its sovereignty surrendered to foreign powers becomes evident when looking at one example of a strategy that enabled

Britain and Russia to pursue their national interests in the country. This strategy can be described as one of 'economic dependency'. With respective diplomatic support, British and Russian entrepreneurs, aware of Persia's economic plight, sought mining concessions and other privileges from its government. By the turn of the century Britain and Russia were exploiting Persia's major resources. In addition Russia tried to increase its influence in Persia by intensifying trade, while Britain tried to counterbalance Russian efforts by taking an interest in the development of communications and the oil industry. To this end the British, who had initiated the Indo-European Telegraph Company, started developing ambitious railway construction plans which, for strategic reasons, included Persia.

All this points to the fact that Russia and Britain had a genuine interest in the economic exploitation of Persia. However, there is a further factor that should not be ignored: both also had a political agenda that brought them into conflict. Clearly, Britain and Russia were competing with each other in a race for a dominant position or at least for the preservation of a balance of power in Persia. With the visits of Naser ad-Din Shah (1848–96) to St Petersburg in 1873, 1878 and 1889 the Russians had been given an opportunity to step ahead in the race for influence. Russia's hidden agenda becomes clearer when considering Russian financial support for the Shah's third trip to Europe.[2]

Further evidence for Russia's game plan in Persia emerged in the guise of a 22.5 million ruble loan offer. During the late 1890s the Persian government was suffering from a major financial crisis. It required capital to serve its debt and maintain the government's budgetary expenditure. Britain and the Imperial Bank of Persia were reluctant to raise financial resources for the Persian government, but by 1898 the British were contemplating a conditional loan of more than £1.25 million. Simultaneously they were blocking foreign loan offers to Persia especially if they presented a threat to British interests.[3] With the return of Amin al-Soltan to power in 1898 the success of Russian endeavours towards political influence in Persia by means of government loans became apparent.

In December 1899, the Russian foreign minister Count Mikhail Nikolaevich Murav'ev proposed the final conditions for a 22.5 million ruble loan to Persia – a negotiation that took place without British consent.[4] The terms of this loan called for repayment over the next 75 years. By accepting this loan Persia played into Russian hands. On the one hand, one of Russia's conditions was that Persia should not accept any other foreign loans without its approval. On the other, Russia intended to secure its repayment by means of revenues from Persian custom duties except those of Fars and the Persian Gulf ports. If this did not prove sufficient to repay the loan Russia would take over the direct administration of Persian customs.[5] It thus appears that Russia was trying to exercise influence over Persia's domestic as well as its foreign affairs. This loan was agreed to by the Persian government, represented by General Mirza Reza Khan Arfa od-Dowleh, and the Russian Discount Bank, in January 1900, in St Petersburg.[6] Moreover, a further loan of 10 million rubles was granted in 1902.[7]

The Russian loan of 1900 took the British by complete surprise. British Ambassador Sir Charles Scott 'expressed his government's "profound astonishment" that the loan had been negotiated without the exchange of views with England'.[8] It was clear that the loan threatened British interests by allowing for the possibility of Russian control over Persian finances. Russia had secured its position as the main provider of funds to the Persian government. Britain could not allow such moves to go unchallenged. The then British minister in Tehran, Sir Arthur Hardinge, was convinced that the more the Persian government fell into debt to Britain the more would British political influence in Persia increase and Russian influence decrease.

In 1901 the British, encouraged by Lord Curzon, therefore started to negotiate a substantial loan to the Persian government, in return for, among others, all revenues generated by the Persian telegraph lines and the custom duties collected in the region of the Persian Gulf and of Seistan province.[9] Such a loan would strengthen British influence over areas of strategic importance to India. However, the British proposal did not materialise as it failed to comply with the terms and conditions set by the preceding Russian loan. In October 1901 the Political Committee of the Indian Council rejected the use of Indian funds for loans to Persia.[10] Nevertheless, in 1903 and 1904, British loans were successfully negotiated with the Persian government.[11]

As a result, after this breakthrough the Persian government was on better financial footing, although not to an extent that would have covered all budgetary requirements originally projected by the government. On the negative side Persia had sourced out much of its control, particularly over its finances, to Russia and Britain. It is paramount to examine how Persia dealt with its 'economic dependency'.

Persia's Banking Concession for Germany

The loss of financial independence led Persia to believe in the usefulness of approaching a third power that ideally could rescue it from its financial dilemma. One plan of the Persian government to address its financial deficits was to offer a banking concession to Germany in July 1906.[12] From a

Persian perspective Germany had many positive attributes that made it a natural choice for an economic partnership.

However, a Persian banking concession for Germany was not a strategically wise move, since it compromised British and Russian interests. The question arises about the extent to which Britain and Russia would tolerate actions undertaken by the Persian government that might ultimately threaten their national interests in Persia.

Both Britain and Russia were aware of the financial potential of German projects in the Middle East. From a German point of view a bank in Persia would have represented an essential tool for ensuring profitable trade and commerce for German companies.[13] However, what Britain and Russia probably did not expect from a comparatively weak third power was the audacity to enter their historically claimed spheres of interest. This move could have been interpreted as German disrespect for the already established balance of power in the region. Alternatively, such a move might have signalled the rise of a bold contender determined to achieve 'its' objectives.

In both cases the intensity of the British and Russian reactions would have been in correlation with the level of perceived threat to their individual interests in Persia from a competing German bank. Britain feared the loss of power for the Imperial Bank of Persia due to German competition. Similar concerns also alarmed the Russian-controlled Banque d'escompte et de prêts de Perse. In the case of a third power penetrating their spheres of interest, it is reasonable to expect initial discontent and disapproval reflected by general hostility towards any German enterprises, regardless of their inherent value for Persia.

Fortunately for Britain and Russia neither the Orientbank, established in 1906, nor the Deutsche Bank showed any serious interest in expanding their business into Persia.[14] At this stage the decision over a German bank was largely based on economic profitability, overriding any political motives. From the German bank's point of view investments in Persia were considered too risky owing to Persia's political fragility and unpredictability and to the lack of securities for the repayment of granted loans.

This circumstance gave both Britain and Russia time to take some preventive steps, first, against German attempts to establish itself in Persia, and second, in preventing Persia from transferring any control to Germany. It is patent that both powers began to recognise the first signs of a new German Middle East policy. As a consequence the need to secure their power and authority, and to protect their commercial investments in Persia became evident to Britain and Russia.

Fortunately for Britain and Russia the proposed banking project was abandoned, owing to the low commercial viability of a German bank in Persia for the investing German banks and their hostile reception by the Britain and Russia. However, this still remained a serious threat since the success of a German bank in Persia might have had wide-reaching consequences. This threat at least prompted Britain and Russia into recognising Germany as a potential contender in Persia.

In the case of commercial viability, a banking concession would have been an ideal opportunity for Germany to establish itself in Persia. This notion translates to a simple formula that was representative for Germany's Middle East policy during the early periods of the twentieth century. Where there were commercial opportunities, there was German interest; where Germany could not gain financial benefit there may have been a will but little incentive to justify investments.[15] Conceivably this rationale resulted from the controversial earlier German experiences in Africa.

It is of interest to identify what preventive measures by Britain and Russia could have resulted from a German involvement in Persia at this early stage. Both countries must have acknowledged that Persia was using Germany to drive a wedge between their established influence in Persia. As both started to address their Persian problem more intensely, the awareness of a third, rather small but threatening contender contributed to closer bilateral consultations. The German threat called for closer cooperation and provided potentially a viable motive for the division of Persia into spheres of interest, with the goal of deterring other powers from entering Persia, while safeguarding British and Russian activities geographically.

A further consequence resulting from the threat of potential German involvement in Persia was a noticeable shift in the British and Russian 'Persia-policy'. Both powers henceforth started working toward developing Persia's financial and manufacturing industry. The theory behind this shift of policy was that the sympathies of the Persians could be won through the generation of relative wealth. In a more substantial sense this move would provide Persia with a more solid economic base and generate much needed income for the government. Thus the requirement for loans would be less, which also meant less demand for a third power granting loans in exchange for concessions.

Germany's Expansion into the Middle East

Historically, the visit of Kaiser Wilhelm II to the Middle East and his declaration of support, friendship and protection for the Islamic world marked a significant change from the non-confrontational, non-involvement foreign policy of Reichskanzler Otto von Bismarck.[16] This shift became known as *Weltpolitik* or *Neuer Kurs*, and was intended to ensure Germany '*ein Platz an der Sonne*' (a place in the sun).[17]

The main objective of *Weltpolitik* was to seek colonies and turn Germany into a world power by looking for new sources of raw materials, opening new markets for the sale of manufactured products and creating new opportunities for capital investments. The upholders of this colonial policy were the Kaiser and von Tirpitz, the permanent secretary of his navy, together with the organisation known as Alldeutscher Verband. This organisation was created in 1891 as a reaction to the German–British barter agreement of 1 July 1890, whereby Germany exchanged its East African colony Zanzibar for the North Sea island of Heligoland. The main goal of the Alldeutscher Verband was to promote German national interest, reduce the gap between national identity and imperialism, promote Germany as a world power and pursue a more aggressive colonial policy. But it did not take long for the German Empire to realise the marginal economic success it was having with its colonial policy.

At the turn of the twentieth century Germany's expansion policy faced major obstacles. This was partly because by this time the majority of the world was already divided between world powers and partly because Germany's expansion policy, used as a political tool, had created domestic expectations that did not materialise. The German experiences with colonialism and implementation of influence abroad were discouraging. Frustration in this area intensified the desire for success and resulted in more radical policies.[18]

Moreover, Germany's industrial growth made the supply of raw materials progressively important. As the demand for raw materials increased, prices rose and Germany became increasingly dependent on expensive imports of raw materials. In a quest for survival, German industry needed to look for primary resources to secure future supplies for the requirements of a growing population and its overseas markets. In addition, the more German industry was able to produce, the more difficult it became to find export markets for its products. This led to fears of competition from countries that had access to cheap natural resources. Hence, countries that had the potential of supplying Germany with cost-effective natural resources where high on the agenda.[19]

The Middle East was an obvious choice, and one for which Germany at the time was prepared to pay a high political and economic price. The most important Middle Eastern power for Germany was the Ottoman Empire. German interest lay largely in the heartland of the Ottoman Empire, since it alone offered what Germany needed. The reasons for the German attraction to the Ottoman Empire were that it was hardly explored, it was rich in natural resources and provided an ideal export market for German goods. Furthermore, its geographic and strategic location contributed favourably to the German cause. These benefits were complemented by more pragmatic considerations, such as, for example, the practicalities in logistics and the opportunities for investment in areas such as commercial transport of goods. Organisations like the Alldeutscher Verband even had developed plans for the migration of German citizens to the region.

The Baghdad Railway project of 1898,[20] linking Turkey with the Persian Gulf, was the first major German venture that resulted from Germany's expansion policy in the Middle East.[21] This unprofitable commercial enterprise of the Deutsche Bank and its associates was politically significant particularly in light of *Weltpolitik* and the visit of Kaiser Wilhelm II to Constantinople. In the same year, the Deutsche Bank formed the plan to connect Tehran and Baghdad through an additional railroad project.[22] This plan was brought to fruition through the first Baghdad Railway concession on 23 December 1899.

A bank represented a key tool for the promotion of trade between Germany and the Middle East. Based on this notion, almost four years earlier than the Baghdad Railway concession, in 1896, the Deutsche Palästina und Orient Gesellschaft GmbH was founded in Berlin. The mission statement of this enterprise was to promote German economic interest in Palestine and the Middle East as well as actively support ventures serving German objectives.

Accordingly, on 1 May 1897, the first branch of the Deutsche Palästina Bank was established in Jerusalem.[23] In the high spirit of the emerging German Middle East policy, this bank was to meet the regional economic demand for a European merchant bank. In line with the growing business opportunities, the monetary power of the Deutsche Palästina Bank grew steadily throughout its short history.[24] Branches opened in key locations and as one of only four significant banks in the region, it became an integral part of German economic activity and developed a growing interest in investments, commercial penetration and political strategy.[25]

In 1911 Kaiser Wilhelm managed to take Germany's move towards the Middle East a step further. At the Potsdam conference, he succeeded in obtaining Russia's recognition of Germany's economic interests in Persia. This signifies a change from 1910: Russia now not only tolerated the Baghdad railway project but it acknowledged Germany's economic interest in its own Persian sphere of interest as well.

The 1903 establishment of the Baghdad Railway Company, the inauguration of the Deutsche Palästina Bank, and Russian sympathies for German projects in Persia after 1911 were all elements of a German Middle East foreign policy that inherently threatened Britain.[26]

We may conclude that this shift in German foreign policy also resulted in a revitalisation of German interests in the Middle East that ultimately paved Germany's way into Persia.

The British–Russian conflict

In the early 1920s Britain held a dominant position in Persia, despite the Persian government's resistance. Britain aimed at securing its influence in Persia by systematically managing to outmanoeuvre rival powers and thereby also implicitly undermining Persia's sovereignty.

The following sequence of events enabled Britain to effectively protect its interests in Persia. The period until 1907 was marked by Anglo–Russian rivalry and the emergence of Germany as a new player. In 1907 an Anglo–Russian agreement was ratified that aimed to ensure the cooperation of Britain and Russia in pursuit of their respective economic and political interests in Persia. At the St Petersburg Convention of 1907, Russia and Britain decided to resolve their differences and prevent future conflicts by dividing Persia into spheres of influence.

The division of Persia produced questionable results for the British and Russians, Germany's status and the Persian government. There are good reasons for arguing that Persia's division into spheres of influence did not solve many problems in the medium term but, on the contrary, led to frustration, hostility and devastation.

World War I (1914–1918) and Germany's consequent defeat changed the course of international foreign policies. Britain saw the ground prepared for its hegemony in Persia. Because of the February and October revolutions of 1917, the Russians were temporarily forced to neglect their Persian interests, since they were financially and politically weak and too preoccupied with internal affairs to maintain a strong position in Persia. They nevertheless tried to sustain a degree of economic and diplomatic relations with a weak and defeated Germany. But by the end of World War I, despite some economic activity by German entrepreneurs such as Thomas Brown, Germany's diplomatic relations with Persia had also deteriorated.

Ultimately, the decline of *Weltpolitik*, the economic weakness of post-war Germany, the political weakness of post-revolution Russia, and the economic and political weakness of an unstable and ineffective Persian government allowed Britain to be the dominating foreign power in Persia.

These circumstances set the stage for the ratification of the controversial British–Persian treaty of 1919.

Persia's Division into Spheres of Influence and the Role of Oil

We noted earlier that by 1907 Britain was aiming to end its conflict with Russia. It wanted to keep Persia as a buffer zone protecting its interests in India.[27] Both Britain and Russia had strong reasons for maintaining their influence over Persian politics. In this, Britain could not afford to have Russia in opposition. Neither could it tolerate a German–Russian alliance. This led to the 1907 agreement, by which both Britain and Russia aimed at taking control to avoid a possible clash over their positions in Persia.

After the division, the Russian zone stretched across the north and the British zone across the southeast of Persia, maintaining a central neutral zone for the activities of both powers. Wilhelm E. Griffith comments:

> The Russian sphere, which included Tehran, was greater than the British, and Russian interference in Iranian politics was more direct and brutal. Thus, Iran became the victim of détente between its two principal foreign enemies, and its nationalism became all the stronger because it was more frustrated.[28]

At the outset of the 1907 division, Britain and Russia appeared to pursue a policy characterised by a 'peaceful penetration' of Persia. This becomes clearer when considering the following objectives of the British and Russian governments. Russia, with its northern zone, saw a chance of peacefully gaining access to the Persian Gulf and the Indian markets. On the other hand, the existence of Britain's southern zone prevented Russia from achieving this very goal. Britain's objective was to protect British India and to preserve its dominance in the region through a double containment policy. The 1907 agreement was successful to the extent that it avoided a direct conflict between Britain and Russia; notwithstanding Russia's expansionist policy in Persia.[29]

Although the 1907 agreement was largely a political instrument it also had economic significance. We may argue that a further objective behind the division of Persia into spheres of interest was the desire for the development of trade and securing of economic interests in each zone. While financially rewarding, this would have enabled Britain and Russia to establish themselves in Persia as the dominant economic powers, to a degree that would have discouraged the economic participation of a third country such as Germany in Persia.[30]

Nevertheless, Russia, similarly to Britain, largely neglected the economic development of Persia. Russia's economic situation did not allow any large-scale foreign development, and since Britain had a large array of promising colonies and spheres of interest, the political instability of Persia did not encourage greater British investments either, with the sole exception of the oil industry.[31]

Seven years after Wilhelm Knox D'Arcy's oil concession of 1901,[32] the British set up the Anglo-Persian Oil Company, known today as BP, to secure their economic and political influence in the region.[33] Through the efforts of Winston Churchill in 1914, the British government bought a majority of the company's shares. At this time Churchill was First Lord of the Admiralty, and his main goal was to ensure that the Royal Navy had a sufficient supply of oil.[34] Naturally, this added an economic factor to the strategic and political significance of Persia, and made Britain even more dependent on and interested in strengthening its position in Persia. In 1907 the British thus had legitimate reasons for thinking that they could gain control over Persia through its division into clearly defined spheres of interest. Yet, however promising the British plans were, the weak Persian government reacted against British control over the oil industry and Russian influence in the North through an outbreak of nationalist feelings that sought liberation.

The division of Persia into spheres of interest did not leave much space for the involvement of other countries, and accordingly resulted in a setback for German influence in Persia. During this period, also as a result of the Potsdam agreement, Germany was carefully avoiding political confrontation with Britain and Russia, and for this reason made no real attempt even to participate in the financially attractive Persian oil business.[35] A note to the Persian government on 7 April 1910 had also warned Germany that Britain and Russia would not tolerate any concessions to a third party, as this would infringe on their national interests.[36] In this, both Persia and Germany were in a similar situation, since both had to give way to British and Russian influence.

It could be reasoned that the supreme hegemony of Britain and Russia resulted in some Persian nationalists and democrats developing a resistance born out of nationalism. At the same time, these individuals started turning to Germany for support.[37] During World War I a number of Persian members of parliament were already pro-German, and when the Russians marched towards Tehran in 1915 some of these nationalist pro-German parliament deputies left Tehran to set up a defence committee against the Russians.[38] This resulted in the Russians moving more forces to the north, causing the dissolution of the newly elected provisional third Majlis in

Qom. As a consequence, the Persian government was even more paralysed by the existence of two 'governments'. The first was Ahmad Shah's regime in Tehran and the second the provisional government in Qom. Neither of them exerted much authority in a divided Persia.[39] The nationalist pro-German deputies later received financial aid from Berlin to organise tribal forces against Britain and Russia, but they were too weak. Some leaders fled to Germany to continue their propaganda for a weakened Persian government that was caught in the stranglehold of Britain and Russia.

Although in part successful, specifically in the case of British oil interests, the 1907 agreement did not live up to the expectations of Britain and Russia. However, German designs for Persia had to take second place to German relations with Britain and Russia. Nevertheless, the 1907 agreement had provoked hostile feelings among Persians. These feelings were reflected in the objectives of the Constitutional Revolution that aimed at Persia's political independence. The result was a rejuvenation of nationalist feelings in Persia, resistance against foreign dominance and strengthened the desire for economic ties with a 'neutral' Germany.

The Dynamics of German *Weltpolitik*

The increasing disintegration of pre-World War I German foreign relations was to isolate Germany even more after the war. The original architect of German Middle East policy was Marshall von Bieberstein. He served as the German ambassador to Turkey from 1897 to 1912. The entry of Turkey into World War I also ended a chapter of German Middle East policy, which not long before had been perceived as the only way Germany could ensure a friendly political and economic cooperation with Britain and Russia overseas.

The creation of the Anatolian Railway Company in 1889 symbolises the first successful German venture towards a *Weltpolitik*. This railway project also clearly revealed that Germany's involvement in the Middle East was manifested in an economic approach rather than political considerations.

The consequences of Germany's shift from Bismarck's non-involvement policy to a policy revolving around its activities in the Middle East were not well received by Britain. From a British point of view Germany presented a threat not only because of its move into regions that were traditionally British or Russian domains but also because of the uncertainty and unpredictability of future German moves and objectives. This situation added further strain to Germany's relations with Britain in Europe.

It is of interest to see how Britain reacted to Germany's *Weltpolitik*. From a pragmatic point of view Britain had to deal with the difficulties resulting from the Boer conflict in South Africa, differences with France regarding Central Africa, and its ongoing rivalry with Russia. Consequently Germany was not high on its agenda. Thus, Britain's preoccupation with other more pressing issues provided Germany with a window of opportunity to pursue its expansion policy in the Middle East with less resistance from Britain.

Historical developments underline Germany's determination to enter the international scene on its own with the goal of establishing the image of a serious world power. The naval arms race with Britain and independent diplomatic negotiations with Russia confirm this. It can be argued that the events surrounding the Baghdad Railway concession represented a further indication of the determination and scope of German involvement in the Middle East.

The Baghdad Railway Project incorporated elements that illustrate the wide political and economic implications of foreign involvement in the region and the conflicts of interest arising for the major players. The antipathy of the British public in 1903 towards this project may also have translated into British disapproval of German involvement in the Middle East. From a German point of view an initial success in the Baghdad Railway Project was also a German success for expanding influence in the region.

However, new and unpredictable challenges awaited Germany's *Weltpolitik*. First came the fall of Sultan Abdul Hamid in 1909 following the Turkish revolution of 1908. This was followed by Germany's predicament, in the same year, resulting from Bulgaria's declaration of independence, which led to Austria-Hungary's annexation of Bosnia-Herzegovina. Germany as a member of the Triple Alliance found itself faced with a potentially hostile Russia. Furthermore, after Italy invaded Tripoli and Cyrenaika in 1911 Germany had seen itself in opposition to Britain and France. Its involvement in the Morocco crisis of 1911 spurred British and French opposition to *Weltpolitik*. At this point it became obvious that Britain had distanced itself from Germany, but what could result from such a significant British move?

Germany began to consider three principal strategies. It could pursue its *Weltpolitik* with determination and without involving Britain and Russia. As its relations with Britain had reached a deadlock, it could pursue plans to improve its relations with Russia. Germany could also consider its relations with Britain as so important that it could shift its foreign political priorities to a degree that would minimise the tension that had built up between the two countries.

The example of the Baghdad Railway Project highlights that Germany was determined to pursue its foreign political interests, by exerting its economic influence to keep a 'foot in the door' within the framework of its expansion strategy for the Middle East. Germany had developed plans for a commercial expansion in Persia. But Persia was dominated by Russia and Britain, particularly after Persia's division into spheres of interest, which minimised the opportunities for Germany to take advantage of the economic opportunities in Persia.

Evidently Germany had little chance of succeeding on its own. At this time Germany was facing stronger political opposition from Britain than from Russia. At the Potsdam Conference of 1911 Germany reached an agreement with Russia by which Germany agreed not to pursue enterprises in the Russian sphere of interest in exchange for Russian support for the Baghdad Railway Project. This German agreement with Russia, and Russia's support for the Baghdad Railway Project, had naturally increased the tension between Britain and Germany. However, Germany had not managed to resolve its issues with Russia, nor had it managed to negotiate a way out of its political predicament with Britain, as events would show.

Neither Germany's determination to pursue its *Weltpolitik* nor its bonds with Russia were enough to secure its political and economic objectives in the Middle East. Consequently Germany's foreign policy gradually started to shift towards improving its relations with Britain. By May 1914 German–British negotiations finally led to the ratification of several agreements. These agreements regulated shipping on the Euphrates and Tigris rivers, cooperation on the Baghdad Railway Project, the extension of the British Smyrna–Aidin Railway and an oil concession in Mesopotamia.[40]

In summary, during the period from the turn of the century until 1914 Germany had neither the political power nor the financial resources to pursue its *Weltpolitik* in the Middle East without support from Britain and Russia. However, Germany had ambitious plans and was determined to succeed and not to withdraw under external pressure. Germany's initial success with the Baghdad Railway Project, its good ties with Turkey and its enterprising plans for Qajar Persia had proved a source of motivation. German determination and its tense relations with Britain made it turn to Russia in 1911. However, Germany's move towards Russia was largely based on the desire to have a free hand in the Baghdad Railway Project rather than to seek any long-term alliance or even cooperation with Russia. In contrast, Germany tended to hold its relations with Britain in high regard.

Germany appeared to have learned from its experiences with Britain and Russia in the Middle East and its less successful enterprises, particularly in Africa. As a result Germany was prepared to shift its policy of confrontation to one of cooperation. There are two main explanations for this German shift. One is that Germany saw a policy of cooperation with Britain as far more beneficial for its expansionist plans and the objectives of *Weltpolitik*. The other is that a venture like the Baghdad Railway Project involved such high levels of investment, experience and competence that Germany needed support if the project was to be completed successfully. From its long involvement in the Middle East, Britain had the expertise and financial potential Germany was looking for.[41]

The situation Germany faced did not allow for an easy solution. We have shown that Germany broke out of its foreign political isolation by pursuing alone its economic interests in Turkey. The Baghdad railway project would have been an ideal foothold for Germany, if only it had not threatened British and Russian interests. Germany saw itself confronted with such adversaries that it considered surrendering its individualistic approach in favour of achieving better results through international cooperation with the dominant powers in the region.

German Activities in Persia during World War I

At the outset of World War I the ambitious German foreign political plans sought influence in the Islamic world from Lahore to Casablanca. Looking back at these plans and their achievements it is not difficult to conclude that they were less than successful. This may have been because Germany overestimated its own and its allies' capabilities and military strength, and underestimated the resolve and resistance of its declared enemies.[42] We shall henceforth limit our examination to the institutions and personalities relevant to Germany's Persia policy.

A major influence behind the initial separation of Germany's Turkey and Persia policy was Hauptman der Reserve Rudolf Nadolny. He had propagated the idea that if the Turks refused to cooperate Germany should not hesitate to pursue its foreign political goals unilaterally in Persia. The German Foreign Office supported Nadolny's plans as German–Turkish endeavours looked to remain at odds. This conflict resulted in Germany pursuing an independent Persia policy for the first time.[43]

In 1915 Nadolny also backed the idea of establishing a Persia committee following the model of the already existing Germany–India committee. The idea behind this proposal was to create a forum for a selected group of Persians who would cooperate closely with the German Foreign Office in developing a policy programme for Persia.[44]

As a result, the German government recruited Sayyed Hassan Taqizadeh in the United States and with the support of the German embassy in Washington he was brought to Berlin. He was charged with recruiting suitable Persian candidates among expatriate nationalists who had left Persia in the aftermath of the 1911 Russian invasion and the dissolution of the Persian parliament. With the permission of the German Foreign Office Taqizadeh recruited, among others, the former Persian foreign minister, Hussein Guli Khan Nawab, under the code-name S. Hassan.

The Persian envoy to Vienna was appointed as chairman of the committee and in March 1915 Taqizadeh presented the German Foreign Office with a substantial plan. Nadolny felt that the plan represented the ideal of what could be targeted and achieved. According to this plan the patriotic Persian forces were to be encouraged to fight against the enemies of Germany, with the goal of ultimate liberation. To achieve this goal, nationalists were to be sent to cities such as Constantinople, Baghdad, Tehran and Shiraz, to prepare the ground. They were expected, among other matters, to influence public opinion, ensure a pro-German Persian government, support the Persian Gendarmerie forces and the German embassy in Tehran. In exchange the committee demanded the assurance of Persia's independence from Germany, its allies and the Turkish government, as well as provision of financial support and weapons.[45]

To improve the flow of information and coordination of German activities, Nadolny deployed liaison officers to the Turkish–Persian border. These officers had the duty of updating the German military attaché in Constantinople on the situation in Persia. In 1915 Rittmeister der Reserve Sarre and his assistant Leutnant der Reserve Waldman were recruited for this task.[46]

It was questionable whether Germany could maintain its Persian operations, and, furthermore, whether an occupied Persia would be worth fighting for.[47] It was not long before those German government officials responsible addressed these issues through an independent German war policy towards Persia. This policy was influenced by Germany's control over the majority of the Swedish military instructors of the Persian gendarmerie and the break-up of the joint Turkish–German Afghanistan expedition. The emergence of an independent German war policy for Persia was largely also the origin of the German government's official *Persienpolitik*.

A closer examination of German–Persian relations reveals that the German government in Berlin did not have a definite and clear policy regarding Persia. Foreign policy was often a reaction to events and demands rather than the following of a defined strategy.[48] Even after 1915, it is not apparent whether German activities in Persia followed a clear blueprint. It is also difficult to assess whether the German government was aware of the possible results and practicability of its *Persienpolitik*. It is of interest to establish what status Persia held within Germany's expansion policy and where the limits for its strategy, commitment and investments were.[49]

According to Ulrich Gehrke, the records of the German Foreign Office and Großer Generalstab (Great General Staff) did not reveal a detailed or definite German military strategy for Persia. German decisions regarding military operations were based only on bits and pieces of accumulated information. The lack of their clarity and cohesion often contributed to a faulty analysis of the Persian situation.[50]

The responsibility for Germany's Persia policy was split between two government institutions, the Foreign Office and the Großer Generalstab. At the Foreign Office matters concerning Persia were processed through the political department in the person of Baron Langwerth von Simmern and his assistant counsellor of legation von Wesendonk. Neither was very familiar with Persia. The department at the Großer Generalstab dealing with Persia was Sektion IIIb Politik, chaired by the aforementioned Hauptman der Reserve Nadolny, who before the war held the position of counsellor of legation at the Foreign Office. During the early stages of World War I Germany was represented in Tehran through a rather inexperienced young chargé d'affaires, Legationssekretär von Kardorff, instead of the German envoy, Prince Heinrich XXXI Reuß. On leave in Germany, the prince was not able to return to Persia after the outbreak of the war until 1915. Kardorff was joined in February 1915 by the German military attaché, Major der Reserve and counsellor of legation, Graf Kanitz. Thus, Germany was left with a weak link in Persia and an inexperienced superintendence in Germany.

Returning to the wider implications of Germany's Persia policy we have to acknowledge that during World War I Persia did move increasingly into the centre of German Middle East war strategy.[51] This brings us to the obstacles Germany faced in assessing the Persian situation. First, Germany underestimated the logistic and communication problems that resulted not only from Persia's poor roads and rail system but also from the lack of mail and telegraph facilities and from logistical challenges resulting from the political situation in regions on the transit routes between Germany and Persia. The most popular route to Persia went via Baku to the Persian port of Anzali. In the case of Persia's entry into war this route would not have been available, nor were the other alternative routes much more accessible. For example, the railway connection on the alternative route from Constantinople via Baghdad to the Persian Gulf was still under construction. Furthermore, the sections completed could hardly supply the freight capacity the Turks required, and the alternative water and road connections between these sections were time-consuming and less efficient. This posed a serious problem, for if Persia entered the war on the side of Germany it would be dependent on German funding and shipments of arms.[52]

German officials were not fully aware of the implications of these challenges. Realistically, it could take months for shipments to reach Persia from Germany. Conversely, the British and Russians could gain access to Persia effectively and quickly. This takes us to the second obstacle Germany faced in Persia. Through decades of dominance Britain and Russia had devised several measures to secure their interest, including military presence, control over telecommunication, finance and banking as well as influence upon Persian politics.[53]

This leads us to Germany's third major obstacle. Britain and Russia had access to a large quantity of high-quality intelligence accumulated in Persia over the years. German government agencies had comparatively little access to relevant intelligence nor had any significant groundwork been laid in preparation for it. German operation plans testify that its government agencies suffered from insufficient intelligence on Persia, which inevitably led to a misjudgement of the Persian situation. Sizeable German military activities in Persia were almost impossible nor were there any preparations made for military or political activities. Considering the above, it is not difficult to predict only modest chances for success resulting from any German activities in Persia.[54]

Initially, Feldmarschall von der Goltz was assigned to coordinate German–Turkish efforts towards Persia. However, Germany failed to meet its promise for financial support to Persia and its agents based there. Moreover, the combat readiness of tribal forces recruited by German agents was largely overestimated. The lack of funding from Germany resulted in the destruction of Graf Kanitz's West Persian defence strategy. Furthermore, German operations in Persia disintegrated when von Goltz died in battle in 1915.[55]

Wilhelm Wassmuss was one of the best-known German nationals active as an agent in Persia during the war. His persistent protests against British methods of rule in Persia[56] won him the sympathy of some Persian tribes who were disturbed by British disregard for Persia's neutrality.[57] It can be claimed fairly that Wassmuss and the nearly one hundred other German agents in Persia managed to keep Britain and Russia busy throughout the war. They initiated disruptions and troop movements that weakened British and Russian activities elsewhere. These covert operations may have cost the German government approximately 50 million marks. However, the ultimate results achieved in the context of German war efforts were dismissible.[58]

One other reason for the failure of Germany's Persian operations was the Ottoman Empire. As most German initiatives in Persia depended on its links with Turkey, the Turkish opposition to Germany's activities in Persia proved destructive. In addition, the Turks regarded Persia as their 'turf', since it was part of the Islamic world. Consequently, they deliberately undermined any German plans directed towards Persia.[59]

There were, in addition, further reasons for the German failure: the lack of straightforward logistic access of German troops to Persia; misjudgement of the strength, capability and loyalty of the Turkish troops entrusted with German military operations; the lack of Persia experts in key positions in German government agencies or in the field; a shortcoming in coordination between Germany's political objectives in contrast to its military operations; and insufficient intelligence on Persian politics, military and culture.[60]

In his book *Persien in der Deutschen Orientpolitik* Ulrich Gehrke argues that Germany had scarcely any specific and cohesive strategy towards Persia, let alone a comprehensive plan for involving Persia in the war. This argument stands in contrast to the British perception of German operations. For example, Gehrke quotes a telling statement made by the director of the Imperial Bank of Persia, Sir Hugh Barnes, following a talk by Sir Percy Sykes in 1920: 'So immediate, so universal, and so well concerted were the (German) measures taken, that it is difficult to resist the conclusion that everything had been very carefully prepared before the war.' Gehrke attributes this impression to the determination and personal qualities of the same group of individuals who were later doomed to fail because of lack of a common vision, leadership, coordination, funds, and support from Germany.[61]

As a result of a series of shortcomings in German cooperation with the Turkish forces and the collapse of the provisional Persian government of Nizam al Saltane, and in consideration of the success of British and Russian war operations, the German Foreign Office decided to close its embassy in Tehran in mid-1917. Because of the continuing German–Turkish tensions Germany also withdrew in July 1917 from its last stronghold in Persia, the Gendarmerie.[62]

Soon after, as a result of the Russian revolution and the German–Russian armistice agreement of 15 December 1917, Russia promised to withdraw its troops from Persia. This agreement also included terms that led to the removal of Turkish troops from Persian territory. On 27 January 1918 Trotsky annulled the 1907 British–Russian agreement because it violated the freedom and independence of the Persian people. Furthermore, on 3 March 1918, at the Peace Conference of Brest-Litovsk, Germany negotiated terms for Persia that advocated its political and economic sovereignty. These developments not only won Persia's sympathies for Germany but they also contributed to Persia's autonomy.[63]

Britain was left as the major foreign power in Persia, and Lord Curzon's words and actions did not signal withdrawal. The British even used this opportunity to expand their influence into the northern regions of Persia. However, they did meet with resistance. For example, a motorised British expedition led by Major General Dunsterville on its way to Tifflis was held up at the port of Anzali by Bolshevik troops organised under Mirza Kuchik Khan and his Jangali movement.

Mirza Kuchik Khan's troops, supported by German and Austrian soldiers, were resistance fighters in the northern provinces of Persia.[64] However, after the Turkish occupation of Tabriz in June 1918 Mirza Kuchik Khan distanced himself from the Turks and looked to the British. This ultimately resulted in the expulsion of German and Austrian military instructors from his troops.

Mirza Kuchik Khan's radical action did not contribute to Germany's cause. The German government resumed negotiations with the Turks, asking them to comply with the Brest-Litovsk agreement. In October 1918 the Germans succeeded in obtaining a Turkish promise ensuring its withdrawal from Persia and Azerbaijan in particular.[65]

In response to the British request, the Persian government in November 1918 provided a blacklist with the names of 73 Germans, 10 Austrians, 13 Swedes, 5 Swiss and 1 Turkish citizen who were allegedly operating covertly during the war in Persia. Consequently, Britain managed to negotiate for itself the 1919 agreement securing its dominance over Persia. As a result Russian and German initiatives in Persia had been effectively combated. However, the real loser of the conflict was Persia, which was now, as at the outset of the war, occupied by British troops.[66]

From the very beginning, Germany's strategy towards Persia had been based on unstable foundations. Germany's strategy was improvised, displayed limited vision, and had little government commitment. Clearly Germany's Persia policy failed to achieve its objectives. Germany could have achieved a better outcome had it addressed these shortcomings. However, Persia may not have played an important role in German foreign policy. The lack of awareness and financial support by the German government and the rather small contingent of individuals involved in Germany's Persia operations clearly support this theory. Even in the lead-up to the war, German records provide enough evidence to verify that Germany was more determined and willing to make sacrifices in other countries than it did in Persia.

Nevertheless, even with the difficulties of war, finances, and the hostility it met with, Germany genuinely pursued relations with Persia. But the degree and level of these relations should not be overestimated. Germany continued to maintain some level of support for the Persian government immediately after the war. In the following section, we highlight the benevolence and hostilities Germany met with in its fragile but persistent course towards strengthening its relations with Persia.

The Consequences of World War I for Russia and Germany in Persia

The aftermath of World War I brought significant change to the development of German relations with Persia. Four years after Germany's declaration of war on Russia in 1914, the Allied efforts resulted in the defeat of an exhausted Germany and the uprising of the German people against their leadership. The Social Democrats took over government and proclaimed a republic. This resulted in the destruction of Germany's domestic strength and its international influence. The new Weimar Republic was established. In the same year Germany was forced to sign the Treaty of Versailles, which deprived it of land and natural resources. In addition, Germany was obligated to pay high war damage reparations. The treaty of Versailles essentially dashed its hopes for a fast economic recovery. However, Germany was determined to recover from this setback with a careful political approach, one that allowed it to maintain good relations with major powers, while re-establishing itself within its new international political environment.

But how did post-war Russia react to Germany's revived interest in establishing economic relations with Persia? The Bolshevik government had cancelled the British–Russian 1907 treaty, and to compensate Persia for the war damages it relinquished all its concessions and monopoly rights. It also declared that the ownership of the Russian Discount Bank, the Russian railroad and harbour equipment as well as other technical installations should be transferred to the Persian government.[67] These moves show the strong Russian wish to come to terms with the Persian government, while at the same time signalling Russia's withdrawal from Persian trade and commerce. This in turn created the opportunity for other foreign powers to become commercially involved in Persia. Although Britain continued to maintain and protect its concessions and privileges, it did not use its political power indiscriminately to secure further economic advantage until 1920–21.

This situation provided Germany with an immediate opportunity to secure a share of the more profitable projects in northern Persia. Of interest to Germany were the former Russian petroleum and coal-mining concession granted in conjunction with the railway concession of Julfa–Tabriz–Tehran.

Mining concessions in general were promising as the geological conditions of Persia offered many mining opportunities, not only for oil and coal but also for silver, copper, zinc, iron, lead and cobalt.[68]

From an economic point of view, the precondition for the success of such promising German enterprises was a functional transportation system. Hence, profitable railway, motor vehicle and air transport concessions were sought. However, from a political point of view, Germany faced one major barrier. Ideologically, the Russians would not tolerate the idea of Persia's concessions being surrendered to exploitation by capitalist powers. But this objection was directed more specifically towards Britain. The Russians clearly indicated that they preferred concessions to be granted to Persian entrepreneurs or neutral states. From a Russian perspective, Germany qualified as a neutral state. This political shift resulted in less Russian and British hostility in the context of the growing Persian desire for granting Germany north Persian concessions.

This circumstance presented Germany with an opportunity to enter into negotiations with Russia on a problem that had to be resolved before it could consider investing in Persia. Profitable German exports and imports to and from northern Persia relied heavily on their transit through Russia. It was thus crucial for German trade to ensure favourable Russian transit arrangements.[69]

Russia showed itself prepared to tolerate German economic involvement in northern Persia and it moreover started to support German activities by way of cooperation. Accordingly, Russian foreign minister Georgi Wassiljewitsch Tschitscherin asked Sommer, the German representative in Tehran, to investigate areas of possible German–Russian cooperation.[70] On the assumption that British influence in the north was weak ('her wallet could not reach the northern regions of Persia'), the first post-war cooperation initiative between Germany and Russia was a planned northern railway development project between Tehran and Tabriz. This project brought both countries together in pursuit of a common goal.

The predicament was that each country was pursuing a different agenda. Cooperation with Germany in northern Persia would have been in compliance with Russian political ideology, and from a pragmatic point of view it would have provided a level of Russian presence and influence that could have protected northern Persia from a British infiltration. This was something Russia could not financially afford to do on its own. By keeping Britain at a distance Russia would also create a buffer zone, protecting its borders with Persia from immediate exposure to British influence. Germany, on the other hand, stood to benefit from such a joint venture commercially and to improve its potential for securing future projects. From a political point of view Russia's support and cooperation appeared to supply the key to Germany's entry into Persia. This created a German bias towards Russia that was reflected in improved relations between both counties. However, German enterprises could not expect British sympathy, because of the British fear for loss of influence in northern Persia.[71] On the other hand, Britain's post-war hegemony dazzled it into believing that it was able to maintain its control over Persian politics and its oil-based economy. Still, Britain could not have welcomed the emergence of Germany as a third power in Persia, particularly when supported by Russia.

The British, disappointed at such close cooperation between the two countries, vented their resentment against what they perceived as German anti-British activities to the German Minister for Foreign Affairs, Dr Wirth: they pointed out that previously

> Dr. Rosen [had] assured Lord D'Abernon that the primary and essential object of German policy was to establish relations of confidence with Great Britain and that the most stringent instructions had been issued to the German representatives abroad to refrain from any action whatsoever which might run counter to this most dominant objective of German policy.[72]

The German delegation in Tehran was accused of disregarding these instructions by displaying continued hostility to British interests and by supporting anti-British intrigues and agitations. According to one document, 'the German Charge d'Affaires appears at the present moment to be actively engaged in underhand measures to encourage the Persian Government in dishonest and dishonourable designs against British holders of valuable concessions'.[73]

Nevertheless, the Persian government resumed its negotiations with Germany in Moscow, when Minister Ehtesham Homayun approached the German embassy to investigate Germany's position regarding an economic involvement in Persia. This meeting revealed three main challenges that Germany had to address when considering its further involvement in Persia:

1 economic decisions by the Persian government did not involve Germany;
2 the post-war German financial crisis implied lack of funds;
3 the transit problems through Russia.

Consequently, Ehtesham assured the German envoy that the Persian government would endeavour to consider German interests in its future decisions. Regarding finances, he felt that Germany would only require a comparatively small sum for its Persian investments. This left the Russian transit permissions as the major obstacle for Germany's involvement in Persia. In this context it was encouraging that Theodore von Rotstein, the Russian representative in Tehran, and Postuchow, head of the Persian desk and representative of the Russian overseas department, gave verbal assurance that article 20 of the Persian–Russian Treaty of Friendship (26 January 1921) implicitly regulated the transit of German goods through Russia.[74]

The described developments raise the fundamental question of whether Russia had started to shift its foreign policy from just tolerating German presence in Persia to a policy that incorporated and leveraged Germany's involvement in the country in pursuit of ulterior Russian objectives.

In this context it is noteworthy that just a few years after World War I Russia started to work quite closely with Germany in matters relating to Persia. During the early 1920s, on a number of occasions German–Persian relations revealed an obvious Russian link. For example, after the war, an official Persian representative approached the German embassy in Russia, in an attempt to initiate German–Persian cooperation. Moreover, the Russian representative, von Rotstein, played a supportive role in the development of German–Persian relations. Incidentally, the German government replaced its representative in Tehran, Sommer, with its former German representative to Moscow, Graf Schulenberg. Also, the Russian Commissar for Foreign Affairs, Tschitscherin, personally attended to subjects concerning Germany and Persia. This underlines, at the very least, that Russia aspired to having a degree of control over Germany's relations with Persia by ensuring that its counterparts were Russia-friendly. However, there was also the likelihood that Russia was engineering a complex diplomatic strategy for Persia in which Germany played a pivotal role.

Domestically, the German government had to boost morale, create new jobs, and resume its contacts with the outside world to secure its status as a major European power in the eyes of its electorate. Internationally, also largely to achieve its domestic goals, Germany looked for alliances and agreements with other countries chiefly to facilitate its economic goals of securing much needed low-cost raw materials for its industry and export markets for its domestic production.

A major step toward formalising such an alliance was a treaty between Russia and Germany ratified in April 1922. During an international economic conference in Genoa, a Russian delegation was invited to participate for the first time, alongside a German delegation. These two delegations used the opportunity to meet on 16 April 1922 at the neighbouring town of Rapallo for a special dialogue. These talks resulted in the signing of the Rapallo Treaty by Reichskanzler Wirth, the German foreign minister Rathenau, and Tschitscherin.

This treaty with Russia allowed Germany to resume its diplomatic relations and renounce any claims for reparation payments arising from World War I. The Rapallo Treaty came as a surprise to the western powers and was heavily criticised by Britain. Nevertheless, for Germany and Russia this was a first step out of their diplomatic isolation. As a result Germany was now, in cooperation with Russia, also in a position to confidently pursue its political and economic strategy towards the Middle East and more specifically Persia.

Accordingly, in a meeting with Graf Schulenberg, Tschitscherin voiced Russia's concern for Persia. He emphasised that Britain was trying to undermine Russian influence by attempting to obtain north Persian oil concessions through cooperation with an American oil company.[75] It was understood that Winston Churchill had recommended that the Anglo-Persian Oil Company and the American Standard Oil Company should cooperate to prevent a potential British–American conflict in Persia and instead contribute to politically advantageous developments. An upshot of such cooperation would have been increased political stability in northern Persia.[76] The British were simultaneously exercising financial pressure on a strained Persian government by supporting Kurdish revolts. The Kurds, under the leadership of Simko, were taking a stance against the Persian government to gain independence. As a result, government troops, mostly from the Tabriz region, were pressurised into fighting heavy and costly battles against the Kurdish revolts.[77]

Given these circumstances the Persian government was under such pressure that it felt compelled to consider granting oil concessions to the British-American consortium.[78] Russia was not in a position to back the Persian government. Tschitscherin, having recognised the potential threat to Russian influence in Persia, saw the solution to this dilemma in the economic support of Germany. Although the Russians were successful in winning German sympathy for their plans, for Germany the longstanding Russian transit problem for its goods had not yet been resolved. Realising the acuteness of this issue, the Russians contemplated granting Germany a transit concession.

The conundrum here is that it is not clear who was in control of events. In particular, it has not been established whether Germany was pursuing its economic objectives in Persia with the help of Russia or whether Russia was implementing its political objectives through German economic influence – alternatives that do not exclude each other. What is evident is that Persia preferred cooperation with Germany but its weakness forced it to await further developments. There remained still major obstacles for German–Persian cooperation. For one, the republics of Azerbaijan and Georgia were so displeased with Germany's failure to include them in the Rapallo treaty that they vetoed granting permission for the transit of German goods through their territory.[79] Moreover, the Russian publication *Ekonomicheskaya Zhizn* openly and critically emphasised the fact that only German interests appear to be served by a transit permission.[80] Simultaneously, Germany was being weakened by domestic developments. The newly established German parliamentary democracy was hopelessly inefficient due to the large number of political parties that made reaching majority decisions almost impossible. Consequently, lesser forces tried to overthrow the republic. Until the time that German relations with Russia produced tangible results, German entrepreneurs could only gain access to the Persian markets by participating in foreign industrial syndicates.[81] Britain's determination to protect its own interests was not going to make post-war German involvement in Persia an easy task either.

In conclusion, a shift in Russian policy after World War I evidently provided Germany with promising economic prospects in Persia. Through the Rapallo Treaty both countries managed to formally re-establish their diplomatic relations and re-enter the international political arena. Consequently, in the Persian context Russia tolerated German involvement and signalled its cooperation and support for Germany. Inherently, Russian cooperation and support for Germany was not in compliance with British designs for Persia and provoked formal protest. British interests were further challenged by the Persian government's increasing interest in Germany. The situation worsened for Britain when it transpired that Russia intended to leverage German economic and political potential to further its own political interests in Persia. Nonetheless, the demanding domestic developments in Germany, and British opposition, increased the barrier to entry for Germany and severely challenged its strategy of involvement in Persia after World War I.

The Winners of the British Strategy in Persia and the Role of the United States

The British plan aimed at joining forces with the United States in Persia indirectly created economic opportunities for Germany but clashed politically with Russia. The British policy in Persia was also shifting towards a policy of cooperation. As a result of their engagement in Persia, the British had recognised that to maintain influence in Persia they would achieve better results if they pursued a policy of cooperation. In addition such a shift was diplomatically desirable, since the independence movements throughout the British Empire threatened British hegemony, so that Britain had to embark on an alternative policy aimed at securing its overseas interests.

Consequently, in 1919 the British government had expected to secure its interests in Persia through a treaty amounting to a British protectorate.[82] However, it is questionable if this treaty-based approach really succeeded in serving British interest in Persia.

Foreign Secretary Lord Curzon was the architect of British foreign policy in Persia. He gained power in 1918 with the formation of the Eastern Committee of the War Cabinet,[83] which replaced the former Persia Committee. Field Marshal Sir Henry Wilson, the Chief of the Imperial General Staff, an advocate of military rather than diplomatic solutions, had created this committee to coordinate British policy and strategy in the eastern regions. General McDonogh, a high-ranking representative of the British War Office, had backed Curzon's plan for a treaty with Persia. McDonogh believed that Britain's objective should be to take control of Persia 'both financially and otherwise'.[84] When Curzon became foreign minister in 1919, one of his main objectives remained to settle British interests in Persia without foreign interference.

In August 1919, after Curzon successfully kept Persia out of the Paris Peace Conference, he succeeded to ratify the Anglo–Persian treaty, through his negotiations with the Shah, the Triumvirate and Sir Percy Cox, the British minister in Persia.[85] The main objective of this treaty was to secure British interests in the Persian army and state administration, by means of a British loan as well as the appointment of British civil and military advisers to the Persian government.[86]

Werner Zürrer argues that Lord Curzon intended to create a firm partnership with Persia rather than pursue only colonial ambitions. He believes that Curzon preferred a unified and stable Persia, and insists that the terms negotiated in the 1919 treaty did not infringe on Persia's sovereignty. He argues that if the treaty had been implemented according to British intentions it would have helped Persia to strengthen its neutrality.[87]

This is in contrast to W. J. Olsen's standpoint, who maintains that, because it was characteristic of British practice during World War I to rely on personalities rather than politics, Curzon failed to work out a treaty closer to Persian reality and therewith forced upon Persia impossible terms and conditions.[88] The main objective of Curzon's agreement was to prevent any rival power from gaining political or economic influence in Persia.

This resulted in Russia distancing itself even more from Britain, particularly since the support of independence movements in countries such as Persia had become one of Russia's foreign policy objectives. However, in 1921, due to internal unrest and limited resources, the Central Committee of the Bolsheviks shifted its attention from overseas concerns to its own domestic affairs.

The British Foreign Office was sceptical of this change in policy and feared a hidden ideological agenda. British scepticism increased when Russia continued to advocate that Persia should be kept free from foreign influence. Russian sympathies for Persian nationalist movements, such as the Jangali movement and separatist movements in Azerbaijan and Khorasan, posed a continued threat to British interest.

Owing in part to its cost, Britain had lost its determination to maintain large military forces in Persia and to engage in anti-Bolshevik campaigns in Russia. The British India Office had decided that it would be more advantageous for British interest to back the rising nationalist movements in Persia. The British objective was to thereby win public support. It was ultimately hoped that this move would give Britain a better negotiating position than Russia, and subsequently lead to a closer cooperation with the Persian government.[89] This was all the more important, since after the fall of Vusug ad Daula in 1920 and the rise of Reza Khan in the coup d'état of 1921, the 1919 treaty started to lose its significance.

A further explanation for a British shift of policy in Persia was the threatening success of the Irish rebellions. As colonies and protectorates realised that Britain was not invincible, they began to press for their independence. The crisis accompanying the independence movements in India and Egypt gave the British a strong cause for concern regarding the rise of nationalist movements in Persia. This was reinforced by Lord Curzon's statement that circumstances demanded a radical change of British policy because the decline of British hegemony in the Middle East had to be stopped in Persia before it reached the gates of India. As a consequence Britain's strategy verifiably shifted to one that favoured a stable Persian leadership and an organised government.[90] It can therefore be concluded that Britain was pressured into respecting and recognising the patriotic sentiments and nationalist movements in Persia. For similar reasons, Britain appeared more inclined towards accepting Persia's economic sovereignty.

Taking into account Persia's wish for rapid industrialisation and economic growth, the British were faced with accepting the economic activities of other countries in Persia. This shift in British policy benefited German economic interests in Persia. But, mainly because of its unresolved Russian transit problem, Germany could not take full advantage of the available opportunities and concessions that were officially earmarked for Persian and citizens or organisations from neutral states.[91]

A further important competitor for the Persian market, standing to gain from a shift in British policy, was the United States of America. Haji Mirza Hussein Khan Sepahsalar was reportedly the first Persian minister who took the initiative to establish diplomatic relations with the United States. On 21 May 1881 he had successfully approached the United States representative John W. Foster in St Petersburg and had prevailed upon him to convince his government of the economic value of diplomatic relations with Persia. As a result of government approval on 3 August 1882, the United States commissioned Minister Benjamin to the court of Naser ad-Din Shah on 11 June 1883. According to Ramazani, the reasons for approving Bill H.R. No. 6743, were threefold. The United States sought to protect their missionaries in Persia, expand trade and 'establish diplomatic relations with "the oldest government in the world" that was of such "strategic importance"'.[92] The Shah's reason for approving Persia's relations with the United States was fuelled by his expectation of economic support from the United States. This expectation was initially only partially met through the appointment of two American financial advisers. In 1914 Persia had approached the United States with the request for a financial adviser to its government.[93] As a result the American financial expert Morgan Shuster was appointed. Later he was joined by his colleague Arthur Millspaugh.

At the Paris Peace Conference in 1919 the United States had failed to give Persia the support it expected to speak in front of the commission headed by President Wilson and other allies.[94] After infringements on its sovereignty by Turkey, Russia, and Britain during World War I, the Persian government had hoped for more support from the United States. Persia's requests included the following: membership and participation in the Paris Peace Conference; abolition of treaties and agreements violating its integrity; reimbursement of war damages; guarantees of economic independence; reconsideration of treaties and abolition of capitulation rights; and restoration of former boundaries.[95]

Considering the ongoing British–Persian negotiations in preparation for their 1919 agreement, Britain had been made aware that Persia wanted to be heard at the Paris Peace Conference. As Persia's participation at the conference might have raised questions that could have proven damaging to British interests, they did not support the Persian request; neither did the United States. Despite the fact that the United States must have been aware of the British activities and designs for Persia, it nevertheless appeared to be backing Britain.[96] The United States declared such claims to be unsubstantiated. Lord Curzon added that the United States 'had never been kept in ignorance of the (1919 agreement) negotiations'.[97] The official reason provided for not allowing the five Persian delegates to be heard at the Paris Peace Conference was that participation was limited only to the countries that had declared war on the Central Powers. According to the British foreign policy expert at Versailles, Harold Nicolson, the Supreme Council officially rejected the Persian request in order to avoid setting a precedent for other countries that would have liked to present their case before the conference.[98]

Until about 1921, Britain perceived the United States as a threat to its interests in Persia and consequently their relations did not result in much. The subsequent absence of the United States from Persia deprived Britain from an ally that it nevertheless preferred to the Bolsheviks.

As a result of the shift in Britain's Persia policy, the Foreign Office urged the Anglo-Persian Oil Company in 1921 to find ways of involving the American company Standard Oil in the Persian oil business.[99] Churchill, who feared the destabilising effects of an eventual British–American rivalry over oil in Persia, backed up the proposal of the British Foreign Office.[100]

The British were aware of the potential of Standard Oil and its aggressive pursuit of lucrative markets. They preferred to cooperate with the United States and share influence to prevent American oil companies from taking over large sections of the Persian oil market. Britain also expected to benefit from the presence of the United States, especially in northern Persia, as it would avert Russian expansion into the country while at the same time diminishing British–American rivalry for Persian oil.[101] This premise resulted in a cooperation agreement between the Anglo-Persian Oil Company (APOC) and Standard Oil.[102] Both agreed to establish the Perso-American Petroleum Company, in which each owned half of the share capital.[103]

However, the Persian Government rejected the APOC–Standard Oil partnership because it was in breach of a parliamentary decision ratified on 23 November 1921. This regulation maintained that a concession could only be granted to an independent American company. This ruling left Standard Oil, which had already made a payment of $1 million to the Persian government, with the option to reapply for a new oil concession on its own or withdraw from the Persian market.[104] Ultimately, Standard Oil decided to renew its bid for a Persian oil concession, without the APOC, and in competition with another American company, the Sinclair Oil Company.[105]

In 1924, the Persian government awarded the Sinclair Oil Company oil exploration concessions in five northern Persian provinces. The ratification of this contract between the Persian government and Sinclair's representative, Soper, in Tehran, complied with Russian agreements but threatened British–Persian relations.[106]

This concession raised Persia's hopes for long-anticipated loans from the United States and the resulting commencement of American industrial projects in Persia. The American financial adviser to Persia, Morgan Shuster, had been instructed to pursue funding opportunities for such projects. But the British could not accept Persia's decision to award Sinclair with oil concessions counter to British designs, nor did Britain permit Persia to get away with rejecting the Anglo-American joint venture bid. The Majlis were soon to learn that the US State Department and its Persia desk representative, C. van Engert, preferred not to jeopardise America's foreign relations with Britain and Sir Percy Loraine in favour of American relations with Persia. Moreover, after failing to win the bids for the joint APOC–Standard Oil and the Standard versus Sinclair concessions, the US State Department assured the British Foreign Office that Sinclair would not find it 'easy' to meet its contractual requirements crucial to the finalisation of its concession agreement with the Persian government.[107]

A consequence for the Persian government was that even years later Morgan Shuster was not successful in obtaining any loans from the United States. Moreover, Sinclair was forced to abandon its oil exploration projects in Persia, due to the failure to raise the funds required to finalise its concession agreement. Persian–American relations deteriorated further since British anti-Persian media propaganda had penetrated the United States press. Primarily it was alleged that Britain had experienced difficulties with the repayment of loans granted to the Persian government. Furthermore, the tragic death of Robert Imbrie, the United States vice-consul in Persia, erased the last hopes for an American involvement in Persia.[108] By 1925 the United States had almost completely withdrawn itself from Persia. Hence, at first sight, Britain had successfully maintained its dominant position in Persia. The snag with this conclusion is that while Persia failed to win the United States as an economic partner, it did succeed in keeping Britain out of its northern regions. The withdrawal of the United States simultaneously removed a serious competitor for Germany and improved its business outlook in Persia. What's more, the United States withdrawal from Persia marked a victory for Russian foreign policy and its treaty of friendship, ratified on 26 February 1921: 'This was the first big milestone in the relations between the two countries in the twentieth century.'[109] It also was the first treaty of its kind ever to be agreed between a foreign government and the Russian government.

Political and Economic Developments during Reza Shah's Rise

Foreign interest and rivalry, motivated by political objectives or economic influence, as well as the ambition for a physical presence in the region, proved a fertile ground for the rise of the future monarch of Persia, Reza Khan.

Reza Khan was born on 16 March 1878, in a northern Iranian village. He was the youngest son of Abbas Ali Khan, an army officer, known as Dadash Beg, and Nush-Afarin Khanom. At a young age, Reza Khan joined the Cossack Brigade, in which one of his uncles was an officer. He was promoted through the ranks and was assigned as an officer to the machine-gun division. Reza Khan was involved in several military campaigns against northern tribes. At the age of 40, as brigadier, he was in command of the Hamadan Cossack Division, said to have been the only well-trained and effective unit of the Persian army.[110] The Cossack Brigade was established in 1879, by Naser ad-Din Shah after a visit to Russia. Operating as an elite unit, originally at regiment strength, this unit soon expanded into a brigade. By 1920 this brigade had by all accounts grown into an accomplished division of some 8,000 soldiers.

From about 1921 the British started to execute on their strategy of 'cooperation' with Persia. Britain's initial goal was to establish a stable government in the country. Their preferred candidate for the leadership of Persia was Sayyed Ziya al-Din Tabatabai, a pro-British nationalist journalist and editor of the newspaper *Raad*. However, Ziya's chances for being elected as prime minister were not ideal. As a result, Major General Edmund Ironside, head of the British forces in Persia, consulted with Reza Khan, Colonel of the Cossack Brigade and his most favoured candidate. Major General Ironside assured Reza Khan that Britain would not interfere if he took control over the Persian government through a coup d'état.[111] According to Elwell-Sutton, Ironside believed that Colonel Reza Khan, the then co-commander of the Cossack Division, was the only man capable of commanding the Cossack Division.[112] Sayyed Ziya was popular with the British and a friend of the well respected and influential British Consul in Tehran, Howard. Ziya became later known as the architect and driving force behind Reza Khan's 1921 coup d'état. He was interested in Reza Khan as the commander of the military operations supporting the coup d'état. Reza Khan had proven his capabilities and trustworthiness. Reza Khan was amenable towards the proposals presented to him by Ziya. Both shared an anti-aristocratic stand point, despite Reza Khan having served loyally under men like Farman-Farma and Sardar Bahadur.[113] Moreover, Reza Khan welcomed the opportunity to reduce British influence over what he believed was the 'soul' of his country, the Persian army.[114]

After Major General Ironside had failed to persuade Ahmad Shah to agree to Reza Khan as future ruler of Persia, the British military advisers and the Gendarmerie assured Reza Khan of their support for a coup d'état. In February 1921 Reza Khan's Cossack Brigade marched into Tehran under made-up pretences, and as a result some 60 Persian politicians were arrested. Donald Wilber points out that 'Once the march was under way Sayyed Ziya' al-Din went to Colonel Gleerup, Swedish police organiser-general, who were friends of his, and won verbal promises that their men would not be ordered to oppose the Cossacks.'[115] The Qajar monarch was aware of the coup and had ordered the capital's garrison not to resist the intruders. Furthermore, after Reza Khan assured the Shah that the coup d'état was designed to save the monarchy by preventing a revolution, the Shah accepted the coup, and awarded it a degree of legitimacy.[116] On Tuesday 22 February 1921 Reza Khan's declaration of martial law, posted around town, foreshadowed the future. This declaration opened with the words 'I command' and was signed 'Head of the Cossack Division of His Highness of Holiest Divinity and commander of all forces – Riza'.[117] He demanded the appointment of Sayyed Ziya al-Din Tabatabai as prime minister,[118] and progressed from being the commander-in-chief of the Cossacks (Sardar Sepah), to becoming Persia's Minister of War. The Qajar king Ahmad Shah was supportive of Reza Khan. Consequently, when disagreements threatened to split the coup d'état leaders Sayyed Ziya and Reza Khan into two opposing fronts, Ahmad Shah decided in favour of Reza Khan and relieved Sayyed Ziya of office.

The 1921 coup d'état is described by some sources as the 'White Revolution', since it was almost bloodless. According to a number of Persian accounts it was 'the by-product of British post-war diplomacy in the Middle East'. Younes Benab argues that the British financial adviser in Persia, J. M. Balfour, admitted that the British gave their moral support to the protagonists of the coup d'état, and that five years later it transpired that the British adviser to the Cossack division, Colonel Smyth, was involved in the coup. There is little to suggest that Britain was not the dominant influence in Persia.[119] One of the British objectives fuelling the coup was to create a strong Persia that could prevent Russian penetration into the country's northern regions. Britain also believed that the resulting stable, strong and centralised Persian government would provide the requisite level of protection for Britain's eastern colonies.

On 28 October 1923, a few days before he left to remain in Europe, Ahmad Shah (aged 17) appointed Reza Khan as his Prime Minister, while allowing him to retain his post as Minister of War. Ahmad Shah essentially transferred the absolute power over Persia to Reza Khan. At this stage the authoritarian Reza Khan had experienced six cabinets and four prime ministers, Sayyed Ziya, Qavam al-Saltane, Mushir al-Dowleh and Mostofi al-Mamalek, who all preceded him between 1921 and 1923. Although Reza Khan was aware of his 'blank cheque' authority, he continued to cooperate with the Persian parliament and operated within the framework of law. Consequently, except for a minority led by the cleric Sayyed Hassan Mudarres, the majority of the Majlis were supporters of Reza Khan.

The British Foreign Office also provided support for Reza Khan and his wide-ranging reform plans. The then British Prime Minister, Ramsay MacDonald, believed that Reza Khan's leadership would be the most advisable way to secure British interests in Persia. This resulted in a balancing act of high diplomacy, as the British had also to consider their position towards the rebellious Sheikh of Mohammera and the Bakhtiaries in southern Persia, the heartland of British economic oil interests. The Russians exploited Britain's predicament by criticising the duplicity of British tactics in Persia and argued that in contrast the Russian government was a true friend of Persia. Consequently the British had to take action and decide between the Persian Prime Minister and Sheikh Khazal. Sir Percy Loraine met Reza Khan in early December 1924 at Ahwaz to discuss the above situation. He felt reassured by Reza Khan's interest in cooperation with Britain in establishing stability and peace in the southern regions of Persia. British foreign secretary, Sir Austen Chamberlain, was satisfied with the course British–Persian foreign relations were taking, knowing that a stable Persia would provide an ideal buffer zone against a Russian penetration of British colonial interests in India. Inevitably the British Foreign Office's bias for Reza Khan marked a change in British policy in southern Persia. Britain soon adopted a policy of 'watchful inaction', allowing Reza Khan not only to take control over the south of Persia, but also to capture and imprison the Sheikh for life. Officially the British government maintained a neutral position regarding what it perceived to be an internal affair. However, this result signified a level of British influence over Persia's domestic policy that could serve as evidence for British support of Reza Khan.[120]

On the basis of these achievements, Reza Khan was not satisfied with the notion of representing an absent Shah who could return at any time and relieve him from office. Thus, in a strategic move he formally offered his resignation, knowing that this would not prove popular with the majority of the Persian population. When, as he expected, a majority requested his return to office, his standing in Persia became stronger than ever before.

On 12 December 1925, the Persian constitutional assembly voted with 257 affirmative votes against 3 abstentions in favour of amending its 1907 constitution to officially allow the Pahlavi dynasty to succeed the Qajar dynasty.[121] When Reza Khan ascended the Persian throne on 15 December 1925,[122] he was forthwith formally acknowledged by many European countries. The first countries to recognise him were Germany, France, Italy, Great Britain and Poland. On 19 December 1925 Reza Shah appointed his first Prime Minister, Mohammed Ali Forughi and a few days later, on 25 April 1926, he was crowned in Tehran as the new monarch of Persia.[123]

The nationalist movement that had supported the Shah's rise to power demanded a radical transformation of Persia towards economic autonomy and political independence. Since the Persian government's tax income was low, the value of exports minimal, and industrial activity negligible, the Shah's economic ambitions were largely reliant on the oil royalties received from the British oil concessions. Moreover, the British-dominated Imperial Bank of Persia was in charge of Persia's financial administration. This meant that in his quest for Persia's political and economic independence the Shah had to seriously consider ways of bringing Persia's finances in line with his progressive ambitions.

Meanwhile, he started his reforms by introducing a bill for compulsory military service, and a further bill that aimed at using tax revenues from the sale of tea and sugar for the construction of a Trans-Iranian Railway. Moreover, weights and measures were standardised, the pre-Islamic calendar was replaced by the Gregorian calendar, birth certificates were made compulsory, European-style family names were introduced, and Qajar titles of nobility were abolished.[124] The Shah also hoped that by maintaining a neutral status in world politics he could encourage enough foreign inward investment to boost Persia's economic growth. The Shah's vision was to create a western-oriented modern Persia, that was an equal member of the international community.

However, the Shah's ambition to establish a western-style economy in Persia also relied on a well-functioning financial system that could provide the preconditions required for Persia's economic development. Hence, the Shah must have felt pleased with the news that the German representative in Tehran, Graf von der Schulenberg, had assured the British representative in Tehran, Sir Loraine, that Germany had no political ambitions in Persia, but was adamant to pursue economic interests. Accordingly in 1923 the Imperial Bank of Persia had declared itself prepared to assist with German trade interests in Persia.[125]

It could be argued that during the period of Reza Shah's rise to power Persia came to view in Germany an ideal partner for its future economic development. The Shah saw in Germany's advanced industrialisation a blueprint for his own reforms. German individuals were respected in Persia for their 'German characteristics', such as reliability, expertness, and diligence. Accordingly, they were entrusted with high positions of responsibility in the Persian government and economy. Moreover, Germany did not display any evident intentions of dominating or oppressing Persia. From a Persian perspective, German policy stood in strong contrast to that of other major powers with shared interests in Persia. German foreign relations with Persia until 1927 were largely non-political, which would explain why in comparison Germans were popular with the Persian public.

The Shah's progress in centralising power and reforming government, economy, military and culture resulted in a degree of political and economic stability that appealed to the outside world. The impression left was that Persia was determined to become a commercially attractive and politically independent country.

Since the military constituted Reza Shah's power base, his interest in the economy was much dictated by the requirements of the Persian military. The construction of roads and railways would enable rapid deployment of troops, while the creation of monopolies in the agricultural sector enabled a more efficient way of taxation, sustaining the growing military infrastructure. The Shah was aware that to achieve his ambitions he needed the support of industrialised foreign powers.

Germany's economic growth relied on the expansion of its international export and import markets. Persia was turning into an attractive emerging market for German economic interests. The German economy was ideally positioned to contribute to the economic development of Persia, through rail and road infrastructure projects, supply of industrial production plants, the establishing of trade, and the development of the financial services sector. Persia needed economic partners such as Germany for its industrialisation, preparing it for its first experience as a modern economy.

2

GERMAN FOREIGN POLICY TOWARDS PERSIA

In the late 1920s oil exploration and oil revenues played an important role in Persia's strategy of becoming a modern country. However, it was the discovery of rich sources of minerals that influenced the Persian government also to focus on industrialisation.[1] This encouraged the Shah to invite foreign investors to participate in the exploitation and industrialisation of his country.[2]

The German Foreign Office too encouraged German companies to become more interested in Persia; it rejected allegations that claimed it continued to advise German companies against doing business with Persia.[3] The German Foreign Office admitted that, as a result of Persia's instability and its unclear financial status in the years 1921 and 1922, it had recommended that German companies should exercise caution when trading with Persia.[4] But this standpoint had changed. The German Foreign Office was later convinced that the Shah's plan for turning Persia into a modern economy and the country's growing income would prove beneficial for German trade. It revealed that, compared to 1920/21, the value of German exports to Persia had increased fivefold and its imports tenfold.[5]

To advance the economic and cultural relations between both countries, and as a result of the growing interest of German industrialists in Persia, a German–Persian association was revived.[6] In the same symbolic spirit the Shah was presented with a German wireless set. He was so pleased with the performance of the equipment that he immediately wanted to know from the Germans whether it was technically feasible to have the debates at parliament broadcast to his palace.[7]

On 10 May 1927 the Persian government informed the German government that its trade agreement of 11 June 1873 was to be cancelled in one year. Simultaneously, it insisted that it was happy to negotiate a new trade agreement with Germany. Mirza Abdul Hossain Khan Taimurtash, the Shah's Court Minister and one of his closest advisers, personally assured the German representative in Tehran, Friedrich-Werner Graf von der Schulenberg, that the cancellation of the 1873 agreement was not an act against Germany but that all Persian trade agreements with foreign countries including capitulation rights were due to be cancelled as well. Hence, on the contrary, the cancellation of the trade agreement between the two countries created an opportunity for Germany to negotiate an improved agreement with Persia.[8]

Three further seemingly unrelated events proved key to furthering Germany's influence in Persia. First, on 23 May 1927 the Persian cabinet stood down. Second, at the end of July the American financial adviser to the Persian government, Arthur Millspaugh, declared his intention not to renew his contract under its new terms. Third, in July the German entrepreneur, Thomas Brown, met with Persian officials in Tehran to discuss the opportunities for German companies following the modernisation plans for the country.

The New Persian Cabinet from a German Perspective

On 23 May 1927 the Shah accepted the resignation of his Prime Minister Mirza Hasan Mostofi. The German representative in Tehran believed that, while foreign political deliberations were the main reason for the cabinet standing down, it was domestic difficulties and the impeachment of parliament that caused Mostofi to hand in his resignation.[9] Soon after, Mehdi Gholi Khan Hedayat was instructed to form a new cabinet, which he introduced on 3 June 1927.

In fact, as Table 2.1 shows, apart from the changes due to Hedayat becoming Prime Minister and also taking over the office of Minister of Public Interests, only two ministers were replaced. From a German perspective the real significance of the change of cabinet lay in the personality of the new Prime Minister, its signal to Russia and its contribution to the influence of Taimurtash.[10]

Hedayat was regarded as one of the most educated, decent and respected political figures in Persia. He was brought up in Germany and whereas Mostofi was regarded as pro-Russian Hedayat was considered unbiased. Germany considered Mostofi's replacement to be a hint to Russia. It was believed that this change of office signalled the Shah's dissatisfaction with the slow and unfruitful economic negotiations between the Persia and Russia. Germany believed that Russia had to take this hint seriously if it did not want to lose its standing in Persia.

Table 2.1 Changes in the Persian Cabinet after Hedayat replaced Mostofi as Prime Minister, June 1927

Ministers	*Mostofi's Cabinet*	*Hedayat's Cabinet*
Foreign Affairs	Ansari	Ansari
Interior	Fatemi	Samii
Education	Taddayun	Taddayun
Finance	Prince Firuz	Prince Firuz
Justice	Dawar	Dawar
Public Interests	Ala	Hedayat
War	Forughi	Sardar Asad
Post	open	open
Court	Taimurtash	Taimurtash

In Russia this change was interpreted differently. According to Hey, at the German embassy in Moscow, an *Izvestia* article had reported that it was unfortunate that the Mostofi cabinet resigned at a time when the negotiations between the two countries were just about to be finalised. It held an incident between the Shah and the British representative Clive responsible for the change of cabinet. A short time before, Clive had asked the Shah for the dismissal of Mostofi's cabinet. Clive voiced to the Shah his dissatisfaction with Mostofi's refusal to accommodate British transit and development agreements. The Shah apparently broke off this meeting and left the room when Clive made a point of reminding him that he owed his throne to Britain and that there were other pretenders to the throne. Thus, this incident had to be taken into account when considering Mostofi's resignation. Hey reported further that according to *Izvestia* Mostofi's resignation served to keep the British happy. At the same time, the article pointed out that it was in the vital interest of Persia to be mindful of Russian interests in Persia as well. The Russian journalist concluded that since the programme of Hedayat's new cabinet dealt extensively with Persian–Russian relations, and a pro-Russian Persian foreign minister had been reinstated, Russia had little cause for concern.[11]

Domestically the Persian parliament and the cabinet were in constant dispute. The main reason for this was the parliament's dislike of three particular cabinet ministers. Interior minister Fatemi was accused of insincerity. Finance minister Prince Firuz was disliked and never freed of the stigma of signing the 1919 agreement with the British. Justice minister Ali Akbar Dawar was accused of incompetence and corruption. Relations between the cabinet and parliament had reached an inefficient deadlock that begged for a change. Surprisingly, two of the three above-mentioned ministers were reappointed as members of the first Hedayat cabinet (Table 2.1).[12]

According to Schulenberg at the German embassy in Tehran, the reason for this was the omnipotent influence of Taimurtash over the Persian government. Prince Firuz was said to be a good friend of Taimurtash, and Dawar was the person to whom he had assigned the task of cancelling all foreign capitulation rights. Furthermore, the newly appointed cabinet members lacked strong personalities and therefore could undoubtedly be manipulated by him. Except for Prince Firuz all other cabinet members were considered as weak.

According to Schulenberg, Prince Firuz and Taimurtash were both regarded as intelligent and clever. At the same time they did not enjoy any trust, even from the Russians. Schulenberg characterised Prince Firuz and Taimurtash as ambitious, power-hungry men from aristocratic backgrounds, who were patriotic but did not neglect to ensure their own welfare while carrying out their official duties. Considering the described status quo and the discouraging continuation of the vendetta between the new cabinet and parliament, Hedayat personally confessed to Schulenberg that his term of office probably would not last for long.[13] From a German perspective this left Persia with a fragile cabinet dominated by individuals such as the influential but manipulative Taimurtash.

Arthur Millspaugh and American Influence on the Persian Government

In 1922 the Persian government had appointed the aforementioned Arthur Millspaugh of the American State department as Treasurer-General. Millspaugh's assignment was to centralise the treasury, reform finances, establish economic legislation and attract foreign investment and loans to Persia.[14] Five years later, Millspaugh's refusal to renew his contract with the Persian government had implications for Germany.

Besides the major powers Russia and Britain there were two alternative contenders for Persia. The prevailing school of thought is that Persia was subject to a bipolar system of power rivalry. However, Germany viewed America as a contender for economic influence in Persia as well. Hence, although it is indisputable that the two main powers in Persia, Britain and Russia, bore hostilities against each other, the hitherto less important contenders, Germany and America, were also competing against each other and at the same time with the two dominating powers. The difference is that Britain and Russia safeguarded their economic interest mainly through their political power, whereas Germany and America, lacking significant political power in the region, limited their competition to the economic realm.

From a German point of view the Americans were marginally ahead in the race for the lucrative emerging markets of Persia. It was believed that this advantage could partly be attributed to the fact that the financial adviser to the Persian government was an American. This implies that Germany believed that Millspaugh in his role had enough influence to create an American biased economic patronage system in Persia. The German media reported that Reza Shah, having recognised American protectionism, wished to ensure equal opportunities for countries trying to secure an economic foothold in Persia.[15]

Regarding railway construction in Persia, Schulenberg reported that the prevailing feeling among the Persian authorities was that Millspaugh misused his position to draft the terms for railway construction contracts in such a way that it gave only American companies an opportunity to submit competitive bids.[16] Schulenberg also singled out American bias in the draft of a bill concerning the employment of foreign nationals for the construction of the Trans-Iranian Railway. This bill not only specifically required American engineers to be employed for key positions but also stipulated that their wages were to be twice the wages of their European counterparts.[17] Later in the same year a German Foreign Office official, Dr Ziemke, concluded that the American industry was at a clear advantage in Persia regarding the construction of the Trans-Iranian Railway. The reason for this was again associated with the American protectionism coming from the offices held by Millspaugh and William B. Poland, the American national in charge of the construction of the Trans-Iranian Railway. Ziemke recommended that Germany should compete with America in alternative sectors since German companies had a good chance to win contracts for the construction of factories, sugar refineries and power plants.[18]

From a German point of view no other government would have tolerated the unusual degree of power Millspaugh was given by the Persian government. Therefore, it will have come as no surprise to Schulenberg when the Persian government decided to restrict Millspaugh's authority through a new employment contract. Schulenberg acknowledges the good results Millspaugh had achieved by administering the Persian finances. Yet he felt that Millspaugh personally was partly to blame for the curtailment of his powers, because of his harsh, arrogant, bureaucratic, impolite and stubborn character, which had made him many enemies, including the minister of finance Prince Firuz. Schulenberg believed that, since Prince Firuz was a good friend of the all-influential Taimurtash, it was obvious how the Shah ultimately came to agree to limit Millspaugh's powers.[19]

According to Schulenberg, when a displeased Millspaugh finally decided not to sign his new limiting contract the cabinet forthwith proposed to replace him by appointing the American Charles I. MacCaskey. MacCaskey was General Treasurer of the Persian government and had served under Morgan Shuster. He was prepared to accept a possible offer, but the resentment of the Persian parliament against '*Finanz-Amerikanisches*' meant that a final decision was not reached.[20]

At this point Schulenberg reported rumours in Tehran that the Persian government planned to appoint a German expert as its financial adviser. In addition, Schulenberg was informed by a Persian Member of Parliament that his government was positively looking into such a possibility. During the same period, on 31 July 1927, an article appeared in one of the major Tehran newspapers, *Shafaghe Sork*, which admiringly described how German financial experts single-handedly managed to restore Germany's financial status after the devastating war. Although there was no mention of a German financial adviser for Persia, Schulenberg believed that influential parties might have inspired the article, possibly even the royal palace. Hence he recommended that because of the extraordinary economic significance of the office of financial adviser Germany should be prepared to take such a request seriously.[21]

In contrast to German optimism, on 8 September 1927 the Capital City News Association in Washington published an article with the title 'Persian finances to continue under supervision of American'. The article reported that William B. Poland, American Director General of the Persian Railway Administration, was the most likely candidate to succeed Millspaugh as Administrator General of Persia's finances and that his assistant C. J. Carroll was also believed to be under consideration. The article goes on to mention that Millspaugh 'refused recently to renew his contract on the ground that under the terms of the proposed new arrangement his administrative powers would be greatly curtailed and his work hampered'. Yet the article admits that Millspaugh was given in his original contract of 1922 'extraordinary powers that went so far as to make his office independent of even the Persian parliament'.[22]

On 17 September 1927 a further article revealed Millspaugh's own perception of the situation in Persia. He is quoted as having said that the terms of his new contract 'would have substantially altered the conditions and greatly reduced the powers under which he had previously worked'. Millspaugh also pointed out that when he arrived in 1922 Persia was 'in a state of demoralisation, corruption and chaos'. During his term of office 'the American Mission made encouraging progress in reorganising the tax system, revenues increased from twenty million to thirty million dollars, expenditures were placed on a budgetary basis and accounting was established in all departments except the Ministry of War the budget was balanced and in the last two fiscal years a substantial surplus was created'. This article claims to have 'reliably understood' that Persia and the Shah were planning to replace Millspaugh by another American.[23]

Despite Millspaugh's group of twelve American financial experts continuing to assist Prime Minister Hedayat with the Persian finances and the pro-American newspaper report from Washington, a number of factors led Schulenberg to believe that there was still a genuine opportunity for a German candidate to become the next financial adviser to the Persian government. These factors included Millspaugh's telling refusal to renew his contract as financial adviser to the Persian government, the Persian cabinet's decision to cut down the powers of its American financial advisers, the resistance of Reza Shah against American protectionism, and the pro-German propaganda in Persia.

The Entrepreneur Thomas Brown and the German Economic Deal with Persia

Thomas Brown was a German national, a partner of the Hamburg-based German company Woenckhaus & Co., and an expert on Persia. His company had 35 years of experience in the import and export business with Persia. It also represented a majority of large German industrial companies with a commercial interest in Persia.

In 1927 Brown had travelled to Persia with the aim to negotiate contracts for larger industrial shipments to the Persian industry, involvement of German companies in planned Persian railway projects and the expansion of the Junkers airline flight operations.[24] Brown states in a comprehensive report to the Reichswirtschaftsministerium (Reich's Economic Ministry) that on arrival in July in Tehran he had planned to investigate opportunities for German economic involvement in Persia.[25]

Since Brown was aware of Russia's political and economic influence in Persia, he had held a number of meetings with the German representative to Moscow, Graf Brockdorff-Rantzau, and the Russian vice-commissar for foreign affairs L. M. Karachan. The Russian proposals for the creation of a German–Russian consortium for the construction of the Persian railway network dominated these meetings. In fear of the negative foreign political consequences, Brown turned down the Russian proposal for a railway construction consortium. At the same time, however, he succeeded in ensuring Russian support for possible German economic activities in northern Persia.

After arriving in Tehran Brown re-established his close links with prominent Persians and the government. He learnt that as a result of Germany's defeat in the war, Persia did not perceive Germany as a threat. On the contrary, he sensed Persian admiration for Germany's industrial, scientific and organisational achievements. Under such circumstances the opportunity for German companies to establish themselves commercially in Persia was good. Nevertheless, Brown's initial negotiations with the Persian government did not lead to any major breakthrough.

Brown attributed this result mainly to the resistance coming from the American Financial Mission in Tehran. The American Mission, for fear of German competition, appeared to be protective of American business interests. Two weeks after Brown's arrival in Tehran, the crisis between the Persian government and the American Mission had reached its height when Millspaugh formally refused to renew his contract. Brown considered Millspaugh's departure an opportunity for Germany.

Aware of Taimurtash's power and influence over the cabinet, Brown forthwith approached him. In his consultations with Taimurtash Brown re-emphasised German eagerness to participate in the economic development of Persia. Brown also assured Taimurtash that German involvement in Persia would not take the form of exploitation but would take into account the mutual interests of both countries. To prove the seriousness of his cooperation proposal and commitment, Brown offered the Persian government a substantial loan on behalf of German industry. This loan, which was exclusively to be used for the payment of German goods and services, amounted to 40 million goldmarks.[26]

To put the significance of the German loan offer into perspective, we may turn to the Persian government's regular annual budget for the budget year 31 March 1927–31 March 1928. The Persian government's regular budget was estimated at 25 million toman (1 toman ≈ \$1; \$1 ≈ 4 Reichsmark) equivalent to 100 million Reichsmarks, excluding the special budget created for railway construction.[27] On the basis of these figures the German loan would equal about 40 per cent of the Persian government's regular budget and was therefore substantial in magnitude. The German loan also played well into the hands of the Shah who was keen on driving forward his modernisation strategy for Persia. Hence, the German loan offer was what the Persian government had long hoped for and was predestined to win sympathies for Germany.

What proved significant for Germany was Brown's main condition for granting this loan. He requested that the Persian government did not renew its contract with an American Financial Mission that included Millspaugh.[28]

Considering Taimurtash's issues with Millspaugh he must have been agreeable to Brown's proposal. As a matter of priority he discussed Brown's proposal on the same day with Reza Shah. On the next day Brown was invited to the palace where Taimurtash told him that the Shah had accepted his loan offer and that further details should be negotiated directly at cabinet meetings. On the following day Brown attended the first of five cabinet meetings where his plans were examined in more detail. It was subsequently decided that the German loan should be utilised to finance an electricity plant for Tehran, aircraft, and several factories for the production of cement, sugar, textiles and material for the construction of blast furnaces and railways.[29] From a German perspective it appears that Taimurtash genuinely had the authority and influence attributed to him, as he managed to have Brown's proposals approved by the Shah and the Persian cabinet in record time.

After the positive results of the negotiations with the Persian government, Brown consulted the Russian embassy in Tehran to obtain Russian assurance of support for his economic plans for Persia. In Brown's view, Russia welcomed his plans because although Bolshevik foreign policy was aimed at strengthening Persia commercially and politically it could not afford to do so financially. Brown was also pleased to learn that Russia had extended Persia the right of free transit of goods through its territory in a recent trade agreement. Brown had even managed to persuade the Russians to add a term to the agreement that would restrict transit rights only to goods originating from countries that maintained trade relations with Russia. This in term was a significant advantage for German exporters of railway construction material. As a trade-off Brown persuaded the Persian government to grant Russia a long-desired flight concession to Anzali.[30]

During the last two cabinet meetings Brown attended, he participated in the debates discussing the Persian railway project. The entire railway project was to be financed through taxes on tea and sugar. Persia's financial state was comparatively sound as the country had only 20 million goldmark foreign debts. The tea and sugar tax monopoly generated $6 million annually, and a further $1–2 million was being raised through the introduction of a match tax. Through leveraging these taxes the government had already accumulated $16 million for its railway projects. Yet, on the recommendation of the American Financial Mission, the Persian government had intended to manage its railway projects internally, and have its construction contracted out to Americans.

Brown criticised this plan at the cabinet meeting and argued that governments always constructed more expensively than the private sector. As a result of his rationalisation Brown was asked to recommend a better plan. Brown duly recommended that the Persian government should contract out the survey of 600 kilometres of railroad – which began 300 kilometres south of Tehran and stretched to the Caspian Sea – to a German group of companies. After completing the survey of the first 100 kilometres these German companies would then construct the first 100 kilometres of railroad. After the satisfactory completion of this first section the government should open the construction of the remaining 500 kilometres to international bids.

Brown remarks in his report to the Reichswirtschaftsministerium that after the completion of the first 100 kilometres it would be difficult for other companies to compete with the already established German railway construction consortium in a public bid. This was also due to the exclusive support of Russia for Germany.[31]

Since all of Brown's negotiations with the Persian government took place in close consultation with Schulenberg and with Schulenberg's support, his progress was regularly reported to the German Foreign Office. In this context Schulenberg had remarked that leading Persian figures were greatly impressed with Brown and that as a result the Persian government was also planning to employ German experts for the construction of its railway.[32] To Brown's satisfaction the Persian government agreed to accept his proposals as presented.[33] Thus, a few days later Schulenberg forwarded the requests of the Persian government for 22 German railway experts in a telegram to the German Foreign Office.[34] The Foreign Office duly informed the ministry of finance of the Persian government's request for railway experts. In its turn, the ministry of finance forthwith contacted the director of Deutsche Reichsbahn-Gesellschaft with the urgent instruction to propose suitable candidates for all 22 requested positions.[35]

In a next step Brown brought a number of German construction companies together into a partnership. These companies were Philipp Holzmann Aktiengesellschaft, Siemens Bau-Union and Julius Berger Consortium. Representatives of these companies soon after arrived in Tehran to negotiate details of their contracts with the Persian government.

Brown's consultations with the Persian government resulted in even more success for Germany. First, the government agreed to replace Millspaugh through a German financial expert.[36] As a result Schulenberg asked the German Foreign Office on behalf of Hedayat to recommend a suitable candidate to replace Millspaugh. The new German financial expert was expected to control the Persian financial administration and budget, recommend and improve sources of tax revenue, and take charge of loan applications and profit-generating government enterprises.[37] But because of his reduced authority compared to his American predecessor it was expected that he would find it more difficult to secure his authority and exercise the desired influence.[38]

Furthermore, on his return to Germany by way of Russia, Brown managed to gain full support for his Persian plans from the German embassy in Moscow and the vice-commissar for foreign affairs Karachan. He was explicitly assured of the unobstructed and inexpensive transit of German goods through Russia. The newly appointed Russian ambassador to Tehran, Daftian, also officially confirmed this assurance to the German ambassador in Moscow, Graf Brockdorff-Rantzau.

Brown's recommendations, in his own words, provided Germany with the unique opportunity of securing an economic monopoly in Persia. With relatively low risk and with little effort Germany could create conditions that would help it to advance and become a leading economic and political power in the Middle East. The accessibility of the Persian market provided Germany with a great opportunity for the expansion of its economic influence. The unexplored rich mineral resources and large oil fields that covered the north of the country would have been of particular interest to Germany. Through the envisaged industrial exports and the monopoly position thus created in the region, German companies could also hope to secure a continuing demand for their goods. Through the German loan, the construction industry alone was expected to win contracts to the value of at least 150 million Reichsmarks.[39]

In support of the 40 million Reichsmark loan, Brown requested that the Reichswirtschaftsministerium should provide a guarantee against trade cancellation for those German companies planning to export goods to Persia.[40] By this time the Foreign Office was already aware of Brown's request for a trade cancellation guarantee. Brown had approached the Reichswirtschaftsministerium earlier with his request but did not receive a definite answer. Hence, in compliance with Brown's request, the Foreign Office had asked the Reichswirtschaftsministerium to reach a definite decision regarding a 25 million-mark guarantee.[41]

Brown had promised the Persian government to announce the results of his negotiations with the Reichswirtschaftsministerium by the end of September. However, this deadline could not be met since on his return to Germany Brown suffered from a bout of malaria he had contracted in Persia.[42]

After recovering, Brown reported on the state of his negotiations with the Persian government in a meeting with representatives of government and industry at the Reichswirtschaftsministerium. Brown presented to the German government officials and industrialists the Persian government's proposal for the establishment of a National Bank. He explained that such a bank's founding capital could reach approximately 200 million Reichsmarks. Furthermore, while the National Bank would become the official bank of the Persian government, it was proposed that it also should provide banking facilities for regular customers.

Moreover, Brown discussed the Persian government's intention to consider German proposals for the appointment of a director for its proposed National Bank and a new financial adviser to the government. In this context, the director of the German Bank für Industrieobligationen (Bank for Industrial Bonds), Dr Bötzkes, had already been asked to undertake relevant due diligence in Persia.[43]

Besides the National Bank, details of the conditions the Persian government and the interested German companies had to meet to qualify for the commercial loan were discussed. Reportedly all participants agreed to the general terms presented. Thus, Brown announced his intention to return to Persia in December to finalise and close on the initial contracts for German exports to Persia.

At this meeting the German representatives committed themselves to provide an export guarantee covering approximately 60 per cent or 24 million Reichsmarks of the total contracted exports of 40 million Reichsmarks to Persia. The terms and conditions of this guarantee required that of the remaining risk of approximately 40 per cent or 16 million Reichsmarks, 20 per cent was to be directly covered by the companies concerned and the remaining 20 per cent was to be shared equally between the companies and the Reich. The repayment of the loan was to take place in instalments within a maximum of eight years. As a condition interested German companies had to submit their applications for the Reichsgarantie by 1 February 1928. By this date companies had also to submit a binding initial contract with the Persian government.[44]

The results achieved at this meeting were a success and a great source of encouragement for Brown. He not only managed to secure the German government's commitment to supporting German industrial exports to Persia but he also secured a major milestone for Germany's participation in the development of Persia.

German involvement in Persia up till 1928 was largely commercially motivated. It was initiated by the skill and ambitions of Thomas Brown, who managed to negotiate and ensure the backing of the highest levels of government in Persia, Germany and Russia for his commercial projects. The sympathies of the Persian cabinet towards his ideas and the influence of Taimurtash secured his success. The Millspaugh crisis contributed in many ways to the German cause. It created an opportunity for Germany to enter into dialogue with Persia; it allowed Persia to display its resentment against the American Mission; Millspaugh's replacement by a German was a triumph for Germany's rivalry with America; Germany had for the first time in decades a national serving in high government office in Persia. The positive development of Persia's economic ties with Germany soon resulted in the appointment of further German nationals to high offices. One of these was the director of its proposed National Bank.

The Persian National Bank

Brown succeeded in agreeing with the Persian government to appoint a German national as director general of its proposed National Bank. The Persian National Bank was to be primarily financed through the selling of crown jewellery, valued at an estimated 80–100 million goldmarks, and the sale of crown property. Moreover, the German government was to be officially approached by Persia with the request for a suitable candidate for the position of director general of its National Bank.[45]

The history of the Persian National Bank began in 1889 when Naser ad-Din Shah approved a concession for its establishment. A bank was created in the same year under the name 'The Imperial Bank of Persia'. This bank maintained a head office in Tehran and twenty branches across Persia. The Imperial Bank also maintained an international branch in London that served as its main administrative headquarters. It subsequently opened two branches in Iraq and one in Bombay. The British national Sir Hugh Barnes and seven other executive directors managed the bank. In addition a commissioner appointed by the Shah supervised and safeguarded the Persian government's interest at the bank.

The Imperial Bank's balance sheet revealed a reserve of £520,000 on 20 March 1927. According to the terms agreed in its concession, the Persian government received 6 per cent of the bank's annual net profits. The net profits of the bank for the year 1926/27 were £135,367.[46] In 1889 the bank had also secured a 60-year monopoly right for printing money. The highest amount the bank was allowed to print without an authorisation by the Persian government was £800,000. In addition, a 33 per cent cash reserve was always to be maintained. The bank's balance sheet for 20 March 1927 is presented in Table 2.2.

The Russian Banque de Prêts de Perse, later renamed to Banque d'escompte, was a second bank operating in Persia. But in 1921 this bank was handed over from the Russians to the Persian government. The bank was later renamed 'The Bank of Iran' and was affiliated with the Persian

Table 2.2 The Imperial Bank of Persia: 20 March 1927 balance sheet (values in £1,000)

Capital	650	Cash	4,262
Reserves	520	Investments	1,987
Circulation of bank notes	2,155	Bills of exchange and advances	4,565
Deposits	6,483		

Source: Report of statistical department of the Reichsbank in Berlin, 31 October 1927. PAAA, Department III–Economy, R92320, p. 1.

ministry of finance. Furthermore, the Ottoman bank maintained three branches in Persia and a new bank, created with the help of the Russians, maintained branches in the northern provinces.

In 1927 two major banking projects were discussed by parliament that aimed at facilitating Persia's industrialisation. One was to create a government security loan bank and the other was to create a National Bank.[47]

The law relating to the creation of a National Bank was accepted and passed by parliament on 5 May 1927. According to this law the government was obliged to create a bank under the name 'National Bank of Persia'. Article 1 established that the headquarters of the bank should be in Tehran and its operations were to be extended on demand through creation of branches in Persia and overseas. Articles 2, 3 and 13 determined that the initial 20 million toman capital of the bank, as mentioned before, should be raised by the sale of crown jewellery and state property, valued at 15 million toman. The remaining 5 million toman were to be accumulated by advances from the government. Article 4 regulated that government advances were not to come from the railway construction reserve. Article 5 stated that the main purpose of the bank was to support agriculture, industry and trade by granting loans. Article 6 specified that the government, its administrative agencies and the city councils should not be eligible for loans, except with the consent of parliament. Articles 7 and 8 determined that the director of the bank should be an American banking expert whose work could be overseen by an inspector. Article 9 gave the bank the right to accept private customers and pay out interest on their deposits. Article 10 ruled that the bank's paperwork had to be kept in Persian language. Article 11 stated that both the ministry of finance and the directors of the bank should draft the standing orders of the bank. These then had to be approved by the council of ministers and the finance commission before they could become effective. Article 12 expected the Persian government to keep all its financial assets with the National Bank. Article 14 determined that after the American director of the bank was appointed, he should work out a law for a gold-based Persian currency. The draft version of this law was to be presented to the government within one year. Article 15 concluded that the law creating the framework for the National Bank of Persia would come into effect on 6 November 1927.[48]

It is of significance that this law regulating the creation of the National Bank of Persia, specifically had requested for an American national to become its director. The German Reichsbank's explanation for this law was that Millspaugh and his finance commission had prepared its initial draft.[49]

However, many changes had taken place in Persia since March when this law was approved. Specifically, in July Brown had succeeded in gaining the Persian government's approval for the appointment of a German expert as the director of the National Bank instead of an American, yet at first glance either Persia did not see this as a binding promise or the German government had failed to give the matter the necessary attention. In December 1927 the German Foreign Office recorded that the Persian representative had informed them of his government's intention to employ a Swiss national as the first director of its National Bank. Nevertheless, the Persian representative had also added that a German applicant could still be considered if a suitable candidate was recommended without delay.[50] Hence, if Germany did not act fast it would forfeit the opportunity to have a German national appointed as the director of the National Bank of Persia.

It appears that faced with an ultimatum from the Persian government the German Foreign Office started to take the matter more seriously. Dr Bötzkes, the director of the Bank für Deutsche Industrieobligationen, who had already conducted due diligence on the status of banking in Persia, had put forward a Dr Lindenblatt as a suitable candidate for the position.[51] The Foreign Office subsequently tried to contact Lindenblatt via telegram to enquire if he would be interested in the post and if he was prepared to relocate to Tehran for a salary of $12,000.[52]

Lindenblatt was born on 11 October 1885 in Freienwalde. He completed his university education in economics and law in 1912. He was then employed by the Disconto-Gesellschaft, one of four Berlin-based credit banks. He also had gained international experience at the London branch of the same bank. With the outbreak of war he joined the military until 1916. His economic expertise was then put to use by the German Foreign Office and its consulates in Constantinople, Copenhagen and Amsterdam. In 1922 Lindenblatt returned to the Disconto-Gesellschaft, and after a period of preparation in Berlin, he was sent as the first German Director of the Credit Bank-Sofia to Bulgaria. During his six years at the bank he gained relevant experience in domestic and international banking.[53]

On receiving the Foreign Office enquiry, Lindenblatt seemed enthusiastic about the idea of going to Persia and contributing to the development and construction of the Persian economy. To take up what he called 'an important position in the Persian empire', Lindenblatt approached the Disconto-Gesellschaft with the request to consider relieving him from his contract in Sofia. Accommodating the special circumstances, the Disconto-Gesellschaft agreed to support Lindenblatt's appointment as the first director of the National Bank of Persia.[54]

One month later Lindenblatt signed his contract with the Persian government and by the end of April 1928 he left for Tehran.[55] Remarkably his nomination as the first director of the National Bank of Persia was covered in the German press.[56] Lindenblatt's appointment added weight to a new phase in Germany's involvement in Persia, a phase that saw Germany's influence progressively expand.

German National Interest and the National Bank of Persia

When the creation of the National Bank of Persia became intertwined with German involvement in Persia, in other words when the Persian government facilitated Germany's involvement in the founding of the National Bank by providing its director, the bank became effectively a German project, and as such it turned into a vehicle for German economic and political influence in Persia.

However, Lindenblatt and Millspaugh were both employees of the Persian government and not official representatives of their countries. The German Foreign Office acknowledged that the American government did not exercise any influence through Millspaugh and that the Americans employed by the Persian government were not a 'Mission' of the American government. They were officially regarded as independent experts recruited by the Persian government. Supporting this position was the fact that, 'not one American dollar had been granted to the Persian government' as a result of the appointment of American nationals by the Persian government.[57]

The Americans also had made clear that Millspaugh's appointment as financial adviser to the Persian government 'was a private arrangement and was not made on the advice of the American State Department'. With reference to Millspaugh's resignation, it was clarified that the American government 'was interested to see that the services of a competent American adviser were obtained by the Persian authorities, but it was explained that the State Department has no responsibility in the matter and cannot intervene in the matter of Dr. Millspaugh's contract'.[58]

Similarly, the German government also officially regarded Lindenblatt's appointment a private matter between him and the Persian government.

However, we have seen that Millspaugh, as an independent agent, was protective of American interests in Persia. For example, he was inclined to approve new laws passed by the Persian government only if key individuals associated were American nationals.[59] The official stance of both the American and German governments remained similar. Both governments maintained that, while the Persian government had employed one of their nationals, these were not pursuing their government's interest. Yet Millspaugh's case shows that he could effectively operate as an instrument of American influence when dealing with Persia. Both governments seem to have learned from the past mistakes of the super powers Britain and Russia. Instead of focusing resources on political game plans they focused on gaining influence, albeit indirectly by securing strong economic footholds in Persia. Thus, the German perception of Millspaugh facilitating American economic interest in Persia was regarded as a competitive advantage for America and a handicap for the smooth progression of German projects in Persia. How much of a handicap becomes particularly evident when we take into account that Brown thought it worthwhile to persuade the Persian government to have Millspaugh replaced by a German financial expert.

This simultaneously substantiates the contradiction that even though the Germans were dissociating the individual German national sent to lead a Persian National Bank from the German government as an institution, implicitly they were thinking of Lindenblatt as a person who would be in a unique position to advance German interests, in a similar manner to Millspaugh.

Presuming that it was a German aspiration that the National Bank of Persia should provide them with a degree of strategic influence and that Lindenblatt had the potential to influence economic relations between Germany and Persia, how would this affect Germany's prospects in Persia?

3

GERMAN FOREIGN AND ECONOMIC RELATIONS IN PERSIA

Their evolution and the role of the National Bank

The German Approach

Germany intended to set about ensuring its success in foreign policy towards Persia through a radically different approach to that pursued by Britain and Russia. The German government tried to find a political foothold in Persia through the pursuit of economic interests. This strategy of involvement was also being utilised by the United States in Persia. It relied mainly on the notion that a military campaign was out of question and that the new approach towards imperialism should be cost-effective and not resemble colonialism. Neither the German or the American government even attempted to interfere with or influence private enterprise, since from the experiences of Britain and Russia such an approach would have most probably backfired. The British and Russian governments exercised more control over their economic projects in Persia. Thus, it could be argued that even the Anglo-Persian Oil Company was more a British government venture than a private enterprise.

In the German case, instead of the government paving the way for private enterprise, the government's way was paved through private enterprise. It appears that the German government kept its political and economic agendas separate. However, within its economic agenda there was a further division between government-supported initiatives and independent

Table 3.1 Persia's imports and exports. Values in million marks[a]

	Imports	*Exports*	*Total*
1913–14	265	167	452
1919–20	258	151	409
1920–21	198	152	350
1921–22	250	206	456
1922–23	254	301	555
1923–24	279	315	594
1924–25	316	410	726
1925–26	361	434	795
1926–27	323	453	776
1927–28	331	435	766
1928–29	328	607	935

a Figures in Goldmarks are based on official data from the Persian customs statistics for 1928/1929.

German private enterprise initiatives in Persia. Thomas Brown and the Junkers airline, mentioned in the last chapter, are examples of the latter. The National Bank of Persia could qualify as an example of the first. Hence we will first map out German economic influence in Persia before returning to the German political agenda and the role of the National Bank.

German Economic Interest in Persia

In a report on German trade with Persia and its future potential Dr Fritz Hesse explained that by 1927 the public interest in German activities in Persia increased particularly because of the involvement of the Julius Berger Group in the Trans-Persian railway project and the appointment of German experts to high government positions in Persia.[1]

To analyse the premise of Hesse's statement three different approaches will be used when considering German economic influence in Persia. First, we look at German trade with Persia. Second, we survey the scale of German enterprise in Persia. Third, we reflect on Germany's efforts in promoting its business and culture in Persia.

The trade statistics presented in Table 3.1 show the volume and development of Persia's import, export, and total trade between 1913 and 1929. To put the significance of these figures into perspective we shall consider the total trade of Persia's neighbour Turkey, a country that was also important for German trade. Table 3.1 reveals that already in 1927/28 Persia's overall

Table 3.2 Position of countries in Persia's foreign trade. Value in million marks. % = share of market

	Import	%	*Export*	%	*Total*	%
Great Britain	63	19.1	156	25.7	219	23.5
Russia	115	35.5	66	10.9	182	19.6
British India	73	19.3	58	9.6	121[a]	16.0
Egypt	0.04	—	182	—	182	—
France	16	4.8	32	5.2	48	5.1
United States	16	4.8	32	5.2	48	5.1
Germany	19	5.7	16	2.7	35	3.8
Belgium	12	3.5	14	2.2	26	2.7
Turkey	0.3	0.1	16	2.6	16	1.7
Italy	8	2.4	4	0.7	12	1.3

a Figures add up to 131, the original document notes 121.

volume of trade was 766 million goldmarks and therefore potentially higher than Turkey's total volume of trade, which amounted to 738 million goldmarks or 369 million Turkish pounds, during the same period.[2]

In the year 1928/29 Persia's volume of trade, at 935 million goldmarks, was more than 100 million goldmarks higher than Turkey's volume of trade during the same period, approximately 823 million goldmarks or 411.4 million Turkish pounds. Moreover the total volumes of trade for other countries in the region, such as Syria, Palestine, Iraq and Afghanistan, were far behind that of Persia. Therefore, although Persia's elevated trade figures are largely due to its oil exports, which in 1928/29 totalled 415 million goldmarks, these figures show that Persia as an emerging market had become more important for international trade than Turkey.

However, while Germany occupied the third position in the ranking list of countries trading with Turkey, Germany occupied only the seventh position in the ranking list of countries trading with Persia (Table 3.2). Germany's volume of trade with Persia was comparatively small, particularly when compared to Britain, Russia and British India, which together represented over 60 per cent of Persia's foreign trade.[3]

Nevertheless trade between Germany and Persia was growing. Table 3.3 shows that in 1927 Germany's volume of trade with Persia had reached the levels Germany had maintained before World War I. Despite Germany facing major challenges while establishing itself, in 1927/28, it still managed

Table 3.3 German trade with Persia. Value in thousand marks

	German exports to Persia	*%*	*German imports from Persia*	*%*	*Total*	*%*
1913–14	15,185	4.5	1,475	0.7	16,880	3
1919–20	58	0.02	—	—	53	0.014
1920–21	219	0.13	78	0.04	297	0.08
1921–22	1,232	0.49	98	0.04	1,330	0.29
1922–23	3,478	1.21	145	0.05	3,624	0.66
1923–24	7,245	2.74	436	0.13	7,682	1.23
1924–25	9,458	2.99	783	0.19	10,241	1.41
1925–26	13,405	3.71	751	0.17	14,156	1.78
1926–27	16,133	4.43	1,846	0.41	17,980	2.26
1927–28	13,208	4.11	13,801	3.17	27,009	3.52
1928–29	18,894	5.76	16,631	2.67	35,546	3.8

to grow its trade with Persia. Between the years 1920/21 and 1928/29 Germany increased its exports to Persia from 0.13 per cent to 5.76 per cent of total market share. Germany's imports from Persia increased in the same period from 0.04 per cent to 2.67 per cent of total Persian exports.[4]

These rather small figures appear in a different light when considering that about 60 per cent of Persia's imports were composed of cottons, low price textiles, sugar and tea. These are all goods that were from a practical and economic point of view not suitable as German exports to Persia. Britain, India and Russia could produce cottons cheaply in a ways that Germany's quality-oriented textile industry could not compete with. Also, the Persian sugar market was dominated by the Russians, since they exported their sugar at subsidised dumping prices.

The other categories of goods imported by Persia, such as food, petroleum, gold and silver, were not typical German export goods. Hence, they do not feature in the analysis of German trade with Persia. A more objective picture of German trade with Persia can only be obtained when we focus on German exports of manufactured goods. Germany could realistically only compete in this category of exports with comparable goods offered by other countries.[5]

German manufactured goods made up a significant share of the total Persian imports of high-end and quality manufactured goods including steel and machinery. Even though the markets for automobiles, bicycles, supplies for the Persian construction industry, tools and hardware were dominated

Table 3.4 Persian exports. Value in thousand marks

Type of goods	*Total exports*	*Exports to Germany*	*German share in %*
Petroleum	415,042	12,652	3
Skins	4,943	3,375	46
Wool carpets	63,740	596	0.9
Rubber *tragant*	6,340	397	6.3
Dried fruits	19,845	383	1.8
Animal skins	2,298	160	6.9
Other rubber types	1,011	53	5.2
Lambskins	2,886	44	1.5

by American and British exports, Germany successfully maintained a strong position in the export of paints, drugs and chemicals. German exports of electrical goods, precision machinery and optical articles were also well established and provided potential for expansion. Moreover, although Germany's export of power stations and machinery was curbed by the scarcity of skilled Persian operating staff, Germany had the potential of becoming a major exporter of leather, paper, glass and glass products to Persia.

Table 3.4 shows that except oil from the British-dominated Olex Germany imported comparatively little from Persia.[6] Common reasons for the low volume of trade between Germany and Persia were poor logistics and limited access to capital in Persia. Nevertheless, due to the growing importance of Persia for trade and the increase of German trade with Persia, Germany had good prospects in developing relevant opportunities in areas such as agriculture, water, power stations and mining as well as through the establishment of commercial enterprises which required only limited capital investments.

Compared to Britain (the backbone of British economic policy in Persia was its maintaining of large commercial enterprises such as the Anglo-Persian Oil Company and the Imperial Bank of Persia), Germany was still doing little business in Persia. However, due to the growing opportunities in Persia's emerging markets, German companies became increasingly interested in investing in the country.

One such company, whose business was facilitated by both the German and Persian governments, was the Junkers airline established in 1927. Within a short period this company proved profitable and looked to secure further concessions, permitting it to expand its flight operations in Persia.[7]

Another, larger company with business interests in Persia was a construction consortium made up of the companies Julius Berger Tiefbau A.G., Philipp Holzmann A.G. and Siemens-Bauunion. These companies were part of a railway syndicate for the construction of the Trans-Persian railway. Encouragingly, the Persian government's tax-funded railway construction reserves for railway projects had reached a commercially attractive 103 million marks by 23 September 1929.[8]

The involvement of the German consortium in the construction of what was for its time an ambitious and capital-intensive project resulted in a significant increase in trade between Germany and Persia. Furthermore, a number of major German companies such as Krupp, I. G. Farben, A.E.G. and Siemens-Schuckert Werke engaged permanent representatives in Persia. Other German companies, including Wönckhaus & Co., Undütsch & Co., Steffen & Heymann, Riedel & Haen A.G. and Deutsches Magazin (Tehran), maintained business relations with Persia.[9] Supporting German trade were also the shipping company Hansa Line and a newly formed German logistics company Pers-Express A.G. They provided regular freight shipping services between Germany and Persia.

German economic interests in Persia also benefited indirectly from Germans employed in the country. The National Bank of Persia was officially considered a Persian enterprise and constituted the National Bank of the Persian government. Authority over the bank lay exclusively with the Persian government. Its German director Lindenblatt and the numerous German employees working at its branches were officially Persian civil servants and carried out their duties in the interest of the Persian government. Nevertheless, it is certain that it reflected positively on German business, when German nationals working in key government offices achieved good results and were kept in high regard in Persia. Apart from the bank further high offices in the Persian government were held by German nationals such as finance inspector Scheer who was the head of the Persian finance administration, Fry, who was head of accountancy, and Ministerialrat Schniewind who as previously mentioned held the office of financial adviser to the Persian government.

The reportedly devoted services rendered by these German nationals for the development of the Persian economy unquestionably improved Germany's image in Persia and therewith also indirectly promoted the image of the German entrepreneur and his business interests.[10] Germany would have also benefited from officially promoting its culture and business in Persia. It can be argued that the German government did not maintain any cultural institution that could promote German values, ability or capabilities in Persia.

The director of the Tehran trade school was German, but the school was equipped and run by the Persian Government, and the popular 'German School' had been shut down in 1916. The only German organisation in Persia was the *Deutsch-Persische Gesellschaft e.V.*, which was founded by German companies and individuals resident in Persia. This organisation aimed at promoting cultural and business relations between the two countries. Its chairman, Fritz Hesse, believed that however desirable the promotion of German culture and business was, the initiative for promoting it should come not from the German government but from the larger German companies with interests in Persia. One reason for the German government's shortcomings in this area might have been the recommendation by Hesse that investments in the cultural sector, however beneficial in the long term, could not benefit German–Persian economic relations in the short term.

Germany's economic progress in Persia was reflected in growing trade figures. German companies had become increasingly interested in the business opportunities that Persia presented. Other factors encouraging German economic activity in Persia, included a weak improvement in the Persian currency; the exploitation of newly discovered oil reserves in northern Persia by the Russian company Kevir Khourian; the opportunity to construct industrial plants, including a blast furnace, a match factory and an electrical power plant; stable agricultural output with an increased focus on the production of silk; significant improvement of travel times due to improved roads and an increase in motor vehicles; enhancement of air travel and the postal service;[11] and the ongoing appointment of German nationals to key government offices with economic and financial responsibilities in Persia.

Germany's Foreign Political Agenda for Persia and Taimurtash's Role

Germany's designs for Persia become more transparent when examining the official German documents linked to the Berlin visit of the Persian foreign minister Ali Gholi Khan Ansari in March 1928, the visit of the German foreign minister Gustav Stresemann to the Persian embassy in Berlin in April 1928, and the official visits of Taimurtash to Germany in July and September 1928. The objective of such an examination would be to outline the nature and evolution of German intentions in Persia as presented in the documents of the German Foreign Office prepared for diplomatic consultations with Persian government officials. This approach also singles out certain key personalities involved in the policy-making of this groundbreaking period of German–Persian relations.

In the briefing prepared for the German foreign minister Dr Stresemann for a meeting with Ansari it is recorded that in the ten years before World War I Ansari was the Persian representative in St Petersburg. After the war he became Persian ambassador to Angora (Ankara) and thereafter for six years Persian ambassador to Moscow. Although on the occasion cited above Ansari was on a private visit to Germany he attended official meetings throughout his stay, including meetings with Lindenblatt and the director of Bank für Deutsche Industrieobligationen, Dr Bötzkes in Berlin.[12]

Stresemann's briefing documents single out five key items to be negotiated during his proposed meeting with Ansari:

1 the negotiation of treaties between Germany and Persia;
2 a German financial adviser for Persia;
3 railway construction;
4 German industrial exports to Persia;
5 Junkers airline operations in Persia.

It can be deduced that the German Foreign Office had considered these topics to be of major significance for its designs towards Persia. Concerning the first item on the agenda, Germany's political objective was to ratify a number of treaties and agreements with the Persian government. Of prime importance were a treaty of friendship, a settlement agreement and a trade and shipping agreement that simultaneously would grant German exports a most-favoured-nation treatment. The briefing notes emphasise the German government's determination to secure most-favoured-nation treatment.[13]

Concerning German financial advisers, the briefing documents reveal that as a result of Millspaugh's resignation the Persian government had requested the German government's support in identifying suitable candidates for the office of financial adviser to the Persian government, a director for its proposed National Bank and a finance inspector.

Since the Persian legislation for the employment of foreign financial experts did not state clearly the scope of authority of its civil servants, at the request of both the German and Persian governments Dr Bötzkes, the director of Bank für Deutsche Industrieobligationen, had travelled to Persia in November 1927 to investigate the status quo and clarify what was expected from the requested German financial experts. When in Persia Bötzkes also drafted a statute for the National Bank.

Meanwhile, Dr Lindenblatt, director of the Kreditbank in Sofia, had been identified as the main candidate for the post of director of the National

Bank of Persia. Likewise the German ministry of finance had put forward Ministerialrat Schröder as the candidate for the office of finance inspector, mainly because of his expert knowledge in customs and tax matters.[14]

The third item on Stresemann's briefing dealt with railway construction in Persia. The Foreign Office briefing summarises that over the past three years the Persian government's special tax on tea and sugar had accumulated circa 18 million marks per annum, which was deposited at the Imperial Bank of Persia. The cost for the construction of the approximately 1,600 kilometres of railway was estimated to be around 300 million marks. There were three main groups of companies bidding for the construction of this railway. A German group organised by Brown, and a further German, French and Belgian group were competing for contracts for the construction of the northern section. An American group was bidding for the construction of the southern section of the railway.

Although the Persian government had initially planned to manage the railway project without foreign assistance, it was due to a change in strategy that it was prepared to consider having its railway project contracted out to foreign companies.[15] The precondition for the bidding companies was that they had to secure the financing of their project.[16]

Point four of the briefing addressed the question of German industrial exports to Persia. As mentioned in the previous chapters, the German ministry of finance had declared that it would accept an export cancellation guarantee. This guarantee would cover German exports to the Persian government. Hence, Brown was in the process of negotiating details of German industrial exports to Persia, including factories and electrical power stations.

The Foreign Office, under point five, declared itself satisfied with the performance and the scope of operations provided by the Junkers airline in Persia under its flight monopoly agreement.[17]

The following four items dominated a further briefing prepared for Stresemann, by the German Foreign Office, in conjunction with a breakfast meeting at the Persian embassy on 13 April 1928:

1 negotiations regarding German–Persian treaties and agreements;
2 railway construction;
3 German industrial exports to Persia;
4 German financial experts for Persia.

In the short period since Ansari's visit German priorities seemed to have shifted. As the matter of financial advisers was almost settled, commercial questions gained more weight. However, treaties and agreements remained the first topic on the agenda. It is these agreements which would provide the legal basis for solid economic relations between Germany and Persia.[18]

The document points out that the Foreign Office had sent Gesandtschaftsrat (Counsellor) Kolb to Tehran on 7 April 1928 with drafts of a treaty of friendship, a settlement agreement accompanied by a protocol on the legal position of German nationals in Persia, and a trade and shipping agreement. Since Kolb's documents were all in French, it enabled Schulenberg to forthwith present them to the Persian government and start immediate negotiations. The objective was to have these agreements ratified before 10 May 1928, the date of the termination of the German–Persian friendship and trade agreement. Were this to prove not feasible, the Foreign Office's plan was to reach temporary agreements on its most urgent concerns. These were the legal status of German nationals in Persia, and the terms for import-export of goods.[19]

With reference to the second question on Stresemann's agenda, railway construction, the state of affairs revealed that the German group of companies was awaiting the Persian decision over a proposal which could award them the contract for carrying out the initial groundwork for the entire Trans-Iranian Railway and the construction of two trial sections of 100 kilometres each. For the construction of part of the railway the German group had merged with the American company Ulen and a French group. Furthermore, it was believed that after completion of the two trial sections Persia would contract out the 300 million-mark project completely to the German group.[20]

On the subject of German industrial exports to Persia, point three on the agenda, Brown had managed to finalise and sign an agreement with the Persian Prime Minister over the delivery of German industrial exports to the value of 40 million marks. These included railway carriages, factory equipment, machinery and electrical goods.

The question of a German financial expert for Persia was still on the agenda. This was mainly because a suitable candidate for the post of financial adviser to the Persian government had not yet been identified. However, the German national Schröder was about to be appointed as finance inspector of the Persian government and in April Dr Lindenblatt had been confirmed as director of the National Bank of Persia.[21]

The third key meeting of German and Persian political decision makers evolved around the planned visit of Taimurtash to Germany. In July 1928 the German Foreign Office informed Brown of Taimurtash's plan to visit Berlin in July, on his way to Paris and London, and again on his return in August. According to a telegram from Schulenberg, Taimurtash had planned to negotiate with German companies over the purchase of an electrical power plant, a sugar factory, a cement factory, steel production as well as the construction of a small-scale aircraft manufacturing plant.

To make the most of Taimurtash's visit to Germany, the Foreign Office had insisted that the first series of trade negations between Taimurtash and German companies, should be held in July. The official reason for this, as disclosed to the Persian representative in Berlin, was that two key Foreign Office officials had intended to take their annual leave, and therefore would not be able to attend meetings with Taimurtash in August. Brown also had already been invited to join the trade negotiations with Taimurtash in July.[22]

Ministerialdirektor de Haas commented to Staatssekretär von Schubert, with reference to the two-day visit of Taimurtash in Berlin on 19 and 20 July 1928, that Taimurtash was the real person in charge of Persian government business.[23] De Haas further explained that Taimurtash had been trained in Russia and was promoted to be an officer of the Russian army. On his return to Persia in 1912, he was elected as a Member of Parliament. He served as a minister under several cabinets and since 1925 he had held the office of Hofminister (court minister). In recognition of his authority, he had been received by heads of state and foreign ministers during his European visits to Paris, London, Rome, and Bern.[24]

On arrival in Berlin and during his two-day visit in July, Taimurtash appointed Dr Schniewind, Ministerialrat im Preussischen Handelsministerium, as financial adviser to the Persian government on a two-year contract, replacing Millspaugh. Taimurtash also entered into initial negotiations regarding the appointment of a German finance inspector and a medical adviser. Furthermore, he met with the German industrial group led by the German company Krupp to negotiate the development of new industries and the exploration of minerals in Persia. Taimurtash also expressed the wish to talk to Junkers about the expansion of their airline operations in Persia.

According to de Haas, the Foreign Office planned to use Taimurtash's August visit to finalise any business outstanding from his July trade negotiations.[25] He believed that it was of utmost importance that due to the overwhelming significance and status of Taimurtash, a meeting between him and the German Reichspräsident Hindenburg should be arranged. Moreover, he recommended that an official dinner[26] in his honour should be organised by the German deputy foreign minister von Schubert.[27]

In support of de Haas's proposals, a further document originating from the German Foreign Office stated that Taimurtash was the Shah's right-hand man and next to him the most influential person in Persia. He reported directly to the Shah and not to parliament. German Foreign Office officials acknowledged that this left him even independent of the Persian cabinet.[28]

Hence, the visit of Taimurtash was regarded as an ideal opportunity not only for the improvement of economic relations but also for the progress of Germany's foreign relations with Persia through the ratification of treaties and agreements. Consequently, the Foreign Office intended to use Taimurtash's visit to finalise a series of treaties and agreements with Persia:

1 a treaty of friendship and arbitration agreement (*Schiedsvertrag*);
2 a trade and shipping agreement;
3 a settlement agreement (*Niederlassungsvertrag*);
4 a consular agreement (*Konsularvertrag*).

The negotiations on legal guarantees for German nationals in Persia had been almost finalised.

On the economic front, it was reported that as a result of their negotiations with Taimurtash, an international consortium led by the German companies Julius Berger, Philipp Holzmann and Siemens Bau-Union succeeded in winning a major contract for the construction of the Trans-Iranian Railway.[29] Moreover, Taimurtash negotiated with Brown, who was representing a German consortium led by Krupp, over industrial exports from Germany to Persia. Thus, the export contracts totalling 40 million marks were finalised. In addition, a further agreement securing a monopoly position for Junkers Flugzeugwerke A.G. in Persia was reached. In this context Taimurtash had insisted on visiting the aircraft manufacturing plant of Junkers.

After appointing Schniewind, Taimurtash intended to appoint a finance inspector, a geologist, a mineralogist, a director for the state-owned hospital in Tehran and a medical adviser. In a coded message de Haas informed Tehran of the good progress the negotiation of agreements and the economic dialogue were making.[30]

These results underlined the extraordinary importance of Taimurtash for the economic and political relations of Germany and Persia. Government officials were hopeful that a meeting between Taimurtash and Hindenburg could be arranged to further strengthen the bilateral relations.[31]

Taimurtash had initially presumed that the German Foreign Office did not have much interest in meeting him again on his way back to Tehran. He based his impression on the fact that the German foreign minister Stresemann and Staatssekretär von Schubert had been absent during his first round of official meetings in Berlin. Hence on his return to Tehran he had planned to stop over only one day in Berlin. When the Foreign Office became aware of Taimurtash's travel arrangements he was promptly invited to stay a few days longer. Taimurtash was made aware of the Foreign Office's efforts to arrange a meeting between him and Hindenburg, who was expected back in Berlin on 14 September 1928.[32] Taimurtash agreed to extend his stay and honour the attention given to him by German officials. On his arrival in Berlin he was invited to a reception in his honour at the Reichskanzlerpalais to which 80 of the most distinguished personalities from politics, public life, trade and industry were invited.[33]

On the Sunday of his visit Taimurtash was taken for a tour of Potsdam, visiting castles, a golf club and taking a cruise. In the evening he was invited to see the operetta *Casanova* followed by dinner at the restaurant Casanova. On the Monday of his visit he attended a reception at the Persian embassy, keeping the remainder of the week free of formal engagements.

On the Friday of his stay in Berlin, Taimurtash was officially received by the German Reichspräsident Hindenburg. During their meeting, which lasted 25 minutes, Hindenburg was mainly interested to learn about conditions in Persia. According to German sources Taimurtash appeared to be satisfied with his audience with the German Reichspräsident.[34]

During his visit in Berlin Taimurtash also had a breakfast meeting with the board of directors of the Deutsche Bank, and a dinner engagement with Freiherr von Richthofen. Moreover, he attended tea engagements with the Persian consul general and the company AEG. During his stay he was treated as a guest of the German government. He was provided with a Pullman on departure with which he travelled to the border of Poland where a further Pullman expected him.

The German Foreign Office had every reason to be satisfied with Taimurtash's collaboration during the series of meetings held with key individuals. Consequently obstacles that might have impeded German–Persian agreements were considered settled.

As a result of his negotiations with Taimurtash, Brown planned to return to Persia in October to further progress his projects.

Taimurtash appeared pleased with his visit to Germany. He left with the people he had met the positive impression of an intelligent and capable individual. Hence, German government officials trusted that the Shah would also be pleased with the reception of his Hofminister by Germany.[35]

By 1928 the German Foreign Office appeared to have had a clearer set of objectives regarding its intentions in Persia. The diplomatic briefings and the official documents accompanying the German government's objectives highlight the nature and evolution of German designs during the short period of negotiations under examination. On the one hand it would appear that on the German side the positive developments were based on a combined effort of government agencies, officials and representatives of industry. On the other hand it has become evident that Taimurtash was the key political figure who had been able to drive German foreign political and economic designs in Persia forward.

Development of the National Bank of Persia and the Role of Germans

Throughout the late 1920s, the National Bank of Persia established itself to a degree that it gradually, as an instrument in trade, started to contribute to the improvement of the Persian economy. One determining factor for the steady growth of the National Bank was the increasing number of qualified German banking experts employed by the bank.

Lindenblatt, the German director of the National Bank, was given from the beginning a free hand in the choice of his employees. Since he had difficulties in finding suitable Persian personnel he received approval from the Persian minister of finance for engaging foreign experts. Lindenblatt's main objective was to hire German banking experts, preferably with overseas experience. One of Lindenblatt's plans was to train these carefully chosen German nationals as financial experts for the Persian market; such experts were very few and much needed.[36]

However, at the same time Lindenblatt had reservations about the long-term job security for the Germans he employed, as he feared the consequences of possible uncertainties in the future of Persia for his staff. Hence, he had asked Schulenberg to investigate the possibility of a reassurance for his staff which would allow them to return to employment in Germany should it arise that they had to leave Persia. Lindenblatt felt that, given the small number of German nationals concerned (between 6 and 12) and the growing economic and political ties between both countries, it should not be too difficult to get the approval of the Reichsbank, Reichskreditgesellschaft or the Bank für Industrie-Obligationen for such a proposal.[37]

However, this concern was being overshadowed by a more immediate problem involving Schniewind, the new German financial adviser to the Persian government. Schniewind expected the Persian government to provide him with housing, apart from his 25,000 toman remuneration. The subsequent refusal of the Persian government to provide him with housing nearly resulted in a blow to German interests in Persia, since, if Schniewind had further delayed accepting his contract, a non-German expert would have been appointed in his place. To encourage Schniewind to accept his post, Taimurtash intervened and promised to provide him with a motorcar, although this was not a part of his contract. Furthermore, Schulenberg secured for Schniewind the house of the American railway expert Poland for 175 toman per month. The house featured 12 rooms and was in a prime location. Schulenberg called on the German Foreign Office to exercise their influence on Schniewind so that he would accept his contract. Lindenblatt shared Schulenberg's concern and felt that such an important matter should not fall victim to a trivial disagreement.[38]

In late November 1928 Lindenblatt reported that the National Bank had survived the most difficult stage of its initial development. The National Bank had an impressive 50 million marks in funds, of which the Persian government deposited a large percentage. The German employees of the National Bank received notable credit for the good results achieved throughout the start-up phase of the bank.

During these early stages of the bank's development Lindenblatt felt that he could not delegate any major responsibility to his Persian staff. As a result he continued to hire German nationals. He employed Otto Vogel as vice-director of the National Bank, Otto Döcker as the bank's chief inspector, Erich Klemme as supervisor of bureau, and an expert who was put in charge of government pawnbroking (*Pfandleihe*).[39]

For the branches of the National Bank that were about to be established in Bushehr and Tehran two further German nationals were employed: Baron Richard von Bodeman, the former branch manager of Süddeutsche Disconto-Gesellschaft, and Heinrich Rust, a former branch manager of a Bavarian bank. Lindenblatt had great faith in these two experts and believed in their positive contribution to the German efforts. Furthermore, Lindenblatt expected the arrival of Ernst Jedermann, former branch director of a German bank in Constantinople. Jedermann was Lindenblatt's prime candidate for the planned Tabriz branch of the National Bank. If this development was to continue, all major branches of the bank across the country would have been managed by German nationals who also had the opportunity to evolve into business experts for Persia. These favourable developments along with the progress of the railway syndicate and other commercial projects in Persia proved valuable to German industry and trade.[40]

The National Bank expanded geographically by opening its first major branches across the country. On 18 February 1929 the Bushehr branch was inaugurated. In charge of this along with director von Bodeman were vice-director Dr Franz Isphording, and Hran Frendian. The Tehran-Bazaar branch also opened on 18 February 1929, under its director Rust, supported by Ali Chems and Abol-Hassan Meykadeh. The Tabriz branch opened on 20 March 1929 under the directorship of Jedermann. In addition, Ferdinand Voigt was appointed as vice-director along with further key employees, Sarkies G. Apcar and Niko Kühnreich.[41]

By the end of 1929 the bank had expanded aggressively. Fifteen new branches were opened and several more were planned. The number of German nationals employed by the bank rose to over forty. Although, this fact also increased Lindenblatt's concern for the future job security of his German staff, he was convinced that by implication the National Bank was assisting German trade and commercial interests in Persia.[42]

The rapid growth of the National Bank as a major financial institution started to directly benefit Persian trade and commerce. The bank's growth was largely based on the good performance of its German employees, supporting with their growing business expertise Persia's economic development.

German Nationals in Persia Attract German Business

The appointment of a German financial adviser to the Persian government was largely politically motivated. It is most likely that the Shah and hence the Persian government did not want any foreign national involved in decision-making at a high level. However, they accepted the German national Schniewind. The Persian motives behind this appointment may have been similar to the motives of the Shah when appointing Millspaugh. The foremost motive must have been the Persian desire for loans from Germany. But politically the appointment of Schniewind also suggests Persian goodwill and respect towards Germany.

From a German point of view matters appeared more complicated. Personally Schniewind felt that he was effectively contributing less to the development of the Persian economy as a financial adviser than he would have preferred. From a German economic perspective the presence of Schniewind in a high position within the Persian ministry of finance increased the interest of German industry in Persia. The German Foreign Office was convinced of the political and economic significance resulting from the presence of a German expert in such an important position within the Persian government. Furthermore, Schniewind's presence as a German expert was also significant for the expansion of German economic influence in Persia.[43]

Schniewind's position at the Persian ministry of finance along with Lindenblatt's office as the director of the National Bank of Persia and the commercially important posts held by other German nationals contributed significantly to an increased level of confidence and trust in Persia, as a viable and sound emerging market for the economic activities of interested

German companies. The German ambition for economic expansion not only promised improved relations with Persia but also stimulated a host of new German investments. These were further encouraged through: the positive experiences of the Persian government with its German staff; the satisfaction of the Persian government with German economic activity; Germany's growing popularity in Persia in contrast to Britain and Russia; and the respect both countries appeared to maintain for each other.

German industrialists viewed the offices held, particularly by Lindenblatt and Schniewind, as a competitive advantage for German commercial interests in Persia. The case of the American financial advisers to the Persian government described earlier illustrated that Lindenblatt and Schniewind were well positioned to nurture a German bias. The National Bank supported German trade and commerce as a leading financial institution and its German staff installed confidence in German investors. Thus it can be argued that the National Bank was in more than one way turning into a Trojan horse for German economic influence in Persia. Furthermore, by 1930 the National Bank of Persia had reached a high level of autonomy, manifesting itself in its decision-making authority when faced with critical political and economic challenges.

Germany's Interpretation of Persia's Financial Crisis

Although the Persian government had increasingly gained formal control over its finances, from a German perspective the direction developments were taking constituted a serious threat to Persia's financial stability.

Persia's finances entered a particularly critical phase when the government budget for the fiscal year 21 March 1929 to 20 March 1930 was undoubtedly over-inflated. The likely government income for that year was about 25–26 million toman compared to a budgeted 34 million toman. The Persian finance minister Moshir ol Molk officially denied any discrepancies between the expected government income on one side and its expenditure on the other. Nevertheless, he tried to keep the situation under control by cutting government expenditure down to 30 million toman and limiting the remaining deficit by tapping into the Persian government's assets at the National Bank and in Europe at the Imperial Bank of Persia.[44]

Despite the serious deficit in the 1929/1930 budget, the Persian parliament decided to set the budget for the following year again at 34–35 million toman. The original recommendation to balance the budget at 30 million toman by the ministry of finance was outvoted after the intervention of Taimurtash during the assembly meeting. Taimurtash had argued that government income was to improve through a restructuring of the opium monopoly, as recommended by Schniewind, and the introduction of a progressive income tax and of a tobacco monopoly.

Schniewind and Lindenblatt, who both were consulted during the cabinet's budget session, failed to persuade cabinet members not to expect a government income of more than 30 million toman. Both believed that after the losses in previous years the restructuring of the opium monopoly could only increase government tax income to its former levels, and also that the effects of changes in income tax would take years to translate into real income for the government. Schniewind's warnings were disregarded when he tried to explain that the tobacco monopoly, as proposed by the government, was doomed to fail similarly to the way in which the opium monopoly had failed to achieve its projected results. Both Schniewind and Lindenblatt therefore expected a serious government budget deficit for the Persian fiscal year 1930/1931.

Schulenberg believed that Taimurtash was too intelligent to make the same mistake twice and that his motive could not have been an economic one. He believed that the true reason for pushing through an inflated budget was that Taimurtash intended to prove to the Shah the innocence of his friend Prince Firuz, the former finance minister. The Shah attributed the financial problems faced with during the previous budget year to the inability of Prince Firuz. Consequently, he had been held in detention as the person responsible for the 34 million toman inflated budget. Taimurtash's possible intention was to make the Shah believe that the actual reason for Persia's financial problems was that Prince Firuz was jailed and therefore could not pursue his duties as minister of finance.[45]

Schulenberg suspected that Taimurtash believed that extraordinary measures similar to those in the previous year could balance the budget. Information over government budget deficits was successfully shielded from the public. However, there was a new and growing exchange rate problem which could have proved a genuine threat to the Persian economy. The silver-based gheran was rapidly losing its value. Although quite stable at 48 gheran to the pound until March 1929, it had dropped to 56 gheran to the pound in October 1929, and 70 gheran to the pound at the end of January 1930. The gheran's decrease in value had brought public opinion into turmoil. It slowed down imports and negatively affected the gheran-based salaries and scholarships paid out overseas.

In the search for the cause of the crisis it did not take long until the government's money-issuing bank, the Imperial Bank of Persia, was accused. Schulenberg was convinced that on the contrary the Imperial Bank was doing its best to keep the situation under control. He believed that the true reason for the gheran's drop was the fall in the price of silver on the London market. The situation in Persia was becoming progressively worse due to the inevitable decrease of hard currency movements in Persia.

Although, the Persian government had tried to improve the situation by prohibiting the import of silver coins and bars, this measure proved to have no significant effect. A further approach was to base the value of the gheran on gold instead of silver. According to the German financial experts the main problem with this solution was the concession held by the Imperial Bank of Persia that was still valid for 20 years. To overcome this situation Schniewind had proposed that the majority of the shares of the Imperial Bank should be bought. But the government dismissed his suggestion, since such a take-over could not have been executed with the necessary confidentiality. Therefore Schniewind proposed that to stabilise the gheran the National Bank should be assigned a currency exchange monopoly. Such a monopoly would have allowed the bank to balance export and imports through, for example, limiting the availability of hard currency for the import of luxury goods. Yet the government and Taimurtash dismissed this recommendation also, since in their opinion it infringed the sovereignty of the Imperial Bank and would have jeopardised Persian–British negotiations at a sensitive phase.[46]

Consequently Taimurtash presented his own solution to the problem. Unaware of the consequences, he proposed to attach the Persian silver-based currency to a foreign gold-based currency. For this purpose he was determined to enter negotiations with the American government and American banks.

Schniewind believed that it was unlikely for the Americans to consider such a proposal coming from a country like Persia. If the Americans were to accept Taimurtash's proposal, they would do so only on conditions that would provide them with extensive control over Persia. At the very least the Americans would expect to replace the financial adviser to the Persian Government with their own adviser who would expect to have the right of veto in all Persian overseas business. The Americans would most likely also request that the current director of the National Bank be replaced by an American. Hence the Persian government would have to surrender its sovereignty to a degree that also compelled it to consent to America supplying its armed forces, leading the construction of its railway network and exercising control over many other sectors.

Schniewind was convinced that Taimurtash's plan would fail in its initial phases and that the Shah would not give his approval to a plan that would compromise his country's financial independence. Following the Philippine model, Schniewind had proposed that Persia should apply for a 'Gold exchange fund' at the International Bank in Basel.

Schulenberg was convinced that both Taimurtash's and Schniewind's proposals would require a period of lengthy negotiations, and that Persia needed a faster solution to stabilise its currency. He expected the gheran to stabilise without much intervention when its value reached the level of the silver price in London. The outcome of this crisis was also crucial for the continuation of German trade with Persia.[47]

To control this financial crisis, on 25 February 1930 the Persian government finally opted to introduce a law that would give the National Bank control over foreign exchange. Moreover, against the recommendations of Schniewind, it was decided that Persia should introduce a gold-based gheran in one and a half years. The control over foreign exchange meant a significant strengthening of the position of the National Bank, but also a significant loss of power for the Imperial Bank. Britain reacted with protest and alleged that this decision of parliament was in conflict with the monopoly concession granted to the Imperial Bank.[48]

Form a German perspective, Persia's finances were based on robust foundations with a potential for further improvement. However, through mismanagement the government had caused a recurring budget deficit and an unstable currency. The Germans saw, next to a repeatedly inflated budget, the creation of an inappropriate government reserve, misjudged monetary policy, and corruption as further contributing factors to Persia's financial instability.[49]

From a German standpoint Persia's financial instability was largely the result of avoidable financial mismanagement. As described earlier, despite attempted budget corrections, a deficit of about 4 million toman resulted from the inflated budget in the budget year 1929/1930. The government income for the budget year 1930/1931 was also likely to have been overestimated by about 5–6 million toman. Also, since the budget for the year 1930/1931 did not acknowledge the deficit of the budget year 1929/1930, a total deficit of 9–10 million toman was to be expected in 1930. The measures undertaken to cover up this deficit could only defer the effects of Persia's financial mismanagement by one or two years. Particularly in the context of the Persian government's plan to convert the gheran to a gold-based currency, the government's financial mismanagement, which also caused its failure to meet payment deadlines, damaged the trust of local and foreign observers in Persia's financial stability.[50]

For example, in a period when Persia was planning to construct a railway, which was financially an immense project, the government decided to create a government reserve. This reserve was to be financed through the royalties paid by the Anglo-Persian Oil Company. Consequently these royalties were not available for the government's budget anymore and could be regarded as a waste of available foreign currency in a difficult time. It was fairly unrealistic for Persia to implement simultaneously two big projects such as railway construction and a government reserve. This policy further contributed to the devaluation of the gheran.[51]

A number of further miscalculations also contributed to the destabilisation of the Persian economy. Although the government decided to take control over foreign currency exchange to improve its finances, in reality it created a barrier for trade and discredited its exchange policy nationally and internationally. The main reasons for this were the lack of foreign currency holders, deteriorating confidence in the government's ability and the expansion of currency control from a defined list of imports to almost all imports.

In a further questionable move the Persian government decided to base the value of its currency on gold. A preferable approach would have been for the government to try to stabilise its currency through other means and thereby build up public confidence, before attempting such a controversial move.[52]

A final reason for Persia's financial instability was the amount of corruption at all levels of administration and government. To stabilise Persia's financial situation a German report proposed a number of solutions that mainly aimed at increasing the Persian government's overall tax income.

Foremost among these was the recommendation of an improvement of taxation for Persia's most significant tax contributor, the agricultural sector. The tax rate for this sector was 3.5 per cent of the unprocessed harvest. Statistical research reveals that the total annual value of the unprocessed harvest in Persia amounted to approximately 200 million toman. Hence, at a tax rate of 3.5 per cent a tax income of 7 million toman could be expected. In reality this sector only contributed 5 million toman in tax.

The introduction of a tobacco monopoly could also have improved the Persian government's tax income significantly. According to the available statistics farmers generated an income of 1.2 million toman from the production of cigarette tobacco. The sale of the end product, cigarettes, generated about 9 million toman, which left a gap of 7.8 million toman. It was conceivable that after cost a net profit of 3–4 million toman could be achieved from the sale of cigarettes. If the Persian government did introduce a tobacco monopoly it could tap into this profit and without increasing the prices for the end user generate a tax income of several million toman annually.[53]

A closer look at the Persian opium monopoly regulation reveals that it must have been one of the government's most inefficient regulatory policies. The tax income from this sector was 1 million toman whereas the cost for the administration of the opium monopoly was 0.5 million toman. Therefore 50 per cent of the total tax income was spent on administrating the monopoly. The principles on which the collection of opium tax was based were regarded as impractical and prone to fraud. A far simpler method of taxation in the form of a fixed tax based on the area of opium cultivation could have proved far more effective. Thus, a tax of 8–10 toman could have been levied for each 1,000 square metres, generating over 5 million toman in extra tax revenue for the Persian government.

Further considerations to improve tax income were to combat corruption within the civil service, to introduce a form of income tax particularly for companies, and to improve tax income from alcohol and farm animal slaughter.[54]

From a German perspective, it was similarly important that Persian government expenditure was reduced. As a first step it was felt critical that the entire Persian administration was reorganised and bureaucracy cut down. In a next step it was urged to restructure and simplify the budget by changing the budget laws, reorganising accountancy and the tendering and auditing of accounts. It was further recommended to increase the authority assigned to the post of the minister of finance. As a consequence a 25 per cent cut in personnel requirements could have been achieved that would have resulted in a significant cut in government expenditure.[55]

To deal with its economic crisis the Persian government decided to appoint a supreme economic council with the mandate to provide solutions for its economic challenges. The council consisted of the following members: under-secretary in the ministry of industry and commerce Bayat; head of the economic section and former envoy of the Persian legation in Berlin Alamir; Schniewind; Lindenblatt; the legal adviser of the Persian ministry of justice and French citizen Hesse; and the head of Persian customs, the Belgian citizen Dekercheer.[56]

The European-dominated council had no decision-making authority but was solely an advisory body. Schulenberg was sceptical of the effectiveness of such a council regarding its influence over the developments affecting the Persian economy.[57] Ultimately, the state of Persian finances could not only compromise German nationals working in Persia but also damage German–Persian economic relations in their infancy.

Taimurtash's Success Secures the National Bank of Persia as a Foothold for Germany

Taimurtash was instrumental to German–Persian relations. As much as Brown initiated the relations of both countries after the war it was Taimurtash who was key to the development of German–Persian relations on an economic as well as political level thereafter. Taimurtash was part of almost every aspect of German involvement in Persia throughout the late 1920s. This might not be surprising considering his influence within Persia and its government. But just how instrumental he was may become evident after considering a number of political developments associated with him.

In May 1930 Taimurtash officially declared his withdrawal from Persia's foreign policy. Yet Schulenberg was not quite convinced of Taimurtash's intention. He felt that this move just transferred Taimurtash's influence from the front to the back of the stage where he would continue to have the same influence as before. Rumours alleged that Taimurtash had to withdraw from Persia's foreign policy because in the eyes of the Shah and the Persian public he was exercising a degree of authority that should have been the prerogative of the government. Schulenberg speculated that the true reason for Taimurtash's withdrawal was his intention to avoid responsibility for the upcoming and unpopular extension of the concession of the Anglo-Persian Oil Company.[58]

Consequently, the new Persian foreign minister Forughi informed all foreign representatives in writing that they should in future approach the Foreign Office directly with enquiries. This official document implied that Taimurtash was not to be contacted any more in matters of foreign policy. Although, according to German sources Taimurtash personally and repeatedly confirmed his withdrawal from foreign policy, Schulenberg was still not convinced. He was certain that Taimurtash would not only maintain his power over the cabinet but also determine important foreign political matters.[59]

Schulenberg's view was supported by the fact that Taimurtash had just earned the highest level of appreciation from the Shah for persuading the Imperial Bank of Persia to give up its money-printing rights to the National Bank.[60] It had long been a desire of the Shah to transfer the money-printing rights awarded to the Imperial Bank by the Qajar dynasty to the new National Bank of Persia. The Shah's wish materialised when the Persian government managed to buy out the Imperial Bank's money-printing rights for £200,000 in a contract with Sir Sidney Roger, chairman of the governing board of the Imperial Bank. Concessions made to the Imperial Bank for this transaction included the suspension of payment of 60 per cent of the bank's profits to the Persian government, the removal of the

Persian government's control commissioner, and the pledge still to consider including the Imperial Bank in government business. Moreover, both banks promised each other to abandon what had proved to be an unhealthy competition and instead maintain a level of cooperation. The credit for this milestone, which was a major victory for the Pahlavi era and possibly only comparable with the cancellation of the capitulation rights, was given to Taimurtash and Lindenblatt.[61]

The currency exchange monopoly implemented in the early 1930s by Lindenblatt and Schniewind to stabilise the silver-based gheran had also proved successful. New measures introduced kept the gheran exchange rate at about 60 gheran to the pound, despite the silver price falling by a further 25 per cent during that year, which would have meant that the gheran's actual value should have been about 100 gheran to the pound. The exchange rate stability achieved through Lindenblatt and Schniewind's efforts contributed significantly to Persia's economic and trade activities.[62]

However, the currency exchange monopoly was regarded as only one measure among many aimed at ensuring Persia's financial stability, which ultimately was to be achieved through the controversial introduction of a gold-based currency. The date for the introduction of Persia's new bank notes issued by the National Bank was 31 March 1931. Therefore the National Bank had taken preparatory steps to ensure a successful changeover of currency. The Persian parliament had approved on 16 February 1931 a loan to the ministry of trade and industry to meet the capital expenditure required for the establishment of a mint. The machinery and required equipment for this new mint had been ordered in Germany. Moreover, in February 1931 two German experts were appointed to run the operations of the mint. The Persian nickel-based coins were ordered and manufactured directly in Germany and a contract for the manufacturing of the copper-based coins was also expected to go to a German company. However, it was envisaged that the silver-based coins and a limited number of gold coins would be produced at the new mint in Tehran.[63]

Schulenberg believed that although Taimurtash often disagreed and argued with Schniewind he nevertheless respected his advice.[64] Schniewind's contract, which had commenced on 24 December 1928, was due to end on 24 October 1930. According to Schulenberg, the Persian government never granted Schniewind the executive powers he needed to implement his ideas. Moreover, even his advice and suggestions were regularly ignored. Schulenberg was convinced that the Persian government could have avoided financial difficulties if it had complied with the recommendations of its German financial adviser.[65]

In a report Schniewind recounts his term of office, including a list of 44 specific accomplishments, such as his appointment as vice president of the administrative body of the National Bank of Persia. He recounts agreeing at the beginning of his term of office, in an internal arrangement with finance minister Farzin, to co-sign all decrees leaving the ministry. If for any reason an agreement was not reached the matter was to be brought forward to and decided by the cabinet. Yet, according to Schniewind, the cabinet generally had only one opinion and that was the opinion of Taimurtash. As a result, Taimurtash was in real terms running Persia's economic policy and regardless of the agreement between Farzin and Schniewind, he continued to do so. Schniewind considered the economic policies advocated by Taimurtash as unsuitable in many instances, and his unwillingness to consider his advice as counterproductive. Yet it was Schniewind who would have been held accountable for Persia's economic policy in public.[66]

Schniewind came to the conclusion that the Persian government was not yet prepared to give a foreign national any genuine executive authority. To him it appeared that Persia was looking for a foreign individual who could be charged with full responsibility for government decisions on a national and international level, but in reality did not interfere with government business. Therefore, Schniewind felt that more harm than advantage might result for Germany were he to stay in office for any longer, particularly since the Persian government's decision in 1930 to disregard his warnings and introduce a gold-based currency had caused in 1931 the devaluation of the gheran by 50 per cent. Hence, in consultation with Schulenberg, he decided to take no action regarding an extension of his expiring contract with the Persian government.[67] Nor did Taimurtash show any genuine interest in an extension of Schniewind's contract.

In a letter Lindenblatt expressed his regret for the loss of Schniewind, which left him with only Vogel, his deputy, with whom he really could discuss important matters. Lindenblatt described the position of the bank and his office as difficult. German companies such as Siemens and Brünner Maschinenfabrik had failed to win contracts with the Shah who, according to Lindenblatt, must have been one of very few people in the world with the power to control a country single-handedly. During this difficult phase the Shah did surprise the Germans by approaching them with the proposal to construct in joint venture a new cotton factory in Mazanderan. Lindenblatt forthwith tried to appoint a German expert on behalf of the National Bank to survey the feasibility and requirements of the project with the necessary discretion.[68]

According to Grobba from the German Foreign Office this project was of vital political interest to Germany. The Shah had not only without any encouragement approached Germany with his proposal but he also had offered to finance 40 per cent of the total cost of the project privately. The Shah expected a German government loan to cover the remaining 60 per cent of the cost. This was the first time ever that a commercial partnership between the Shah and German investment capital was attempted. Grobba believed that the success of this cooperation could lead to major future economic developments. Therefore, on behalf of the German Foreign Office and on the recommendation of the National Bank of Persia, despite its extraordinary terms of payment, he recommended that a government loan should be granted for this project.[69]

On 5 November 1930 the seventh legislative term of the Persian parliament ended. During the last ceremonial meeting parliament's president Dadgar praised the legislative work of the assembly by presenting an account of its achievements. According to Schulenberg, these included the creation of the National Bank of Persia and an agricultural bank, the granting of loans for new military equipment, the introduction of a gold-based currency, the acquisition of the money-printing rights from the Imperial Bank of Persia, the introduction of a national dress code, the creation of a major wireless station, the setting up of factories, the abolition of capitulation rights, the ratification of agreements on terms of equal rights, the construction of railways and roads. and the creation of a ministry for trade and commerce.[70]

Many of Dadgar's legislative triumphs had not yet been finalised. This included the establishment of an agricultural bank, the introduction of a gold-based currency and the setting up of factories. At the same time Taimurtash, who also was the leader of the majority party, Progress, which claimed 124 of the 128 parliamentarians as its members, could be credited with being the leading figure behind the majority of the already implemented projects.[71]

Taimurtash used among other means also the National Bank of Persia as a vehicle to drive forward what he thought was best for Persia's progress. Since it has been established that on a regular basis parliamentary decisions revolved around the person of Taimurtash, considering the degree of German involvement in the National Bank, he actually facilitated Germany's access to and participation in what were some of the most central decisions for Persia. This becomes clearer when we consider that the National Bank played directly or indirectly a role in the majority of what parliament president Dadgar praised as the achievements of his legislative term. Accordingly, Germany had access to intelligence regarding and participated in the creation of the National Bank of Persia, the granting of loans for new military equipment, the introduction of a gold-based currency, the acquisition of the money-printing rights from the Imperial Bank of Persia, the creation of a major wireless station, the setting up of factories, the ratification of agreements on terms of equal rights, the construction of railways and roads, and the creation of a ministry for trade and commerce.

Self-evidently German relations with Persia had come a long way. The German move toward Persia had therefore succeeded in achieving results that were rewarded through improved economic relations with Persia. The National Bank showed that it had the potential to become central to Germany's interest in Persia, in the same way it had become central to Persia's national and overseas interests and activities.

With its status as the National Bank of the government of Persia and the privileges acquired thereby, the National Bank had reached a status that was beyond competition.[72] In pursuit of its objectives the National Bank, and therefore its German experts, had managed to avoid major conflicts with Britain, Russia and America. As a result we could conclude that now for the first time Germany had a relatively safe foothold in Persia. From a German perspective this meant that a National Bank entertaining German interests had the potential of turning into a Trojan horse for German foreign political and economic influence in Persia.

4

CHALLENGES FOR GERMAN FOREIGN POLICY TOWARDS PERSIA AND THE NATIONAL BANK

It has been argued that the National Bank in its short history had become central to many of the Persian government's major achievements, which proved advantageous to German interests, albeit indirectly. It has also been documented that, by employing German nationals in key positions, the Persian government had on the one hand gained know-how but on the other hand had elevated Germany into a privileged position within its government apparatus. Therefore, although the Bank's staff were employed as civil servants of the Persian government and formally did not represent German economic or political interest, it is plausible that they were biased towards Germany, in the same way other foreign nationals with posts within the Persian government had displayed their national favouritism. The conclusion reached was that this bias indirectly contributed to an increase of German trade and economic activity in Persia.

It is arguable, however, whether the German government did have a coherent foreign political agenda towards Persia, since it was the business interests of German entrepreneurs that mainly prompted the Foreign Office's interactions with Persia. Lobbied by these entrepreneurs, the German Foreign Office had little alternative but, for example, to endorse the employment of its nationals by the Persian government.

German projects in Persia were mostly either co-financed or dependent on a financial guarantee or on bank loans. Since the National Bank was becoming the key foreign trade facilitator in Persia its German bias assisted German entrepreneurs in pursuit of loans to more easily secure contracts.

However, the German government's interest in Persia did not seem to increase with its growing economic ties. German entrepreneurs who lobbied the government only occasionally received what was perceived as superficial support from the German Foreign Office for their projects. The acknowledgement letter of Kommerzienrat Berger from the company Julius Berger Tiefbau A.G., one of the larger investors in Persia, for the assistance received from the Foreign Office and Schulenberg with respect to a bid for the construction of the Persian railway, is a rare example for official support received by a German company.[1] At the same time, there were very few initiatives originating from the German Foreign Office, providing an insight into official government policy.

The 'cooperation' between German entrepreneurs and the National Bank proved more fruitful for German economic ties with Persia. For example, the National Bank agreed to provide a loan of 250,000 marks to the concession holders for the construction of electrical power stations in Rasht and Pahlavi. This loan was guaranteed by the German company AEG, which was the main supplier of the power stations. Similar arrangements between the National Bank and AEG were also envisaged for projects in Tabriz and Isfahan. The main advantage of this type of agreement for German industrial companies was that the National Bank could directly settle their accounts through cash payments. Thus it was not necessary for the German companies to rely on loans secured in Persia for financial transfers.[2]

A more in-depth understanding of German foreign policy towards Persia can be gained by investigating a series of incidents that originated in Germany. These were centred around left-wing propaganda directed against the Shah and his regime, which in 1931 culminated in a political crisis between Germany and Persia. It is of particular interest to see how this crisis came about and how the German Foreign Office dealt with it.

On the Verge of Political Crisis

In 1931 one of the first hints of impending political trouble between Germany and Persia came from Mayer, an official of the German embassy in Tehran. Mayer reported to the German Foreign Office that as a result of the appearance of several revolutionist leaflets, including *Paykar* and *Setarehye Jahan*, the Persian government had expressed its concerns over the indoctrination by communist influences of its students studying in Germany. As a result the Persian Foreign Office had looked at relocating its students to other, less risky countries, in the event Germany's action against the perceived threat proved ineffective.[3]

As a direct response to Persia's concern the district court of Berlin-Central issued a court order against the publishers of *Paykar*, Dr Carl Wehner and his affiliates.[4] As a result of this court order of 29 May 1931, the complete issue number 6 (1 June 1931) of the leaflet *Paykar* was to be confiscated and serve as evidence. The main claim against *Paykar* was that it contained several insults against the Shah of Persia. These included the allegation that the Shah was to blame for allowing the future interests of Persia to become a 'toy' of the Imperial Bank and the British. A further passage alleged that the Shah was more concerned with the purchase of goods than the progress of his country.[5]

After the Persian government's request for his deportation, Grobba identified the Persian student Morteza Alawi as the main character behind the trouble. Grobba consulted in this matter with the Prussian minister of interior, who, together with the Berlin chief of police, was investigating Alawi's case. Grobba explained that Alawi had admitted to the police headquarters that he belonged to a group whose stated mission was to express and further their resentment against Persia's current political rule, and to promote Persia's economic development according to a cooperative model. The publication of this group, which was also known as Revolutionäre Republikanische or Kommunistische Partei Persiens, was the monthly leaflet *Der Rote Stern* (The Red Star). From February 1931 this leaflet was renamed *Paykar* and appeared fortnightly. Moreover, Alawi had admitted that he was a supporter of *Paykar* and that he had invested 8,000 marks in its publishing house, Orientverlag.[6]

This evidence led Grobba to believe that Alawi was not, as he had claimed, a socialist but a communist and the intermediary of a German-based organisation which aimed at overturning the Shah. Alawi's political activities also violated the conditions of his asylum status.

Grobba was convinced that Alawi's activities were severely damaging Germany's relations with Persia. The Persian government had repeatedly insisted on Alawi's deportation while criticising Germany's reluctance to take any serious action. Similar complaints were also brought to the attention of the Foreign Office by the Persian ambassador in Berlin, to the attention of the German ambassador in Tehran, and to German ambassadors resident in other countries. In this context the Persian government had argued that the French government had complied with its request for the deportation of several activist Persian students from France and, moreover, had managed to prohibit the distribution of *Paykar*.

The ill feeling of the Persian government was beginning to have a most unfavourable influence upon economic relations between Germany and

Persia, which until then had been developing slowly but amicably. Persia's discontent with Germany manifested itself in the termination of negotiations with German companies over significant commercial contracts. The anxiety of the Persian government over the activities of revolutionary Persian organisations in Germany became even more apparent in a telegram received by Grobba from the German ambassador in Tehran. According to the ambassador's report the Persian heir to the throne, who was accompanied by Taimurtash, had decided not to interrupt his trip to Switzerland with a stopover in Germany. Grobba felt that, in view of the offensive material spread by Asadoff, a member of the same revolutionary organisation as Alawi, during Taimurtash's visit to Germany in 1928, the anxiety of the heir to the throne was justified.[7]

Grobba also described it as intolerable that the political activities of a single Persian asylum seeker in Germany, who had violated his asylum terms, were threatening both the political and particularly the important economic relations between Germany and Persia. The Foreign Office had forthwith to insist on Alawi's deportation, for which it had already been appealing since March 1931. Grobba asked Severing, the Prussian minister of the interior, to comply with the wishes of the Foreign Office in a way that would enable him to inform the Persian government of Alawi's deportation before the heir to the throne left Persia for Switzerland. Grobba also made it clear that if Alawi was not deported he would not be able to accept responsibility for the consequences. He feared that non-compliance could cultivate a deep and long lasting ill will in the Persian government, which would result in a severe damage to Germany's economic relations with Persia.[8]

In a telegram, Blücher, the newly appointed German ambassador to Tehran, reported the Persian reaction to an article by Leo Mattias published in the German paper *Münchener Illustrierte*. This article triggered off a malicious campaign by the Persian press against Germany for tolerating such articles and for its failure to prohibit centres of anti-Persian propaganda in Germany. The newspaper *Iran* reported in its lead article that either Germany had one of the most incompetent governments, since it was not capable of preventing insults directed at another country, or the German government was prepared to watch the reputation of another country being dishonoured.[9]

The Persian foreign minister made the strength of the Shah's feelings known to Blücher, who tried to put things into perspective for the Shah. Blücher asked the Foreign Office to demand that in their future editions German newspapers, including the *Münchener Illustrierte*, should publicly distance themselves from Mattias and his convictions. Blücher also requested that the Foreign Office should remind the Prussian minister of the interior of the urgency of decisive action against *Paykar*.[10]

An article published in the reputable and government friendly newspaper *Iran* reflected the Persian government's resentment against Leo Mattias's abusive publications and the handling of the *Paykar* affair by Germany. Referring to the temperament of the Shah, Blücher worried that it was conceivable that after reading such an article the Shah could become so infuriated that he might implement decisions that would destroy at once all German accomplishments and achievements to date.[11]

Background of the German–Persian Anti-Shah Propaganda Crisis

This German–Persian conflict originally centred on three individuals, Asadoff, Leo Mattias and Mortaza Alawi, as well as the publications *Der Rote Stern* and *Paykar*. Since 1926 there had been evidence of the activities of a Persian organisation in Germany, seemingly connected with communists, whose objective was to work towards a coup in Persia. The intermediary of this organisation was originally the Persian student Asadoff. Asadoff, who was also a member of the International League against Imperialism, was later joined by other Persian students known to the Persia embassy in Berlin, including Alawi. This group called itself Revolutionäre Republikanische Partei Persiens, Sektion Deutschland and later Kommunistische Partei Persiens. The group printed and distributed its first propaganda leaflet from a small Berlin-based printer in 1927. During the visit to Germany by Taimurtash in 1928, Asadoff had initiated a German-language leafleting campaign. His plan was to protest against any kind of official reception for what he called a '*gemeinen Mörder*' (common or mean murderer).[12]

A short while later a second leaflet appeared which contained personal insults against the Shah, his government and Taimurtash. This leaflet advocated a coup in Persia. As a direct result the Persian embassy asked the German Foreign Office to deport Asadoff and his collaborators on behalf of the Persian government. On 15 November 1928 the then Prussian minister of the interior, Grzesinski, ordered the deportation of Asadoff. However, since a Member of Parliament, Dr Breitscheid, had intervened, this deportation order was not executed. Breitscheid had been approached by a group of Persian students who had argued that since Asadoff was a socialist he therefore had the right of asylum in Germany. In an article the communist newspaper *Die Welt am Abend* also spoke in support of Asadoff. Breitscheid criticised what he called the Foreign Office's endeavours to please the Shah, '*Liebedienerei für den Shah*', during a session of the Reichstag and in an article published in *Vorwärts*. He pointed out that the German Foreign Office was allowing itself to become the henchman of a foreign government and that such a stance was not consistent with the honour of Germany and the spirit of a democratic republic.

In November 1928 the Shah sent Bahrami to the Foreign Office, with the task of emphasising the Shah's personal interest in the deportation of Asadoff. Despite this and other similar attempts the Prussian interior ministry declared on 18 December 1928 that it could not justify Asadoff's deportation, since according to its findings Asadoff was cleared of the claim of causing domestic political disorder or engaging in activities against the German government. Nevertheless, because of the Foreign Office's fear of serious foreign political implications following this ruling, the interior ministry was prepared to negotiate.

When Taimurtash was informed of the German interior ministry's readiness to negotiate, he requested that the Shah's personal opinion on this matter should receive serious consideration. He pointed out that the Shah was temperamental and unforgiving, and that he was convinced that any government should be able to prevent revolutionary activities aimed at the leaders and civil servants of a befriended nation.[13]

By this time Asadoff already had decided to leave Germany voluntarily for Moscow. However, the Foreign Office was determined to prevent his return to Germany. On 22 February 1929 Stresemann appealed in a letter to Grezinski to reconsider the interior ministry's decision. Before a final judgement could be reached, a new immigration decree of the Prussian police, dated 1 January 1930, made it officially possible to deport foreign nationals on grounds of threatening the relations of Germany with another government. The Foreign Office viewed this decree as a satisfactory formal solution for Asadoff's case.

In July 1929 a new publication, *Der Rote Stern,* gave the Foreign Office cause for concern. This leaflet depicted itself as the organ of the central committee of the communist party of Persia. It was printed by Haag-Drugolin A.G. in Leipzig and distributed by the communist-friendly publisher Peuvah in Berlin. The German Foreign Office repeatedly intervened to stop the publication and distribution of this leaflet, but failed. The Persian embassy, which had found Alawi and a group of students responsible for the publication of *Der Rote Stern*, requested their deportation. The police headquarters, however, rejected this request when it was put forward by the German Foreign Office. Soon after, a further leaflet printed by Haag-Drugolin A.G. entitled *Communiqué der kommunistishen Partei Persiens* appeared in Paris.

The suicide of a Persian student by the name of Atai at the Persian embassy in Berlin resulted in further tensions among Persian students in

Germany, adding to the problems of the Foreign Office. In May 1930 the inspector general in charge of all Persian students studying in Europe travelled from Paris to Berlin to investigate the matter. He requested that the German Foreign Office should assist in maintaining discipline among Persian students, and if necessary emulate their French counterparts in showing their support by deporting problematic students. On several occasions the Persian ambassador to Paris successfully presented similar requests for the deportation of problematic students to the German ambassador in Paris, von Hoesch. Yet the Prussian police headquarters still maintained that it did not have a legal justification by which it could warrant the deportation of Persian students active in Germany.[14]

In late 1930 an article by Leo Mattias was published in the newspapers *Montagspost* and *Wiener Freie Presse*. In his article Mattias claimed to have witnessed the brutal execution of the son of a Ghashghai Khan. Allegedly the victim was tortured to death by being walled in with fresh clay on top of a hill. This article caused a storm of anger in the Persian press. Further investigations by the German embassy in Tehran revealed that the Mattias article was completely fictional. When confronted, Mattias admitted that he had heard the story from reliable sources.

On 17 February 1931 a group by the name of Aktionskomitee der Persischen Republikaner gathered for a conference in Köln. On this occasion a leaflet was prepared and sent to a number of left-oriented newspapers across Europe. This leaflet contained protest against what it called the terror regime of Reza Khan. The police headquarters in Berlin disclosed that this group had intermediary agents outside Persia, in Berlin, Prague, Lemberg, Zurich, Geneva, Köln, Brussels, Paris, Haifa and Delhi. The objective of this left-wing group was to influence Persia's intellectuals overseas by upholding the idea of a republic as the ideal model for Persia. Wehner, the publisher of *Paykar* was closely affiliated with this group and Alawi.

The first issue of *Paykar* was published in Berlin on 15 February 1931. *Paykar*, like earlier revolutionary publications, attacked the Shah, his government and Taimurtash in an offensive way. It also called for a coup and combined propaganda for Russia and communism. The Persian ambassador in Berlin had legally taken an injunction against Alawi and other individuals who had been involved in *Paykar*, which resulted in the first six issues of the leaflet being officially confiscated. Yet, only in one case did the police succeed in confiscating a complete edition of about 2,000 copies. The Berlin police refused to confiscate further issues of *Paykar* without a court order issued by the prosecuting attorney. As a result further copies of *Paykar* regularly appeared in several countries including Persia. The continuing publication of *Paykar* and the increasing offensiveness of its articles left the Persian government and Shah to believe that the German government was not seriously interested in taking action against the disruptive activists.[15]

As mentioned earlier all efforts of the Foreign Office to persuade the Prussian ministry of interior to deport Alawi proved fruitless. The Berlin police headquarters were not prepared to deport Alawi on grounds of violation of immigration laws. Moreover, although Alawi had admitted to the police that he sympathised with *Paykar*, and although the police had discovered that Alawi was involved in the distribution of the leaflets and even was a shareholder of its publishing house, they argued that they were not convinced of Alawi's collaboration with *Paykar*.

On 4 October 1931 a further article by Mattias appeared in the *Münchener Illustrierte Presse*. His article, entitled '*Der Kaiser ohne Herkunft*' (The emperor without descent), outraged a Shah who had been exasperated for the past four years by defamatory publications originating in Germany. The fact that this article claimed that the Shah had been a porter at the German embassy in Tehran and had received a slap in the face by the former German ambassador was particularly insulting and abusive for the Shah. In actuality Reza Shah had been commander of the German embassy guards. Grobba believed that it was quite inconceivable that a foreign ambassador would physically assault the host commander of his embassy guards. Accordingly, he concluded that the entire article was pure fiction. The Foreign Office had at once contacted the Persian embassy in Berlin to explain the mendacity of the article. However, it was too late since the publication of this article caused a conflict that essentially not only jeopardised German–Persian foreign and economic relations but also threatened to end them.[16]

Consequences of the German–Persian Political Crisis

On 23 June 1931 Taimurtash's Armenian wife, Tatiana, arrived in Berlin to enrol her son at a German boarding school. On the grounds of the overwhelming political power of her husband in Persia and the influence of Taimurtash over commercial contracts, the German Foreign Office recommended a social programme to be organised for her on arrival.[17] Since the heir to the throne, Mohammad Reza, was to be educated in Switzerland, Taimurtash accompanied him on his voyage to Lausanne in September 1931. Soon after he rejoined his wife, who was undergoing surgery in Berlin. During his stay in Europe Taimurtash had also planned to visit Italy, France and Britain before returning to Persia in December. During his absence from Persia Taimurtash was represented by the Persian minister of defence.[18]

It was during Taimurtash's absence from Persia that the Shah became so incensed by Mattias's article that in an outburst of rage he commanded all personnel of the Persian embassy in Berlin to return without delay to Persia.[19] The Persian foreign minister confirmed the Shah's decision to Blücher and added that the Shah's command was given in such a decisive manor that he, the foreign minister, did not dare to contradict him. The Shah's standpoint was that if he could not protect himself and his government from attacks through the German press, the least he could do was to break off diplomatic relations with Germany by ordering the return of his diplomatic representatives to Persia.[20]

By consulting the Persian foreign minister, Blücher tried to investigate the implications of the Shah's decision for German–Persian relations. The Persian foreign minister repeatedly declared that he was not in a position to explain the Shah's decision. Yet, he made clear that he did not regard relations between Germany and Persia as ended. For him Persia's withdrawal of its diplomatic representatives from Berlin was only a temporary measure. Blücher was convinced that this crisis was the direct result of the capricious decision of an autocratic and ill-tempered Shah, whose decisions none of his ministers dared to challenge. The question here is whether this crisis might have been prevented if Taimurtash had not been in Europe. This leads to the further issue of Taimurtash's status and role in German–Persian relations. It is most likely that he was the only minister who could challenge the Shah and thereby possibly inject a level of rationality into his more controversial decisions. Blücher believed at the least that had Taimurtash been in Tehran at the time, he could have prevented the recall of the Persian embassy staff from Berlin. In search of a solution and in the knowledge of Taimurtash's influence, Blücher instructed the German Foreign Office in Berlin to find Taimurtash and ask for assistance in the matter. From Blücher's point of view it was encouraging that the Persian foreign minister appeared to be interested in a solution to the crisis that would enable the continuation of relations between the two countries.[21]

In a first step, the publisher Knorr & Hirth GmbH agreed that regarding the defamatory article by Leo Mattias, it would voluntarily print a retraction of Mattias's article in its forthcoming issue of the *Münchener Illustrierte Presse*. It also explained that it had decided to publish a series of articles favourable to the Shah and the state of affairs in Persia. Knorr & Hirth's intention was also to publish these articles in other newspapers owned by the publishing house, including the *Münchener Neueste Nachrichten*.[22]

One such exposé was written by Sebastian Beck, a teacher of Persian language in Berlin. He dismissed Mattias's article as a product of fantasy with numerous inaccuracies. In an account of the Shah's life he portrayed him as an able and ambitious man from a military background who provided an example for every Persian. He painted the Shah's achievements in the brightest colours, pointing out the creation of the extraordinarily fast growing National Bank of Persia as just one in a seemingly endless list of noteworthy accomplishments.[23]

The Foreign Office had recognised and warned of the potential of a political crisis developing between Germany and Persia. However, its warnings had not been taken seriously for some time by other government agencies. The preceding series of incidents also indicate that the Foreign Office was not well enough equipped to stand up against other government institutions, let alone enforce its own policy in Germany's national interest. From the moment Germany's relations with Persia threatened to break down it became clear that Germany risked not only losing diplomatic relations with Persia but also a significant export market for its industrial goods. Quite clearly the 1931 crisis provided Germany with the opportunity to take action and address its deteriorating relations with Persia.

On the afternoon of 22 October 1931 Dr Prüfer from the German Foreign Office met with Severing, the minister of the interior. He impressed upon Severing the urgency of issuing a deportation order for Alawi as a sign of German goodwill to the Shah. In contrast to the earlier occasion, Severing issued a warrant against Alawi on the same day, and the Persian ambassador to Berlin, Farzin, and Blücher in Tehran were informed right away of the interior minister's decision.

On 23 October 1931 the Persian ambassador to Germany declared that he was no longer authorised to negotiate with the German Foreign Office.[24] On 24 October 1931 the Prussian interior ministry, through the Berlin police headquarters, enforced the total ban of the leaflet *Paykar* in Germany. In a note Grobba personally and officially informed the Persian embassy in Berlin that in compliance with the decree aimed at preventing political riots the police president of Berlin had outlawed *Paykar*.[25]

On 25 October 1925 Blücher had informed the Foreign Office of his endeavours to keep the Persian government informed of all efforts that had been made in Germany, to address the Persian government's criticism in the interest of an accord. Additionally, in a quest to persuade the Shah to reconsider his decision and send his embassy representatives back to Germany, Blücher made it understood that if the Persian government were to maintain its position, the German Foreign Office would be forced to withdraw its diplomatic representatives from Persia in a counter move.[26]

German efforts to resolve the political crisis resulted in an interim success, when in view of the status quo and faced with a vicious circle, the Persian government agreed to send its embassy representatives back to Berlin, except for the Persian ambassador and his legation secretary.[27]

Immunity of the National Bank

With reference to the German presence in Persia, just before the peak of the political crisis a Russian economic journal published an article with the title 'German imperialism in Persia'.[28] This article propagated the story that the Persian press was commenting almost on a daily basis about the activities of Germans in Persia. It claimed that, as manifested in the growth of trade figures, the objective of German activities was to strengthen and expand German economic and political influence in Persia.

The article further claimed that the popularity of German technology and the sympathies of the Persian public for German culture had helped Germany to outrun its competitors. By then, German influence was evident through the accomplishments of the Junkers airline, the German financial experts active in Persian banking and the large number of railway experts involved in the construction of the Persian railways. The article concluded that despite British, American and French resistance Germany had succeeded in securing an economic and political stronghold in Persia and moreover was happy to rely on the Persian *bourgeoisie* to maintain its influence.[29]

While the Persian press turned against Germany a short time later during the political crisis, the above article confirms the notion that Germany had at least to some extent succeeded in securing a foothold in Persia. It also was no secret that Germany's success was much associated with the National Bank, the Trans-Iranian Railway project and Junkers. It is of interest to see how the German-friendly National Bank was affected by the anti-German campaigns in Persia.

Despite the growing anti-German publicity in Persia, it appears that the National Bank of Persia, as an economic and political institution as well as a German stronghold, was barely affected. The crisis does not even seem to have had serious repercussions for the German staff of the bank. It is surprising that the Shah had taken no action against the National Bank or its German staff. At a time when he had broken off his diplomatic relations with Germany and put commercial contracts on hold, one might have at least expected steps directed against the German staff of the National bank.

Interestingly, the number of available German archival documents dealing with issues relating to the National Bank during 1931 is fewer than during the previous and immediately following years. It is of interest to briefly pay attention to the possible reasons for what appears to be the 'immunity' of the National Bank.

Regarding the bank's German staff we could once more argue that these German nationals were employed as Persian civil servants, and the Shah as well as the German government respected this fact. Also the German employees were successfully running the operations of the bank in all key areas, and therefore were indispensable to the Shah. The Shah must have been aware of the importance of the bank as a financial institution for Persia. By taking action against the German staff of the Bank, he would have harmed Persia commercially more than he could have gained politically.

Throughout the German–Persian political crisis the National Bank appeared unaffected. The bank maintained its operations and continued to expand its influence. We could further argue that the more established the National Bank became as a financial institution the more independent it became from political influences. Interestingly, at the height of the crisis the president of the National Bank's board Gharagozlou was replaced by Hussein Gholi Khan Nawab, the former Persian ambassador to Berlin.[30]

In conclusion, the most likely explanations for the National Bank's 'immunity' during the German–Persian crisis in 1931 were first that its German staff were Persian civil servants who were respected for their professional skills and therefore not questioned, and second that, in conjunction with the National Bank, political and economic matters were kept separate, i.e. the bank as an overall functioning financial institution had reached a status by which it stood above the intergovernmental political crisis which affected German–Persian relations. Hence the crisis did not have an immediate negative affect strong enough to influence the operations of the National Bank or the status of its German staff.

5

THE NATIONAL BANK CONTROVERSY AND THE END OF THE TAIMURTASH ERA

An unexpected and surprising decline in Germany's standing in Persia, its loss of influence over the National Bank, the unforeseen removal of Taimurtash from Persia's political scene, as well as Britain's aggressive attempts to reassert its national interests in Persia, characterise the next phase of developments affecting German relations with Persia and its National Bank. Initially it was not at all clear where events were leading. Without warning German nationals working for the Persian government had been made redundant or their contracts were not extended. This trend also began to affect the foreign staff of the National Bank to such an extent that by the end of 1932 a great number of them faced redundancy.

Looking at each case individually makes it difficult to understand the background and the motivation behind what appeared like a campaign aimed at driving the Germans out of Persia. Therefore we shall focus on the German interpretation of the anti-German propaganda spread in the Persian media, and the allegations made against German nationals serving the Persian government and particularly the National Bank. Furthermore, it is of interest to discover why in early 1932 Germany became the victim of such a wave of unforeseeable and irrevocable setbacks.

What had gone so badly wrong? Was it the German government's indecision in dealing with Persia's concerns that caused the turmoil, or were German individuals directly responsible for the setbacks? The analysis of these questions begins by considering a series of at first sight unrelated events involving Germany and German nationals working for the Persian government and the National Bank. This approach should reveal a possible pattern linking the separate events, and the way they affected the German employees of the National Bank and particularly its director Lindenblatt.

Since the eventual removal of Taimurtash from Persia's political scene would be of such relevance to the future of German involvement in Persia and its National Bank, it is essential also to briefly describe the shattering events surrounding this chief promoter of German interest in Persia. The second part of this chapter therefore addresses the events and intrigues that resulted in the death of this most influential Persian politician. Chapter 6 will more directly address the repercussions of Taimurtash's demise for the National Bank and Lindenblatt.

Threats to the German Status Quo in Persia

While the German–Persian diplomatic crisis should have been symbolically settled through Persia's reinstatement of its diplomatic staff in Germany, one of the first signs of continued Persian anti-German propaganda came in the guise of an article entitled 'We and the German press', published in the government newspaper *Iran* on 19 October 1931. This article argued that either Germany was ruled by an incompetent government that was not able to take care of its own interests or, alternatively, the German government was prepared, with cunning and intrigue, to damage the image of another country to gain even the smallest advantage. The Persian article criticised both Germany's economic state and the anti-Persian propaganda originating from Germany.1

Persia's relations with Germany were described by the author as not 'so necessary'. It was alleged that German political leaders had run down their country to the point of bankruptcy. Moreover, Germany was viewed as the only country to gain from bilateral relations with Persia. Germany would sell goods, set up factories, generate profits, and appoint its nationals to high government positions in Persia, while securing natural resources for its industry. Since Germany was perceived as not being capable of stopping the defamatory publications against Persia, its government was described as the most incompetent ever.

The article went on to criticise what it called the German government's 'stupidity' and 'idiocy', since it did not appear to understand that it should not tolerate the defamation of the dignity of a country it maintained friendly relations with. The author suggested that Germany, by facilitating the activities of a propaganda nest against Persia, could only have been using its political relations, maintained through its representatives, to pursue its ulterior motives in Persia. Hence the question was posed whether it was at all desirable to maintain relations with a Germany which was behaving so suspiciously.[2]

As a consequence of this anti-German propaganda the Persian government passed a motion to reduce the number of foreign nationals it employed. This also directly affected the employees of the National Bank of Persia. The chairman of the board of the National Bank, Nawab, in the presence of the Persian minister of finance, Taqizadeh, approached the president of the National Bank, Lindenblatt, with the demand to cut down the number of his non-executive foreign staff.[3] Hence the administration of the National Bank of Persia was forced to inform about a quarter of its 82 foreign staff that their contracts were not to be renewed. The majority of these employees, 40 in the provinces and 42 in Tehran, were German nationals.[4]

Moreover, according to a Persian source, the dissatisfaction with the way German authorities dealt with the anti-Persian campaigns had provoked an irreparable degree of resentment against everything German among the highest Persian ranks. This was also regarded as the main reason for the decision to replace the German director of the arsenal and all his staff with Swedish experts.[5] The technical director of the Persian arsenal, Hartmann, and the supervisor of the machine-gun section, Haase, were formally asked to leave their posts within three days. Hartmann was surprised, particularly because no reasons were given and the Shah himself had issued the instructions for their dismissal. Later Hartmann was told that cost-saving was the main reason for the termination of his contract. The German envoy to Tehran, Blücher, interpreted the manner by which Persia dealt with the German staff of the arsenal as inconsiderate and brutal. This is particularly evident when considering how well Hartman had built up and managed the arsenal for the Persian government, in over eight years of hard work. Haase also had been employed in Persia for over 25 years, and had been highly decorated for his services.[6]

Blücher considered three possible reasons for the dismissal of Hartmann and Haase. First, it could have been a direct reaction of the Shah to the release of the individuals detained in Germany connected with the *Paykar* affair. Second, there might have been genuine financial reasons responsible for the termination of foreign contracts. Third, the Persian government might have had entered negotiations with Czechoslovakian companies, who offered their machinery cheaper than Germany. Hence it is conceivable that the Persian government had plans for replacing the German staff of the arsenal with Czechoslovakian nationals.[7]

Later it transpired that the Persian government had decided to manage the arsenal without foreign assistance. Nevertheless, the government intended to rely on the services of Swedish engineers for a gunpowder factory. Moreover, the Shah was about to instruct a Czechoslovakian company to construct a gun-manufacturing factory near Tehran.[8]

The Persian government also had plans to take over or reallocate all aspects of railway construction from German hands.[9] As a result Taimurtash had suspended his negotiations regarding the engagement of German experts and instead initiated negotiations with Swedish experts in Stockholm.[10]

These manoeuvres by the Persian government clearly threatened Germany's position in Persia. The initial victims of this shift of policy in Persia were German individuals and companies working on behalf of the Persian government.

The National Bank's Loss of Industrial Projects

The National Bank of Persia's operations included the financing and management of industrial projects next to its banking operations. The Persian government had instructed the National Bank to set up production facilities all over Persia. Unexpectedly, in April 1932 the National Bank began to lose control over most of its major industrial projects.

In Kahrizak a sugar factory had been established on 28 April 1931 with a share capital of 300,000 toman. The project's target was to take over and rebuild the old sugar factory in Kahrizak, which had been shut down for 35 years. The National Bank of Persia held 180,000 toman of the share capital invested in the project. The factory was reconditioned and complemented by machinery supplied by the German firm Grevenbroich, Magdeburg. In March 1932 the Persian government bought the shares held by the National Bank and thereby became the majority shareholder. As a result the general administrator of the department of Industry, Farrokh, replaced the chairman of the board of the factory, Lindenblatt.[11]

In Karadj a sugar factory was commissioned by the Persian government, and construction started in September 1931 under the management of the National Bank of Persia. By the end of 1932 the Persian government had decided to take over the management of the factory from the bank.

The Kerman yarn-spinning factory in Rafsanjan was commissioned by the Persian government in December 1931 with a share capital of 400,000 toman. One-third of the share capital of this factory was underwritten by the National Bank. The management of this project was formally in the hands of the National Bank of Persia, which included Lindenblatt as one of its board members. Yet plans existed to cut out the National Bank from this project.

Similarly to the Kerman factory, the Yazd yarn-spinning factory was also commissioned in December 1931 by the Persian government. One third of its 400,000 toman share capital was underwritten by the National Bank, and the remaining shares were held by local entrepreneurs. But, as in the case of the Kerman factory, plans had been drawn up possibly to join both projects, cut out the National Bank, and appoint a new general manager from the department of industry.

In Kermanshah the plan for the establishment of the Kermanshah wool spinning factory was abandoned by the National Bank of Persia; in Mashad the plan for the establishment of the Mashad cotton factory was also abandoned by the National Bank; and in Mazandaran the plan for the establishment of the Mazandaran linen factory was also no longer pursued by the National Bank.

In Shahi a cotton and fabric factory was founded in 1930 with a share capital of 500,000 toman. The main shareholders of this factory were the Shah and the National Bank of Persia. The following supplying German companies held the remaining shares: Deutsche Spinnereimaschinenbau A.G., Ingolstadt, Siemens-Schuckert-Werke, Berlin, and Unionmatex Gemeinschaft Deutscher Textilmachinenfabriken, Berlin. The factory was officially opened on 11 February 1932. According to the German experts from Ingolstadt under full capacity the factory could produce 900,000 metres of yarn, using 286,000 kilos of cotton. The Shah's designated expert, Hossein Khan Veillard, believed that the realistic capacity of the factory was only about two-third of the German estimate. Veillard also reported that he felt that the machinery supplied to the factory was priced 30 per cent higher than the bids submitted by a British and a further German company. Veillard's report was compromising for the National Bank of Persia since it had been in charge of ordering the machinery. The commercial director of this factory was the German national Hartmann, who was also the director of the Sari branch of the National Bank of Persia. Hence plans existed to replace Hartmann's with a Persian national.[12]

The situation became more critical for Lindenblatt when rumours began to circulate alleging irregularities concerning the Karadj sugar factory. These allegations resulted in the National Bank being officially investigated by the department of industry.[13]

Lindenblatt was convinced that he was being set up, particularly as the investigations commissioned by him did not reveal any irregularities in the bank's conduct. Lindenblatt viewed this case as an obvious intrigue planned against him from the Persian side. Furthermore, other sources suspected that influential Persian personalities who wanted Lindenblatt's resignation had infiltrated agents into the bank with the intent of uncovering evidence that could be used against Lindenblatt. When alerted to the allegations against Lindenblatt and the National Bank, the Shah is reported to have been furiously angry.[14]

The German company Robert Wönckhaus & Co. was also convinced that Veillard had instigated acts of sabotage against the machinery they supplied to prove their inferiority compared to Swiss or British products. By claiming that the German machinery was overpriced, Veillard also aimed at replacing the already delivered German models through his preferred non-German manufacturers. Since Lindenblatt and the National Bank had become cautious about appearing to favour German companies or products, they limited their support for German companies. This consequently resulted in a sharp fall in exports of Robert Wönckhaus machinery to Persia.[15]

Blücher and Lindenblatt had for some time been aware of the vulnerability of the National Bank regarding its industrial projects. They had planned to transfer the National Bank's overall responsibility for industrial projects to individual directors. However, it was too late, since their Persian counterparts were already planning to remove the responsibility for the management of industrial projects from the National Bank. Hence, what was planned as a voluntary transitional withdrawal had turned into a compulsory removal of responsibility.

Blücher was more than surprised when Lindenblatt informed him of his intention to resign from his post. Lindenblatt evidently felt that he could not withstand his adversaries, chiefly Nawab and Taqizadeh. Blücher believed that a change in the directorship of the National Bank at such a critical time should be avoided at all cost. He thus managed to persuade Lindenblatt to remain in office until the final date of his employment contract.[16]

The situation for Lindenblatt and the National Bank had become tense. In a short period the National Bank of Persia had lost nearly all of its influence over its industrial projects.

The Political Reasons for Germany's Loss of Influence

Since the coronation of Reza Shah in 1925 the economic influence of Germany in Persia had grown steadily. German financial advisers worked for Persian ministries. German Junkers aircraft provided an accident-free and much appreciated flight schedule. German engineers and experts had managed the arsenal and gunpowder factories. Multiple sections of the Persian railway had been constructed and commissioned by a German consortium. The National Bank of Persia had also grown in its first years of operation to a network of 32 branches. Under the supervision of the National Bank German companies had, with considerable results, constructed factories and supplied German machinery to the

Persian industry. In only six months the German firm in charge of setting up the Kahrizak factory, which had been shut down for 35 years, managed to start production. It comes as no surprise that after such accomplishments Germany was commended for its competence. As late as 28 January 1932 the Shah himself was praising Germany in a speech given on the occasion of the inauguration ceremony of the Kahrizak factory. The Shah is quoted as having said that he could entrust the industrial development of his country in to German hands with ease of mind, since they instituted success.[17]

Two weeks later the wind had started to blow from a different direction. Taimurtash had arrived back from London one day before the Shah had given his speech. The British high commissioner from Iraq arrived a short time later to prepare the state visit of King Faisal. Four days later the director of the arsenal, Hartmann, was expelled and the contracts of other Germans working for Persia's defence industry were not extended. Reducing government expenditures was repeatedly cited as the official reason for the termination of contracts. Blücher firmly believed that, although the Persian government had legitimate reason to cut its expenditure, the main reason for the dismissals must have been the Shah's anger over the Mattias *Paykar* and Farrokh affairs.[18] Subsequently, the Shah ordered that the National Bank should surrender all responsibilities for industrial projects. It looked as if what was accomplished in over a decade of hard work by Germans was being forfeited in less than four months.

Hardly any Germans doubted that the Mattias article and the *Paykar* affair provided a strong motive for Persia's unambiguous attempts to distance itself from Germany. However, there is a further hypothesis worth considering, which places the *Paykar* affair into the context of an overriding strategic plan. According to this hypothesis Britain was the main strategist behind what was happening to Germany in Persia.

Kurt Weil, managing director of Junkers Luftverkehr Persia, personally initiated negotiations with the German Foreign Office, the German ministry of defence, the ministry of trade and commerce, Lufthansa and Junkers, with the result that, considering the unpredicted restrictions imposed on Junkers in Persia, all participants accepted that every effort should be made to reinstate and expand the flight operations of the airline. It is interesting in this context that the German ministry of defence played a leading role in trying to reinstate Junkers. It had not only been subsidising Junkers but was also prepared to continue its subsidies if Junkers could secure flight concessions through Iraq that would guarantee an efficient route from Germany to Persia and maybe even Afghanistan.

The German entrepreneur Thomas Brown, who was on business in Iraq, had also been asked for his support in the Junkers matter. Brown backed the notion that the cancellation of the Junkers flight operations in Persia and British machinations did possibly result in the deterioration of flight operations in the region. However, he was confident that a solution could be negotiated, since Junkers was not only mindful of the British position but was also receptive to British opinion. Yet he felt that it would still take some time for negotiations to yield any concrete results, so that it remained uncertain whether Junkers would be allowed to resume its flight operations in the near future.[19]

Consequently, it appears that to safeguard its national interest Britain had chosen to engage in indirect diplomatic initiatives rather than opt for an open confrontation in Persia. Next to its central strategic goals of securing the Tehran airfield for its own requirements and removing Germans from Persia's defence industry, it would have been only rational for Britain also to have devised plans for reclaiming its economic dominance in Persia. Under German supervision Persia had managed increasingly to distance itself from Britain's economic hegemony. The transfer of printing rights from the Imperial Bank to the National Bank of Persia must have played a major role in Britain's strategic thinking, particularly because, from a financial point of view, before the transfer of rights Britain had no need to assign sterling funds to its operations in Persia. Whenever funds were needed the Imperial Bank, with its printing rights, was at hand. However, the Persian government had bought the money-printing rights from the Imperial Bank in 1930. Yet the Imperial Bank's money-printing rights formally expired as late as September 1932. If Britain intended to launch a campaign aimed at regaining its economic power in Persia as well it had to do so before September 1932.[20]

Nevertheless, from a German perspective, even though the British political and economic motives may have been obvious and rational, Persian and foreign circles failed to believe in a British offensive aiming at regaining power in Persia. The negative economic experiences with Britain and the strong nationalist movements in Persia were perceived as too strong a barrier for Britain to overcome. Yet this overlooked some crucial points. First, it was not the nationalists but the Shah and his ministers who determined Persia's policy. Second, we can be reasonably sure that the Shah and his aides possessed sufficient foresight to consider the consequences for Persia arising from a possible conflict between Britain and Russia. A monarchy such as Persia was likely to gain more from taking the side of Britain in a possible conflict.

The British could have recognised Persia's predicament and expertly turned it into an advantage by embarking on its exploitation. First, the British placated the nationalists by appearing to generously relinquish privileges that had actually become superfluous. This included the monopoly over telegraphy, which had lost its strategic importance due to the arrival of radio telecommunication. In a second step, the British secured, through retaining the Imperial Bank's money-printing monopoly until September 1932, the financial resources required to start a diplomatic campaign, which ultimately would have enabled Britain to regain its lost power in Persia. This plan was labelled by a German source '*verwegen kühn und genial billig!*'.[21]

According to the available intelligence, the British launched their offensive in July 1931 by organising a Persian art exhibition in London. It was alleged that Britain's motive for organising this event was to flatter Persian vanity and to create a Persia-friendly image for Britain. Of course, the British had ensured that the money paid out by the Persian government for the transfer of printing rights of the Imperial Bank to the National Bank of Persia was transferred to London before the exhibition and before the fall in the exchange rate of the pound. On the other hand this exhibition served as an ideal forum for inviting Taimurtash and other Persian political leaders to London. On arrival, in autumn 1931, the British Foreign Office officials had a good opportunity to brief the Persian political leaders on the advantages that an anti-Russian, Britain-friendly policy would present for Persia. Moreover, it was made clear that Britain could not genuinely trust a Persian anti-Russian policy as long as Germans oversaw the Persian defence industry and economy. This was explained mainly by arguing that from a British point of view, Germany was under the suspicion of being Russia-friendly, particularly in view of the Rapallo Treaty.

It appears that by this time the British strategy was starting to take shape. The British strategy's success becomes evident, for example, when considering Taimurtash's revised return travel arrangements to Tehran via Berlin. Taimurtash had planned, to the surprise of the Germans, such a brief stopover in Berlin that it effectively made the anticipated meetings with German officials and negotiations with German industrialists impossible. This could be regarded as a symbolic assurance by Taimurtash to the British that he had understood their message. Taimurtash's stay in Berlin was later only extended because of the prospect of the aforementioned meeting with the German Reichspräsident.[22]

A further, private reason for Taimurtash's visit to Europe was to enrol his son at a Swiss school, having taken him out of a German school.[23]

The first signs of a change in the Shah's disposition towards Germany appeared a few weeks after Taimurtash had returned to Persia. As we have pointed out, the first major victims of this change were the German experts running the Persian defence industry. A short time later the ground was being prepared for a Persian treaty with British-dominated Iraq. To emphasise and underline this Persia–Iraq 'alliance' a visit of King Faisal to Persia was being prepared.

A possible reason for Britain's phased strategy in removing Germans from Persia's economy and the National Bank was that Britain was determined to accomplish a much more urgent political goal before the summer 1932. The British felt that their economic objectives, particularly regarding the National Bank, had time until September 1932, the month of the transfer of the Imperial Bank's money-printing rights to the National Bank. Although by now German authorities had already deported the 'Persian communists' and convicted the individuals responsible for the Mattias and *Paykar* article, the closer September came the more Britain increased the intensity of its offensive against Germany in Persia. For a German source, this was a clear sign that the Mattias and *Paykar* affair had never been just a coincidence but was a vehicle of the British offensive.[24]

The analysis of evidence indeed shows that the theme and timing of the publication of the anti-Persian articles in Germany may not have been a pure coincidence. Mattias's article, for example, appeared exactly at the time when Blücher in Tehran replaced Schulenberg as the new German envoy. It can be argued that such 'coincidences' could be the result of carefully executed operations by British operatives. Similarly suspicious was that immediately after Taimurtash left London, the Persian communist Farrukhi appeared unexpectedly in Berlin, and thereafter the *Paykar* articles became more radical. Farrukhi, who had escaped Persia without possessing a passport, surfaced in Berlin with an official passport issued at the Persian embassy in Moscow. Again, this took place during the period of Blücher's appointment as German ambassador to Persia. This notion also implies that the circumstances of Farrukhi's appearance and the timing of it were staged, and that Persian government agencies or a number of its civil servants were implicated in the inherent British strategy.[25]

From his safe position in Berlin, Farrukhi actually attempted to blackmail the Shah and Taimurtash into paying him money. Farrukhi's audacity triggered even more resentment by the Shah against Germans in Persia. Blücher feared that it was only a matter of time before this resentment would also prove detrimental to German nationals employed by the National Bank. The bank's employees proposed to appeal to Adolf Hitler to intervene by deporting Farrukhi from Germany. Blücher likewise was convinced that the only way to remove the threat to German nationals in Persia was by deporting Farrukhi. He suspected that in the interest of provoking anti-German Persian sentiment, 'tiresome foreigners' backed Farrukhi's destructive activities. Blücher suggested that if the formal deportation of Farrukhi should fail, he should be offered a financial incentive and be sent to Paris in the same way he was sent from Moscow to Berlin.[26]

By announcing Schulenberg's departure a month in advance, the German government agencies had made it easy for the British potentially to plan their first strike. This also made it increasingly difficult for Blücher to effectively pursue his responsibilities. As a result, Blücher had to wait for an unusually long time before the Shah granted him an audience to acknowledge him as the new German representative to Persia. During this period Blücher was paralysed concerning his official duties.[27]

Blücher's situation was not enviable. First, in contrast to Germany, Britain had political and economic instruments at its disposal with which it could put Persia under pressure. These included the Shah's fear of the Bolsheviks and the imminent threat of tribal attacks on southern oilfields that could result in a reduction of government oil revenues. Second, Britain was pursuing high-priority interests for which it could deploy its significant political and economic power. Germany, on the other hand, was protecting an important but not vital position in Persia.[28]

However, the implementation of the British strategy was not as straightforward as its planning might have suggested. The pro-British strategy in Persia, as was to be expected, ran aground with nationalist groups. It also appeared that Taimurtash, who had stimulated Persia's pro-British stance, had become hesitant in submitting to British demands. The British had so far failed to come to an agreement with the Persian government over the strategically important Tehran airfield. As the British appeared to have failed to achieve a number of important political objectives they resolved to use pressure tactics on the Persian government. With a strategic move they cut the Persian government's share of the all-important oil revenues by £1,000,000, and started fomenting turmoil in the oil-rich southern regions of Persia.

Under such pressure, which hit the Shah at his most vulnerable spot, the previously united front of Persian politicians split into two factions. Since the British exercise of power and the survival instinct of the Shah supported it, the pro-British faction, under the leadership of finance minister Taqizadeh, were the stronger party. The main objective of Taqizadeh's faction turned out to be the elimination of Taimurtash, who had become the leader of the opposition. It is conceivable that Taimurtash was genuinely interested in making concessions to Britain but he was not prepared simultaneously to cut all his ties with Russia. The problem faced by Taimurtash's fraction was that Russia could offer nothing that might counter British pressure.[29]

Taimurtash must have recognised the weakness of his position and therefore had probably envisaged a more long-term strategy. He most likely counted on the strength of the nationalist movement in Persia and the support of the Persian military. Nevertheless, Taimurtash was engaging in a questionable gamble with the potential of a controversial outcome.

Although Germany was rapidly losing considerable ground, the National Bank of Persia was still under the control of Lindenblatt and his management team. Rumours surfaced, however, which alleged that all German nationals working for the bank were to be replaced by non-German foreign nationals. As with the hypothesis of a British plan to regain power in Persia, there was some evidence for these rumours. Apparently the Persian government had tried to recruit new bank personnel in Paris. However, the request of the Persian government was not endorsed by the French legation. Hence the Persian ambassador in Paris reported that he was not able to recruit suitable individuals and that he had forwarded the government's request to the Swiss embassy in Bern. Since a Swiss national had just arrived in Persia as the chief consultant on railway matters to the government, many believed in the strong possibility of Swiss nationals replacing the Germans at the National Bank.[30]

A delegation of merchants and government officials conferred with Taimurtash about the negative implications of a possible sudden change of the staff of the National Bank. Taimurtash assured the delegation that the government was aware of this issue and was not planning to take any hasty decisions. Taimurtash also pointed out that he intended to recommend to the Shah to retain the German staff of the National Bank, although the final decision, naturally, remained the prerogative of the Shah.

It is of interest to return to the initial hypothesis by considering Brown's impression of the causes of the German crisis in Persia. Brown confirms the rumours that alleged the existing crisis in Persia had a political background. He also confirmed that there were those who went as far as to imply that Mattias's articles were motivated not by journalistic ambition but by British pounds. Yet Brown felt that this was a too easy justification that he could not share in full.

It is certain that Germany's relations with Russia and its position within the western powers' structure was monitored with great interest in Persia. The Shah's decision about keeping the German personnel of the National

Bank was very much linked to the question of Germany being already 'infested by Bolshevik ideology' or not.

Persian government circles formally denied that the recent removal of German nationals from key positions was politically motivated. They argued that the dismissals were exceptional cases which had occurred for a variety of different reasons and only affected a limited number of individuals. Brown and, in his opinion, Blücher shared the view that prevailing political presumptions were exaggerated. However, they agreed that the Persian political and intellectual elite paid close attention to Germany's standing in Europe. It was of critical importance to Persia to see if Germany would sway pro-west or pro-Russia.[31]

This makes the hypothesis that Britain wanted to protect its interests against Russia and to regain its lost influence in Persia all the more plausible. As Brown and Blücher pointed out, the motives and extent of British operations may have been exaggerated to some degree. Yet it is unlikely to have been just a coincidence that German nationals were losing their influence in Persia on all levels of responsibility within months of each other. As previously, Taimurtash appeared to hold the key to the current and future developments with regard to German political and economic relations with Persia.

The Crisis Surrounding Taimurtash

The way events were developing set in motion a serious challenge for Taimurtash. Moreover, he faced a crusade against his status, in which the National Bank of Persia and its director played a notable role.

Until now the available archival evidence has been unable to provide more than an ambiguous description of Taimurtash's position within Persia or his role regarding the National Bank of Persia. On the one hand he was regularly described as being pro-Russian and on the other hand, he was suspected to be pro-British. In one instance it was even alleged that he was an agent of the Anglo-Persian Oil Company.[32] Elsewhere he is characterised as the father to the idea of creating a National Bank for the benefit of his country, and the strongest supporter of its German director. Yet he is seen to harm the cause of the bank and even portrayed as abusing the bank for his own personal profit. Moreover, Taimurtash is described as the indispensable aide, all-powerful implementer, and right hand to the Shah, whereas the Shah is portrayed as not being fully appreciative of Taimurtash's significance.[33]

Therefore, to be able to judge the subsequent implications of the developing crisis for Lindenblatt, his staff and the National Bank of Persia, it is necessary to take a closer look at the threatening circumstances surrounding the main figure, on whom Germany's faith in the early 1930s Persia appeared to rest.

For years Taimurtash had been exercising powers that went beyond his legitimate duties as court minister. Taimurtash had not restricted his activities to the royal household but had participated in all ministerial meetings, as the quasi representative of the Shah. Cabinet decisions reserved to the Shah were presented by Taimurtash, which gave him considerable influence over their outcome. Taimurtash's point of view was often determining to a degree that he was seen as the actual leader of the cabinet.[34]

Blücher saw Taimurtash's personal qualities as the prime source of his success. The Shah spoke no foreign languages, was generally regarded as afraid of people and therefore increasingly isolated himself from his environment. The Persian Prime Minister was well educated and respected, but he was old and did not possess much political determination. Taimurtash on the other hand was a spring of vitality, intelligent, and was regarded as a born decision-maker. He also spoke several foreign languages and flourished in public. Therefore, he complemented the Shah in various ways and stood in for the Prime Minister on many occasions. Taimurtash was often described as being indispensable to the Shah. Many of the achievements of the Pahlavi era were associated with him. This had reassured the Shah that Taimurtash was the right man for the execution of his ambitious modernisation plans. The cooperation between the Shah and Taimurtash thrived for years without any noticeable difficulties and the cabinet also willingly accepted the latter's domination. This was until Taqizadeh became minister of finance and started going his own ways, which ultimately placed him into opposition against Taimurtash.[35]

Because of the economic crisis Persia experienced throughout the early 1930s, opposing Taimurtash had become easier than it had been previously. Taimurtash had tried to halt Persia's economic downfall by introducing a foreign trade monopoly and a trade agreement with Russia. Neither measure achieved the desired results. On the contrary, Persia's economic situation worsened. Hence Taimurtash became the scapegoat for the crisis. Moreover, Taimurtash, with his passion for gambling and an exorbitant lifestyle, offered an easy target for his enemies. He was allegedly spending far more money than he could have legitimately earned.

Taqizadeh concentrated his offensive against Taimurtash on exactly this weak point. He suspected that part of Taimurtash's illegitimate income was acquired through an institution over which he had indisputable influence, the National Bank of Persia.[36] In a first step, Taqizadeh succeeded in infiltrating his close friend Nawab into the executive management of the National Bank. In a second step, Nawab, as chairman of the board, ordered the re-examination of all open and secret accounts held at the National Bank.

Within a short time it was revealed that irregularities had been discovered regarding Taimurtash's currency transactions. It was alleged that, at a time when currency transactions were banned, Taimurtash had sold foreign currency at a black market rate, after acquiring the funds at the lower official exchange rate from the National Bank. Nawab directly reported his findings to the Shah, who became furious. The Shah asked Taimurtash to see him immediately, and it was reported that he got so angry that he attacked Taimurtash physically. As a result Taimurtash suffered a heart cramp and was taken ill, withdrawing from the battlefield for the following two weeks.[37]

Taimurtash's absence created the opportunity for his enemies to launch further attacks against him. After the initial success of their campaign, not only members of the closer circle surrounding Taqizadeh joined in but also publicly respected politicians who had been politically incapacitated by Taimurtash. A number of them used the opportunity to consult with the Shah during Taimurtash's absence. It is maintained that these men tried to increase the doubts in the mind of the characteristically suspicious Shah regarding the most recent designs of his ambitious court minister. They mainly campaigned for a return to constitutional values and independent parliamentary elections.

The religious leaders also started their vengeance against Taimurtash for what they perceived as his loose life detached from Islamic values. Taimurtash's future faced a critical phase during which he could have been stripped of all his powers and privileges, or worse.

However, the situation shifted slightly in favour of Taimurtash. This was mainly because Nawab, who was investigating the accounts held at National Bank, had come across irregularities concerning numerous other important public figures, some lower but some also higher in status than Taimurtash. The more these people felt threatened by Nawab's investigative findings, the more their opposition to his activities grew. When Nawab began to realise the level of discord he had caused, his activities slowed down rapidly.[38]

Precisely at this moment Taimurtash returned and attended to his duties as if nothing had happened. Yet he was obviously furious. Blücher points out that in Europe these events would have led to a public confrontation between the two rival camps but in the Orient this affair took a different route. Having been faced with such opposition Nawab decided to change camps. Hence he had a four-hour meeting with Taimurtash after which they were seen embracing each other. Whereas Nawab had initially held Taimurtash responsible for the irregularities discovered at the National Bank, he now argued that the entire affair had resulted from the ill-formulated documents of the bank. Smartly enough, Taqizadeh had managed to keep himself in the background during the entire campaign and therefore did not need to be reconciled with Taimurtash.

However, Blücher felt that no one could predict whether or not the crisis surrounding Taimurtash was over. The Shah was known to treat the individuals whom he wanted to overthrow with utmost politeness until the moment he ordered their arrest. Blücher was convinced that none of Taimurtash's adversaries could match him in intelligence and vigour. At a time when the Shah's popularity was declining and the nation was increasingly dissatisfied, it was essential for the Shah to keep his most capable deputies at his side.[39] Although the Shah is undisputedly regarded as Persia's reformer, he had neither exposure to foreign countries nor did he speak any foreign languages. It is reported that before the construction of the Trans-Iranian Railway he had not even experienced a train. In contrast, his European-educated court minister, who was well travelled and regularly consulted European-qualified experts, was in the position to inspire and implement many of the Shah's reforming ideas. Hence in the long run Taimurtash had good reason to consider himself indispensable.[40]

The Persian-British Oil Conflict and Taimurtash

It did not take long for Taimurtash to be tested by a further political manoeuvre instigated by his plotting opponents. This time the former Persian ambassador to Moscow and the then ambassador to London, Ansari, was the key suspect. Taimurtash knew Ansari as an adversary long before he had decided to launch his Anglo-Persian Oil Company conspiracy against him.

Two unidentified Armenian nationals had made Ansari aware of the window of opportunity for Persia to distance itself from the disadvantageous Anglo-Persian Oil contract. Britain was predominantly preoccupied with maintaining its international status quo. Ansari saw in this a chance first to impress the Shah and appeal to his nationalist feelings by suggesting the cancellation of the above-mentioned contract, and second to overshadow Taimurtash. Consequently Ansari sent to Tehran a proposal letter for the attention of the Shah. Taimurtash, whose anti-British feelings were cunningly hinted at in Ansari's letter, felt railroaded into endorsing the recommendation to cancel the Anglo-Persian oil contract.[41]

On 27 November 1932 Taqizadeh informed the resident representative of the Anglo-Persian Oil Company in Tehran of the Persian government's decision to cancel the D'Arcy concession.[42] In protest, the Anglo-Persian Oil Company questioned the legality of the Persian government's decision. The British ambassador to Tehran declared on behalf of his government that Britain would take every step deemed necessary to protect its legitimate national interest. A similar declaration was also voiced in the House of Commons in London on 5 December 1932. Yet the Persian government remained determined in its objective to remove British influence from its most important national resource, oil.[43]

The two main arguments for the hard line the Persian government was pursuing with the Anglo-Persian Oil Company were, first, the company's failure to increase the Persian government's share of its profits to above its current 16 per cent and, second, the failure to include Persian nationals in the management of the company. Further reasons included the Anglo-Persian Oil Company's reduction of the Persian government's share of oil income, based on falling oil prices, alleged irregularities in the company's accounting practice and a weak pound sterling exchange rate affecting the Persian government's national reserves deposited in pound Sterling. Besides these factors there was also a nationalistic motive, which held that the Anglo-Persian Oil Company was a threat to Persia's sovereignty and prestige.[44]

A German government internal news bulletin compared the effect of the unexpected arrival of the news over the 1932 cancellation of the D'Arcy concession from Persia with the impact of a bomb. This was because the Persian government's cancellation of the D'Arcy concession affected the Anglo-Persian Oil Company, which was one of only two institutions on which British influence in Persia was based. The Imperial Bank, being the other British institution, had already lost in significance, while the 13 million marks capital investment in the bank could not rival the 230 million marks invested in the Anglo-Persian Oil Company.[45]

At this point many putative explanations for the Persian government's action were circulating. It was alleged, for example, that the Russians had initiated the government's move against Britain, or that Taqizadeh, out of his hate for Britain and under the influence of his German spouse, had persuaded the Shah to end the Anglo-Persian Oil Company's hegemony. It was even rumoured that Taimurtash had initiated this affair to outsmart Taqizadeh.[46]

Blücher was convinced that none of the above-mentioned factors described the real reasons for the cancellation demand. Blücher gathered that the idea must have been the brainchild of the Shah himself. Evidently, on a visit to the south of Persia on the occasion of inspecting his newly delivered Italian-built gunboats, the Shah could not fail to see for himself the might of the Anglo-Persian Oil Company. The Anglo-Persian Oil Company with its impressive facilities, ranging from schools to airports, factories, roads, hospitals and settlements, resembled a state within a state. Blücher was convinced that the Shah's decision was formed after seeing the Anglo-Persian Oil Company's omnipotence in southern Persia. On returning to Tehran the Shah supposedly demanded that his cabinet cancelled the concession held by the Anglo-Persian Oil Company. As usual none of the ministers dared to question the Shah's decision. Only after the Shah left did Taqizadeh and his colleague, the foreign minister, add a section to the Shah's instructions that expressed the Persian government's willingness for negotiations with the Anglo-Persian Oil Company.[47]

The Persian Prime Minister and the foreign minister clarified to Blücher that they had no intention of instigating a conflict with Britain. Hence the objectives of the Persian government were reformulated to reflect that not the cancellation of the concession was intended but its renegotiation. The Persian government tried to give credence to its position by not interfering with any aspects of the Anglo-Persian Oil Company's operations.[48]

Blücher never believed in the theory that Ansari was behind the idea of cancelling the Anglo-Persian Oil Company concession. However, one of the main sources on which he based his opinion was Taqizadeh.[49]

Recognising the force behind the British reaction to the Persian government's initial demand, Ansari planned to deflect responsibility for its possible failure by making Taimurtash responsible for its implementation. Hence he compiled a report in which he concluded that the cancellation of the Anglo-Persian Oil Company's contract, as recommended by him, was beyond doubt a politically sound decision. Yet he criticised the process of implementation of the cancellation agreement as arguably damaging to Persia. Ansari had his report directly delivered to the Shah. In the Shah's eyes Taimurtash was responsible for overseeing the implementation of the cancellation of the concession, and he again became intensely angry with Taimurtash, for whom his respect was continuously fading.[50]

The Shah at once placed Taimurtash under house arrest. Taimurtash's house was surrounded by armed forces who prevented him even from meeting his family. Newspapers already predicted the launch of a court case against him. Yet it was not clear what the charges against him would be. The press predicted that he would be charged with having had treacherous relations with the Anglo-Persian Oil Company, which would ultimately be damaging for Persia. For Blücher this was a clear indication of the Shah's methods at work. He felt that the Shah inflated the Taimurtash affair to this degree to distract attention from the fact that he alone was responsible for the challenges accompanying the oil conflict.[51] In a telegram Blücher reported to Berlin that the Persian court minister was discharged in an offensive manner. He concluded by pointing out that he expected wide-ranging political implications, the consequences of which could not yet be foreseen in detail.[52]

Ansari likewise was removed from his post in London and replaced. The formal explanation for this change was that the Shah believed that Ansari was not representing Persia's position strongly enough vis-à-vis his British counterparts. Consequently Ansari decided not to return to Persia on grounds of serious illness. Yet he felt well enough to travel to Paris.[53]

The fall of Taimurtash, who had dominated Persia's domestic and foreign policies for seven years, was a sensation discussed at all levels of Persian society. Blücher differentiated a number of further elements contributing to the downfall of Taimurtash. Starting with his last trip to Europe, during which he was instructed to accompany the crown prince to his new school in Switzerland, it was alleged that he did not pay enough attention to the prince. The Shah was informed that Taimurtash was overshadowing the prince and that when both appeared it always looked as if the prince was accompanying Taimurtash rather than Taimurtash accompanying the prince. Moreover, when in London, Taimurtash had entered negotiations with the Anglo-Persian Oil Company over an increase in the Persian government's quota of the company's oil income. These negotiations failed to achieve any immediate result. Hence, in consultation with the Shah, Taimurtash's opponents were able to use this lack of success against him. The Shah was also secretly informed that Taimurtash, on his way back from London, had stopped over in Moscow and celebrated Persia's relations with Russia in a conspicuous way, neglecting to stress the Shah's omnipotent role in a speech he gave to honour the occasion.[54]

On his return Taimurtash had managed to regain ground but by this time the Shah's distrust for him was already deeply seated. This was followed by the already described campaign launched by Taqizadeh and Nawab and the discovery of the account irregularities at the National Bank of Persia. Nawab had successfully managed to tarnish Taimurtash's standing in the eyes of the Shah. [55]

Moreover, Taimurtash had faced a further pitfall that involved a good friend of his, the Shah's treasurer Diba. Both Diba and Taimurtash were alleged to be passionate gamblers. During a card game Diba had won the phenomenally high sum of 25,000 toman from the Shah's father in-law. In a tragic turn of events resulting from the high debt, the Shah's father in-law suffered a stroke and subsequently passed away. The Shah became angry over this incident and immediately dismissed Diba from his post. To the Shah's dismay, however, Taimurtash continued to uphold his close friendship with Diba and his family.[56] This behaviour by Taimurtash brought the Shah's frustration to culmination.

Taimurtash's continued friendship with Diba, together with the conflict Persia faced with Britain regarding the Anglo-Persian Oil Company's contract, and Persia's generally weak economic situation for which he was also held responsible, made the Shah's decision to part from his court minister final.[57]

Taimurtash, who was kept under house arrest, was completely cut off from the outside world. He received medical treatment at his house for a spell of angina pectoris and a wound to his head, over which Blücher refused to speculate.

In the meantime publications singled out Ansari as the main reason for the Shah's dismissal of Taimurtash. Ansari was purported to have addressed three reports directly to the Shah long before the Persian government's official cancellation of the Anglo-Persian Oil Company's contract. In these reports Ansari described the positive progress of his negotiations with the Anglo-Persian Oil Company. When Taimurtash's negotiations with the Anglo-Persian Oil Company in London had failed to yield any positive results, Taimurtash was accused to have omitted, out of resentment, to forward Ansari's status reports to the Shah. In a further report regarding the cancellation of the Anglo-Persian Oil Company's contract Ansari reported to the Shah his reservations over the consequences resulting from the Persian government's decision to cancel the agreement. He reported that, despite the satisfactory progress of his own contract negotiations with the oil company, Taimurtash had decided to insist on the cancellation of the agreement and thereby was responsible for the negative consequences. This account enraged the Shah who believed he had discovered how deceiving Taimurtash was in his ways. Ansari, although successful in his plan to damage the reputation of Taimurtash in the eyes of the Shah, in the long run not only lost his post but also his honour when he decided not to return to Persia.[58] These results satisfied Taimurtash's worst opponent Taqizadeh, who had most probably exploited Ansari as part of his plan to bring down Taimurtash.

In Blücher's words, Taimurtash's fall meant that Persia faced a new era in its history. With him not only the helmsman of Persia's domestic and foreign policy was leaving the bridge but also the only politician who had been able to guide the often angry and unpredictable Shah.[59]

The End of the Taimurtash Era

In February 1933 Taimurtash was transferred to prison, where he awaited his trial. It had been difficult to find solid evidence that could lead to his prosecution in court. Hence the preliminary judiciary investigation looked into alternative ways by which it could find evidence to prosecute Taimurtash for high treason. With a fresh line of investigation it aimed to prove that Taimurtash was a mercenary of the Anglo-Persian Oil Company.[60]

The Anglo-Persian Oil Company had been paying the tribal leaders in Persia's south for years to ensure the safety of its operations. More than twelve months before the investigation the Anglo-Persian Oil Company had deposited £25,000 into the accounts of the National Bank of Persia for the tribal leaders. This transaction took place at a time when the Bazaar exchange rate for one pound sterling was 9 toman and the official exchange rate 6 toman. The chief prosecutor's line of argument was based on the fact that the tribal leaders only received the equivalent sum derived by applying the Bazaar exchange rate to the transaction. This left, in comparison to the sum derived from applying the official exchange rate, a discrepancy of 75,000 toman. The chief prosecutor's objective was to prove that Taimurtash was on the receiving end of the 75,000 toman. He alleged that it was premeditated that the Anglo-Persian Oil Company had deposited the £25,000 in pound sterling and not its equivalent in toman. Moreover, it was argued that it was part of the plan to execute this transfer through the National Bank of Persia, which in turn would provide Taimurtash with the above-mentioned illegal income.[61]

To this end the prosecutor interrogated Lindenblatt for more than ten hours in one session. The interrogation must have been highly unpleasant for Lindenblatt since the prosecution had discovered on a number of foreign exchange receipts the letter 'T' for Taimurtash inscribed.[62]

Consequently, the court succeeded in convicting and imprisoning Taimurtash based on the evidence uncovered. Blücher observed significant changes after Taimurtash's removal from the public and diplomatic scene. For example Taimurtash was known to have accomplished a great number of the modern reforms in Persia in an uncomplicated and timely manner. Instead, issues now had to be first brought to the attention of the relevant ministry, resulting in ineffective deliberations. Likewise, important matters had to be brought forward for discussion in cabinet meetings, which were chaired by the Shah himself. Since the Shah was known for his temper and volcanic outbursts, out of fear none of the cabinet ministers ever ventured to challenge him. Ministers also lacked the courage to recommend anything unless they already knew it had the full approval of the Shah. This resulted in unsatisfactory delays and obstruction of official matters ranging from governing the economy to the construction of railways and the award of monopoly concessions.[63]

This affected also Germany's situation in Persia, which, despite the Shah's positive reassurance that Germany was now cleared of communist influence, remained in suspension over recent events.[64]

Taimurtash's treatment in prison became systematically worse, to a degree that he was put in a cell together with thieves and murderers. Finally, on 3 October 1933 Taimurtash was found dead in his cell. No autopsy was performed, yet it was rumoured that two prison wardens who had eaten the same food as Taimurtash were taken severely ill. In compliance with instructions coming from the highest ranks, no one besides Taimurtash's attorney and one of his sons was allowed to attend his funeral. It seemed to Blücher that the Shah not only appeared to have disliked Taimurtash from the outset but that he must also have feared him, possibly unjustifiably, until his last moments.[65]

The inescapable conclusion that emerges from the events described is that Lindenblatt's future at the National Bank of Persia was seriously in danger. He had not only lost one of his strongest promoters but he was implicated in the investigation accompanying Taimurtash's prosecution. Moreover, the National Bank of Persia had already lost significant influence over its industrial projects; many of Lindenblatt's German colleagues had been removed from their posts; he had clashed with Taqizadeh who did not appear to be particularly German-friendly; the British had still not managed to achieve their political and economic goals, and therefore posed a threat for him. Furthermore, the Shah's attitude towards him, the bank and Germany was at the least unpredictable. Since Germany's involvement in Persia was predominantly of an economic nature and therefore had increasingly relied on Lindenblatt and the industrial projects of the National Bank of Persia, Lindenblatt saw himself faced with problems that not only jeopardised his future as a person but also the future of German relations with Persia.

6

THE LINDENBLATT AFFAIR AND THE NATIONAL BANK

Following the discovery of the irregularities revealed during the investigation of the National Bank of Persia in June 1932 by the Persian authorities, Germany's relations with Persia had come under even greater pressure. The National Bank's director Lindenblatt had moved into the forefront of allegations of fraud and was held responsible by the Persian authorities for their findings.[1] However, the focus of the authorities unexpectedly shifted towards the German vice-director of the National Bank, Otto Vogel. It is necessary to examine why Vogel suddenly became the prime suspect for the Persian authorities and why the investigation of the bank led to his suicide. Vogel's death refocused the authorities' attention on Lindenblatt and the other German nationals working for the National Bank. While examining the circumstances Lindenblatt was subjected to throughout the Persian authority's investigations, and the events that accompanied his resignation as the bank's director, it is important to see if Lindenblatt and his German colleagues had just become the victims of a political conspiracy, or if they were genuinely involved in dishonourable fraudulent activities.

Director Lindenblatt and the National Bank Crisis

Because of the continuing build-up of tension in 1932 Persia, Lindenblatt had decided to apply for a three-month leave of absence from his post as the director of the National Bank. Predictably, Lindenblatt's decision met with resistance from the Persian minister of finance Taqizadeh as well as from the chairman of the board of the National Bank, Nawab. Before they considered Lindenblatt's application for leave, both demanded from him detailed accounts for the National Bank's financial transactions and statements regarding established factories.[2]

Nevertheless, they soon realised that their harsh attacks against Lindenblatt, and indirectly the National Bank, had mobilised the opponents of the bank, including the Imperial Bank of Persia and its sympathisers. As a result of the perceived threat to the existence of the National Bank they toned down their investigation insofar that Lindenblatt was granted his leave.

Before leaving for Germany, Lindenblatt made it known that he had understood the purpose of the investigation and the fact that his hitherto dominant role in the bank had become a point of criticism. Hence, according to Blücher, he concluded his last meeting with the board of the National Bank by stating that

> Since the first phase of organisation (of the National Bank) was now completed, it was to be followed by an epoch focusing on the regular day to day running of the bank. Until this time it had been necessary to centre responsibility on one person, but now the time had come to contemplate a more relaxed approach.[3]

The bank's board agreed that the National Bank's vice-director Otto Vogel should represent Lindenblatt during his absence. According to Blücher, Vogel tried to approach his responsibilities in a radically different way from Lindenblatt. Vogel had intended to keep regular contact with Taqizadeh, and to allow Nawab to have permanent control over his activities. He also planned to transfer the responsibility for granting substantial bank loans to Nawab. Moreover, Vogel pledged not to resist employing Persian nationals in responsible positions within the bank. He also aimed, by granting competitive loans to factories, to settle the remaining arguments between them and the National Bank. Vogel's approach led to what appeared to be a moderate relaxation at the bank.

Blücher had remarked that Lindenblatt's departure had initiated a historical change of course for the National Bank of Persia. He held that under Lindenblatt the National Bank was actually a German bank in the same way that the Imperial Bank had been an English bank. Blücher was confident that an aware Persian government would not tolerate such a state of affairs over a longer period. Blücher was convinced that there was no other solution for the German employees of the National Bank than for them to become accustomed to sharing their responsibilities with Persian nationals.[4]

Regarding Lindenblatt's future, everything he was doing indicated that he was planning to leave Persia permanently. He had sent his children back to Germany and had dissolved his household. For the Persian authorities

Lindenblatt's departure provided an opportunity to see how the bank would perform without him. From their perspective success in this trial would have seriously circumscribed Lindenblatt's future prospects at the National Bank.[5]

On his arrival in Germany Lindenblatt contacted the German Foreign Office in Berlin with the request for a meeting during which he could report on his assessment of the existing state of affairs in Persia. Subsequently, he reported to the Foreign Office that German nationals resident in Persia were suffering because of the reluctance of German authorities to deal effectively with the anti-Persian press campaigns originating from Germany. Lindenblatt added that as a result he was also expecting to lose his job at the bank. He explained that he was under the impression that the Persian authorities had only granted him his leave so he could return to Germany and personally clarify the Persian government's standpoint on the matter. Lindenblatt further explained that he felt that this was his last opportunity to save his own career and that of about sixty other Germans still employed by the National Bank of Persia.[6]

In the meantime the Foreign Office had received a number of reports highlighting the anti-German atmosphere in Persia. Next to the poor economic situation and the import restrictions imposed by the Persian government, the political stage also looked unfavourable for German interests. Some German nationals felt a distinct hostility directed against them. One of them reported that after Lindenblatt's departure most of the National Bank's German employees were convinced that the end of their short-term contracts also signified the end of their careers in Persia. As an example, the Persian medical administration, whose success owed much to the contribution of German nationals, felt obliged to bow to the anti-German propaganda by looking for alternative non-German, European suppliers of medical goods.[7]

An employee of the German company Schering-Kahlbaum A.G. speculated that the majority of the German colony believed that all problems had resulted from the rivalry between the National Bank and the Imperial Bank. Hence he was convinced that Leo Mattias, the main cause of all the trouble in Persia, was on Britain's payroll. He described the situation in Persia as intensely hostile towards anything German. He urged his company to contact and alert the Foreign Office in Berlin of the situation in Persia. He remarked critically that it appeared to him that the German Foreign Office did not pay the necessary attention to the events taking place in Persia, nor did it seem to appreciate the sensitivities of the Persians.[8]

Back at the National Bank, Vogel had come under pressure from Nawab. Nawab had pointed out to him that during his revision of the bank's accounts he had discovered inadequately secured loans. But Nawab had also made clear that his main intention in revealing the irregularities at the National Bank was to prove that Lindenblatt was following the instructions of his long-standing enemy Taimurtash. Hence he demanded a written statement from Vogel, in which Vogel was expected to state whether Lindenblatt was involved in foreign exchange speculations for his own benefit or for that of other clients. Moreover, Nawab wanted Vogel to testify whether key documents concerning transactions had been destroyed at the bank. Vogel's initial reaction was to counter Nawab with his resignation. It was only in consideration of appeals made by Blücher that he did not resign. Blücher had tried to advocate patience in order not to allow the rivalry of Persian politicians to be carried out on the back of Germans.[9]

However, it looked as if Blücher's efforts had come too late. Vogel managed to update him confidentially on the allegations brought against Lindenblatt, which comprised the following:

1 Manipulating bank balance sheets
(a) through improper account entries;
(b) misappropriating the bank's profits, by deducting funds from a loan granted two years earlier to a merchant named Kaseruni.
2 Engaging in foreign exchange speculations. While foreign exchange speculations were prohibited in Persia the National Bank granted foreign currency at an official rate to senior government civil servants, who sold the currency at a profit on the black market. In individual cases there were no bank slips that documented the receipt of foreign currency by these individuals. The bank also had provided, at a loss of £25,000, currency for Taimurtash's trip to Europe. Moreover, it accepted a fictional sum of £2,000 from the president of the Persian parliament in Germany, and paid him out the equivalent in Persia.
3 The discovery of unexplained extra payments to former members of the National Bank's staff led to speculations that hush money was being paid out by the bank in an attempt to cover up tracks.[10]

The most solid claim resulting from Nawab's investigation centred on the alleged foreign exchange transactions. Not only did much evidence appear to be available for this claim but it also implicated influential individuals. As described earlier similar claims had already contributed to the downfall of Taimurtash. Since they had to authorise foreign exchange transactions, it is conceivable that both Lindenblatt and Vogel had some insight into these irregularities. As for the investigation, both had to expect their Persian clients to reject any claims of wrongdoing or knowledge of illegal foreign exchange transactions. This would have left Lindenblatt and Vogel as the prime suspects of Nawab's investigation.

In light of the findings likely to result from the bank's investigation, Vogel unexpectedly disappeared from Tehran. Rumours added to the weight of the allegations against Vogel and Lindenblatt, claiming that Vogel had fled the country because he had not been able to explain the absence of 50,000–70,000 toman that had been withdrawn from foreign banks by means of five cheques. Moreover, before leaving Vogel apparently had also removed from the bank the receipts for the missing funds that had been authorised by him and Lindenblatt. Nawab investigated the whereabouts of the missing funds by obtaining information from the overseas banks from which the funds had been withdrawn. At this stage of the investigation Blücher and the German employees of the National Bank suspected that Lindenblatt and Vogel might have both been partners in crime by conspiring to embezzle the missing funds.[11]

Having considered the unfolding events and predicting the potential of further circumstantial evidence to support Nawab's allegations, Blücher requested the Foreign Office to inform Lindenblatt in Germany that probably he was to become the centre figure of a scandal of unimaginable scale. He added that such a scandal would not only destroy him morally but also would cause irreparable damage to Germany's reputation in Persia, and make miserable the lives of sixty German members of the National Bank's staff and their families. Hence Blücher requested that the Foreign Office prevail on Lindenblatt to pay back the missing funds and thereby avert the worst repercussions. He further suggested that since Vogel had put himself in a weak position by escaping the country, it might be advisable to make Vogel the main scapegoat for the prosecution. As a result of this proposal and to distract attention from Lindenblatt as prime suspect, he recommended that Lindenblatt should repay the missing funds to the National Bank in Vogel's name and return to Persia, in compliance with the Persian government request for his return.[12]

Unfortunately for Vogel and Lindenblatt, a confidential report by a German member of the National Bank's staff revealed that both could potentially face charges not only for personally profiting from illegal foreign exchange transactions but also for misappropriating 200,000 Reichsmarks forfeited from the bank's currency correction reserve accounts. The board of the bank had in addition embarked upon an investigation into forged commission payments of more than 45,000 guilders to the Dutch company Hochheimer Transandine Matschappy of Amsterdam.[13]

Faced with mounting evidence, Blücher repeatedly urged the Foreign Office to prevail on Lindenblatt and Vogel to repay the funds they had misappropriated. Blücher anticipated that this strategy would increase the likelihood of the board of the bank settling the misappropriation case behind closed doors.[14]

However, Blücher's proposed strategy for Vogel and Lindenblatt would have proved inapplicable, since after his escape Vogel had been arrested in Beirut for possessing a forged passport, and Lindenblatt's signatory authority at the National Bank had been transferred to Schneider, a German employee of the bank.[15]

In Tehran the board of the National Bank had indicated to Blücher that it was prepared to negotiate over possible solutions to the National Bank crisis. However, because of the mere fact that Vogel had escaped from Persia it felt it was impossible to continue without publicity. Hence, in the apparent absence of any other solution, Blücher ascertained that if Lindenblatt were to return to Persia and be cleared of all charges in court this would leave Vogel as the sole accused. On the other hand if Lindenblatt was proven guilty, as strongly predicted due to the strength of the circumstantial evidence, and was not prepared to repay misappropriated funds, it was most likely that he alone would be prosecuted and sentenced. In either case, the adverse publicity and consequent damage to Germany's status in Persia would have been unavoidable. Nevertheless, Blücher believed that the expected damage could be limited were Lindenblatt to return the misappropriated funds to the National Bank. He believed that this could persuade the board of the bank to consider less publicly damaging ways to settle the case.[16]

The Persian government had not raised any formal allegations against Lindenblatt. The official reason for asking him to return to Persia was that his assistance was required to clear up the irregularities uncovered through the banks investigation. Since Lindenblatt had informed the German Foreign Office of his intention to consider returning to Persia, efforts were increased in search of a rapid solution. The matter became even more urgent when the British press started exploiting the German aspect of the events surrounding the National Bank crisis to promote British interest in Persia. The German Foreign Office maintained that it was also in the Persian government's interest to work towards a quick conclusion of the crisis to protect its National Bank from further damage. Thus the Persian government that had been relying heavily on the expertise of German nationals within its financial services industry approached the German government with the request to assist in identifying a suitable candidate to replace Lindenblatt.[17]

Conceivably, the Persian authorities concurred that an end to the National Bank crisis would not only benefit Persia but also allow it to maintain its arguably beneficial relations with Germany.[18] While a timely and amicable conclusion to the National Bank crisis would also have proven beneficial for Lindenblatt's case, Vogel's case presented a totally different challenge for the German authorities.

The Charges Against National Bank Vice-director Vogel

While much effort was put by Blücher and the German Foreign Office into concluding the National Bank crisis, the board's investigation was busy uncovering more evidence against Vogel. It was discovered that on 29 January 1930 Vogel had fraudulently prepared five cheques to the total value of 70,000 toman to be drawn out of the National Bank's foreign currency reserves account. He had utilised the services of the Commerz und Privatbank in Berlin, the International Acceptance Bank in New York, the Midland Bank in London, the Amsterdam Bank in Amsterdam, and the Commercial Bank in Milan, for his transactions. After the discovery of the missing funds, Vogel had not been able to explain why these cheques were paid out, where the funds had gone to, or where the documentation for these transactions was kept.[19]

Of the above mentioned banks two had already confirmed that Vogel had credited one cheque amounting to $10,000 on 27 February 1930 to his private account, followed by a further cheque during the same month. Since this was the first conclusive evidence for fraudulent misconduct which according to Persian as well as German law constituted a crime, Blücher appealed to the Foreign Office to support the extradition of the apprehended Vogel from Beirut to the Persian authorities.[20]

Events took a turn for the worse when the Beirut authorities confirmed that Vogel had identified himself as a Bulgarian national. Subsequently, Sofia officially confirmed the authenticity of Vogel's Bulgarian citizenship. Vogel, who had completed his prison sentence in Beirut and had remained under police supervision, did admit that he had obtained Bulgarian citizenship without the obligatory permission from the German government. Hence, technically, Vogel had forfeited his German nationality at the time he had accepted his Bulgarian passport. Lindenblatt apparently knew about Vogel's unlawful dual nationality. Considering this revelation, the German representative in Beirut, Ziemke, asked the German Foreign Office whether to treat Vogel as a German national or withdraw all assistance.[21] At the request of the Persian government he had already contacted Vogel in prison to ascertain whether he was prepared to voluntarily return to Persia or not.[22]

Despite the discovery that Vogel also held Bulgarian nationality, Blücher feared that if his trial were to take place in Tehran it would cause significant damage to the status of German nationals in Persia. A trial in Tehran would have inevitably triggered numerous other investigations and intrigues against the remaining German staff of the National Bank. According to Blücher even the Persians had acknowledged the damage a local trial could do to the National Bank and felt that it was not inappropriate for the trial to take place in Berlin. Therefore Blücher recommended that the Foreign Office should demand Vogel be extradited to Germany instead of Persia. He also recommended that Vogel should be charged for fraudulently crediting a cheque to his own account at the Commerz und Privatbank in Berlin, since this would justify a trial held in Germany without the need of taking into account Vogel's Bulgarian nationality. Furthermore, Blücher was anticipating that Vogel would be charged for the unlawful application for a German passport on 25 April 1928.[23]

The evidence uncovered and strategies pursued by both sides led to the following provisional conclusions:

1 There was genuine evidence that criminal and fraudulent activities were taking place at the National Bank.
2 These activities did not only appear to benefit Persian nationals, such as Taimurtash, but also implicated German nationals.
3 The alleged illegal activities took place over a period of years and involved a range of deceptive activities.
4 It is more than likely that the directors of the National Bank, Lindenblatt and Vogel, both had knowledge of the irregularities at the bank. Hence the possibility of a pure set-up engineered by the enemies of the bank can be discounted.
5 Both directors appear to have abused their positions for personal gain.
6 Authorities on both the German and Persian side were interested in concluding the investigation of the National Bank rapidly and with as little publicity as feasible. Their main objective was to prevent further damage to Germany's reputation overseas and to the National Bank as Persia's key financial institution.
7 The Persian authorities, familiar with dealing with situations involving abuse of power for personal gain, never publicly charged Lindenblatt or Vogel.
8 The Persian authorities appeared either genuinely interested in maintaining the presence of German experts at the National Bank, or in requesting the German Foreign Office to assist with identifying a replacement for Lindenblatt, aimed at maintaining diplomatic

continuity. The rationale for this decision was either not to upset the German authorities further, or to maintain for the outside world an illusion of stability within the bank by playing down the events through re-employing a German director.

9 At this stage evidence suggests that director Vogel was the principal character behind the irregularities uncovered at the National Bank and that Blücher was trying to minimise damage to Lindenblatt's reputation by incriminating Vogel.

Vice-director Vogel's Suicide and the German Envoy to Lebanon

A further unexpected turn of events must have set shockwaves in motion for Blücher, if not for all affected. On Monday 26 September 1932 a body was discovered on the shore in Beirut and identified on the following day as that of Vogel. Ziemke, who was entrusted with the Vogel case by the German government, appeared confused. He was not sure if he should act on behalf of his government by accepting responsibility for Vogel or if he should delegate all responsibility to the French consulate that officially represented Bulgaria in Lebanon. When the Beirut police authorities formally contacted Ziemke with the news of Vogel's suicide, he told them that the German Foreign Office in Berlin had insisted that Vogel was a Bulgarian national and not German. Although he had received no official instructions from Germany, Ziemke refused to accept responsibility for administering Vogel's estate. The explanation Ziemke provided subsequently to the Foreign Office was that he did not want to interfere with the French authorities, since they were responsible for Bulgarian nationals.[24]

In a joint meeting with the French authorities and the police, Ziemke was told that the police had discovered a sketch describing the location where Vogel had committed suicide, plus two envelopes addressed to him and three additional envelopes intended for his next of kin. One of the envelopes, addressed to Ziemke, contained money that Ziemke immediately turned over to the French authorities. The other envelope contained three letters. The first indicated that Vogel planned to take his own life, and in the other two letters he acknowledged his errors.

To prevent the police from confiscating the original letters for their investigation, Ziemke offered to have the letters translated into French before handing them back to the French authorities. While he later handed over the translated suicide note, Ziemke opted not to hand over Vogel's two confession letters to the French or police authorities. When asked about their whereabouts, Ziemke's plan was to state that he had already mailed the letters to the German Foreign Office in Berlin without keeping copies.

After Vogel was laid to rest at the former German Protestant cemetery in Beirut, Ziemke requested the German consulate in Sofia to inform his next of kin of his death. He also notified Blücher of Vogel's suicide but did not disclose anything about the discovered envelopes. Considering Vogel's confession letters Ziemke suspected that Vogel and Lindenblatt were to be blamed for the serious irregularities at the National Bank of Persia. However, what also became evident to him was that Vogel was not the main character behind the irregularities. As a result Ziemke confidentially informed the Foreign Office that he had left out the following revealing paragraph from Vogel's suicide note in the translation prepared for the French authorities: 'The gold I had received from Dr Lindenblatt, for which I had also signed a receipt (for Dr Lindenblatt), I delivered through Mr Klemme to Gesandtschaftsrat Mayer for Dr Lindenblatt.'[25] Ziemke appeared to have launched a cunning and unofficial cover-up in Beirut to protect German interests and implicitly Lindenblatt.

Vogel's Insight into the Irregularities at the National Bank

To gain a more objective view of what Vogel really wanted to communicate and its wider implications, it is necessary to carefully examine the original letters left by him including his suicide note, confession letter, a letter addressed to his wife and a letter addressed to Lindenblatt.

In his suicide note Vogel mainly disclosed that he was not able to protect Lindenblatt as before and that he felt that Lindenblatt had to stand up for his own mistakes. In addition Vogel referred to Lindenblatt's gold before requesting in detail what should happen with his remaining possessions, followed by instructions for his funeral. He further appealed to Ziemke to inform his family of his death but ask his wife not to come to Beirut. Vogel continued to explain that he had already considered committing suicide in Tehran but believed that he could escape from his problems by leaving Persia. He stated to regret having to end a life of hard work in such an undignified way, but that he saw no other solution.[26]

By turning to Vogel's confessional letter we may discover what led him to commit suicide and why Ziemke decided to conceal this letter from the French authorities, from the police authorities in Beirut, and from Blücher in Tehran.

Vogel admitted that on two occasions he had received large bonuses from Lindenblatt for extraordinary duties. He explained that Lindenblatt had repeatedly assured him that as the only person responsible and as director of the National Bank of Persia he was authorised to approve such payments. In his letter Vogel pointed out that he had no insight into Lindenblatt's contract or into his dealings with the board of the bank. He knew only that Lindenblatt had also approved bonuses of the same or higher amounts for himself. Vogel admitted that he had knowledge of these transactions and that he knowingly assisted Lindenblatt by, for example, running the funds through his own accounts before returning them to Lindenblatt by writing out a cheque or transfer, or by signing off the relevant receipts. Hence, if some receipts only carried his signature it did not mean that Lindenblatt was left in the dark. All the measures he took were taken with Lindenblatt's approval and under his supervision. Vogel further stated that all the foreign transactions were managed from the National Bank's secretariat in Tehran and went through a foreign exchange fluctuation account, also known as Konto Trans.[27]

Moreover, Vogel admitted that he had become so confused by the events of the past months that without relying on his files in Tehran he could not remember the exact amounts he had received as bonuses for extraordinary duties. This was partly because Lindenblatt's share of the funds had to be deducted from the total sums transferred from the National Bank's Konto Trans account to Vogel's overseas accounts. Vogel lastly pointed out that Lindenblatt generally transferred his own funds directly to his overseas bank.[28]

In a last letter to his wife Vogel explained to her that the Persian authorities were trying to charge him for embezzlement of the bonuses he had received from Lindenblatt for extraordinary work. From his letter, in which he described in some detail the nature of his financial transactions, it appears that he believed himself not to have done anything wrong. He held that if a German court was to judge the case he was certain that his innocence would have been confirmed. Likewise he appreciated that regarding the circumstantial evidence it would have proven not easy to clear himself of all allegations particularly in the absence of his insight into the arrangements made between the board of the National Bank and Lindenblatt.[29]

Vogel addressed a further final letter to Lindenblatt. In this letter he tried to describe why he had fled and what had happened after he had taken over the bank. Vogel explained that what he had to go through since Lindenblatt's departure had been beyond his powers. He believed what he had suffered was not merely testing him to the limit but that it constituted a form of torture. He explained that this was why he had lost his sanity, leaving him with only one solution, which was to leave Persia at all cost. Since all foreign staff of the National Bank were under police observation, he could not have left Persia with his own passport. Hence, with the objective of travelling to Berlin to try to clarify the situation in a meeting with Lindenblatt, he bought a false passport and left the country. Vogel himself suspected that someone had tipped off the authorities so that he was arrested in Beirut and sentenced to fourteen days in jail. His jail sentence ended on 22 September 1932. However, he still was not permitted to continue his journey because he was asked to remain in Beirut and report to the police on a daily basis until completely vindicated.[30]

Vogel continued his letter to Lindenblatt by pointing out that he had become completely perplexed because despite the German embassy in Sofia confirming to the German embassy in Beirut that he was a Bulgarian national, not only had the Persian authorities asked for his extradition but the French courts wanted him transferred to Paris. He was also surprised to hear that he was being charged for embezzling 200,000 marks and performing account balance manipulations at the National Bank. At this stage Vogel had decided he had to take action, and that it was not realistic anymore to count on meeting Lindenblatt to discuss a solution. Vogel had further explained that the investigation of the bank covered not the last business year of the National Bank's operations but the entire period since its existence. Likewise, Vogel made a point of disclosing that two bank employees, Clavier and Movat, were well acquainted with all transactions, including his bonus payments, made through the Konto Trans accounts at the secretariat.[31]

Vogel described into what detail the investigations of the National Bank had gone, which included criticising every aspect of out of contract payments to companies and clients of the bank, and particularly his and other employee's unconventional bonus payments. Vogel suggested to Lindenblatt that the two of them should jointly try and explain all transactions, despite lacking documentation, and consider paying back part of the funds personally received to clarify and settle the case with the Persian authorities.

The only explanation Vogel had for the Persian authorities' claim that he had embezzled 200,000 marks was that all the transactions throughout the years that had been credited to his account had been added together. Since this total amount was not equivalent to what he had received, as the transfers often included Lindenblatt's share of bonus payments, he felt unjustifiably accused. Moreover, since Lindenblatt was responsible to the board of the bank and had full knowledge of the account movements within the bank's balance sheets, Vogel felt not guilty as charged.[32]

In his letter Vogel regretted the way in which a period of sacrifice and hard work for the cause of the National Bank of Persia had come to an end. He continued by describing how the bank employee Movat tried to justify all irregularities by accusing Taimurtash for his unauthorised interference in the bank's businesses. Soon, encouraged by Clavier, both Movat and Clavier had changed their tone and developed an antipathy against the German staff of the bank. Vogel also pointed out to Lindenblatt that the privileges granted to Taimurtash and other Persian nationals had also been uncovered by the Persian authorities. However, he saw a major difference between the accused Persian nationals and himself. Vogel was convinced that had he stayed in Persia the Persian nationals would have come to some sort of arrangement between themselves, leaving him exposed to be crushed between the mill-stones of the political and personal intrigues of the opposing parties. The most threatening aspect of the situation for him was that he did not believe in Persian justice. He quoted Movat, who had stated that although Persia had a legal system, and even a parliament, nothing could rival the will of the Shah. Vogel knew of ample cases that proved this statement and therefore had little confidence in the Persian legal system. He was devastated by the notion that all the effort, hard work, overtime, and personal sacrifice made by German employees for the advancement of National Bank, was over-looked by individuals such as Movat and his colleagues. These were chasing every impropriety, however minor, that could stain the achievements of German nationals. Vogel concluded his letter to Lindenblatt by writing that he felt he had turned into an ideal candidate for a sanatorium.[33]

It transpires that Vogel saw himself faced with an unstoppable flood of accusations resulting from the investigation of the National Bank and the fear of an inadequate system of justice in Persia. We also may conclude from his letters that Vogel felt victimised and not responsible for what he was accused of. Since Vogel had knowingly accepted irregular and exceptional payments from Lindenblatt he was consequently implicated in the financial irregularities. Therefore his confessions come across as disingenuous or almost impossibly naive. If his statements were taken as read, this would shift the main focus of responsibility for the destructive irregularities at the bank back to Lindenblatt. Hence, when Blücher and the German Foreign Office, in all likelihood influenced by Blücher's reports, tried to single out Vogel as the main person responsible, this may have proven unjust. Their assessment would have undoubtedly been tainted by Vogel's escape and later by his suicide.

If the German Foreign Office was aware of the likelihood of Vogel's minor role in the events, its modus operandi would have been motivated either by the goal of bringing the whole matter to a quick and quiet end at any price, or of covering up Lindenblatt's mistakes. In both cases the limitation of damage to Germany's reputation could have been the only main objective of the Foreign Office. What remains verifiable is that there was a serious body of evidence supporting the accuracy of some of the accusations brought forward by the investigating committee against the German directors of the National Bank. Lindenblatt's early decision to leave Persia, to bring his family and property into safety, and Vogel's suicide, despite his possible minor involvement, are realities supporting the above deductions. The questions that remain are how seriously the German Foreign Office took the loss of face surrounding the National Bank crisis, and what the consequences of the crisis were for those National Bank employees accused, including Lindenblatt.

Policy and Reality Surrounding Corruption Allegations

Director Dieckhoff of the German Foreign Office had agreed with Lindenblatt that he should follow the request of the Persian authorities by leaving Berlin for Tehran. Consequently Lindenblatt travelled to Tehran on 11 October 1932.[34] It would be justified to assume that life for the remaining German employees of the bank must have become increasingly arduous. Realistically, Lindenblatt's return to Persia could have only worsened the situation for himself and for them.

One of the employees of the National Bank at the Borudjerd branch, H. E. Altenburg, reported that his German staff at the bank were suffering from an intensifying and severe influx of harassment and agitation originating from the Persian side. Moreover, Altenburg felt that he could not rely on any protection or support for his provincial branch from the remaining German staff at the National Bank's headquarters in Tehran. Altenburg even suspected that he was being victimised by his German colleagues in Tehran who were trying to save their own necks. As a result he handed in his resignation so he could leave the bank for Germany as soon as feasible. Altenburg justified his decision by arguing that since every effort had been made by the Persians to rapidly remove all Germans from office, he did not intend to wait and further render himself a victim of the unpredictable moves of his counterparts. Although he did not expect a smooth departure from Persia or an easy transition into work back in Germany, he was determined to leave, as were his German colleagues Arndt and possibly Cleinow.[35]

As noted earlier, the Persian authorities had up to this stage never officially formulated any charges against German individuals. Nor did the Persian side hold the German Foreign Office accountable for any of its findings at the bank. The Persian authorities did not even come up with any type of formal disciplinary measures against the remaining German staff of the National Bank. Yet, as a result of the indirect consequences and the tensions created, a large number of the German bank employees had either left or were planning to leave the country. What is noteworthy is that, as in Altenburg's case, many German individuals believed that they had been abandoned by their own nationals and government and left to survive on their own.

In short, the events surrounding the National Bank of Persia did not cause a diplomatic crisis between Germany and Persia, but could have led to an economic crisis, accompanied by a loss of face for Germany. It is worth noting that Germany itself was navigating through difficult times with an economic crisis and high unemployment. Moreover, the sharp-minded Shah was likely to make this circumstance and the whole National Bank crisis work to his advantage before long.

To gain an insight into the official position of the Persian government regarding the National Bank crisis, it is of interest to turn to an interview given by the Persian foreign minister Foroughi to a Turkish publisher. Asked about the relations between Germany and Persia, when simultaneously presented with an outline of recent difficulties both countries had to deal with, Foroughi responded to the Turkish journalist by explaining that the word 'difficulty' was far too extreme when used to describe the recent events. He emphasised that he had no knowledge of any difficulties. At most, he continued to explain, there had been some disagreements between Persian authorities and a number of German newspapers that had occasionally printed material that had offended the Shah. He emphasised that this matter, which meanwhile had been resolved, had no bearing on the essentially good relations maintained by both countries and their people.[36]

The interview made clear that Foroughi, when asked about the National Bank, was formally satisfied with its administration under the management of director Lindenblatt. But he pointed out that he did regret that the news of Vogel's flight and suicide came as such a surprise during the legitimate routine review of the bank that it led to speculations alleging a link between Vogel's suicide and the National Bank's review. However, Foroughi stated that he was confident that the almost completed investigation of the bank would deliver reassuring clarity in this matter. Foroughi moreover re-emphasised that, particularly in view of the Persian authority's endeavours to replace Lindenblatt, who had resigned from his office, with a German national, this issue also had no bearing on Persia's relations with Germany.[37]

Foroughi added that reports alleging that the Persian government was dissatisfied with German railway construction, or was trying to distance itself from German construction companies, were unjustified. He concluded his interview by reassuring the readers that the Persian government was not only inclined but also determined to employ the excellent German technical expertise to advance Persia's development, wherever the opportunity and possibility arose.[38]

On the basis of Foroughi's interview the impression is given, although it is difficult to verify, that the Persian government was officially trying to play down the National Bank crisis as incidental, while internally continuing with vigour the investigation of the bank's business. This dichotomy caused a possibly deliberate degree of tension and anxiety for German bank employees that culminated in many cases in their resignations. Hence, to a certain extent policy and reality were contradicting each other. One possible reason for this contradiction might have been an ongoing and personally motivated manoeuvre of the Shah against the National Bank and its directors. The Shah, who identified himself closely with Persia, or in other words, as often described, who perceived Persia as 'his' country, must have felt cheated and robbed by the same German nationals he was previously known to have admired a great deal. This possible personal perception of the Shah, however, appeared to be in sharp contrast to the official position of the Persian government. Nevertheless, since the two fronts did not clash publicly, there is little evidence to substantiate the above hypothesis.

The German Foreign Office on the other hand did not formally compromise its fragile relations with Persia by applying political pressure for the benefit of its nationals left stranded in the country. Informally, the Foreign Office appeared to maintain an approach of indecisive idleness when confronted with the specific predicaments of its nationals implicated in the National Bank crisis. Ultimately, this stance of the German government risked the livelihood and safety of its nationals in Persia and established its inability or unwillingness to take concerted action.

Lindenblatt and his German Colleagues Face Formal Prosecution

On 26 September 1933 Lindenblatt received a formal letter of invitation from the Persian embassy in Berlin requesting his return to Persia. He had already requested government protection from the German embassy in Tehran, in case he did comply with Persia's request and returned to Tehran. The official reason stated for the request for his return by the Persian embassy was that Lindenblatt's presence was required to provide information on the controversy regarding the management of the National Bank and to prepare the hand-over of the bank's commercial projects. Since Lindenblatt's invitation to return was issued by the Persian government, the Persian authorities declared themselves prepared to reimburse Lindenblatt for his travel expenses and to continue paying his salary. A copy of this invitation was sent by the Persian embassy in Berlin to the German Foreign Office with the request that they prevail on Lindenblatt to return to Persia soon.[39]

When Lindenblatt was invited to the German Foreign Office to discuss the matter he was told that he alone had to make the decision whether to return to Persia or not. However, if he decided to go, the Foreign Office promised to ask the German embassy in Tehran to request from the Persian authorities his unhindered entry and exit out of Persia, as well as immunity from prosecution when in Persia. Before reaching a final decision Lindenblatt had hoped to formally clarify the true nature of the Persian government's request. Thus, aided by the Persian ambassador in Berlin, Ala, he contacted the Persian government with his concerns. The response of the Persian government, which had been endorsed by the Shah and parliament, was communicated to Lindenblatt via Ala in presence of representative Samiy as follows:

> Personne en Perse n'a l'intention de vous faire du mal ni de vous traduire en justice ou de vous arrêter, il s'agit plutôt du transfert des comptes et donner de renseignements sur les affaires de la Banque et le temps de votre séjour en Perse sera celui que nécessitera le règlement de ces affaires.
>
> [No one in Persia intends to do you harm or bring you to justice or to arrest you; it is a matter rather of transfers of accounts and information about the Bank's business, and the period of your stay in Persia will be what is necessary to resolve these matters.]

Lindenblatt felt so reassured by the Persian government's response that he decided before leaving not to follow up and apply for guaranteed entry and exit visas or insist on an official immunity from prosecution when in Persia. After notifying the German Foreign Office of his decision he left for Tehran accompanied by his legal representative Hirschowitz.[40]

However, even after six months in Persia, Lindenblatt felt that not much had resulted from his and Hirschowitz's efforts towards clarifying and settling his prevailing disagreements with the Persian authorities. He isolated as his major challenge the concentration of the bank's investigation on personality matters rather than facts. Lindenblatt saw in the person of Nawab his main enemy. Lindenblatt recalled that he had been informed by a reliable source that Nawab was an agent of a third power, and that during a court session in Berlin Nawab's own legal representative had labelled him as mentally unfit. These were certainly no preconditions for a healthy settlement of Lindenblatt and the bank's case. When in Tehran Lindenblatt was meeting regularly with representatives of the National Bank including Nawab and

Clavier. He felt that both were on the one hand displaying their willingness to bring the prevailing disagreements to a positive end, but were on the other hand obstructing progress by, for example, forestalling Hirschowitz's access to documents crucial to the resolution of the inquiry.[41]

On 10 April 1933 Lindenblatt formally handed over the directorship of the National Bank of Persia. However, he was informed that just a few days before the hand-over either the bank or Nawab had referred his case for further investigation to the Persian judiciary authorities. This meant that Lindenblatt could expect to be arrested at any moment. His house had been put under observation by the secret police. In a desperate attempt, Lindenblatt requested the German embassy to explore every possible avenue to secure the immunity from prosecution he had initially been promised. Lindenblatt was conscious of the fact that in the course of the trial proceedings against Taimurtash, as a result of which Taimurtash was convicted, Lindenblatt himself had in reality emerged as the main suspect implicated in the findings of the judiciary investigation, the only difference being that at the time he was not on trial.[42]

Meanwhile, consultations were in progress at the German ministry for trade and industry that aimed at determining the status of the German companies whose payments from the National Bank were overdue. The former financial adviser to the Persian government, Schniewind, as well as the former representative of the National Bank and manager of the Shahi factory, Bertram, were also invited to the meetings. During these consultations it became evident that, for example, in the case of the Shahi factory, the Shah, after discovering the profitability of the factory, had decided to take over the ownership of the factory without considering the rights of the remaining shareholders. Therefore the National Bank was left to deal with the consequences and had to promise the Shah that it would deal with the problems expected in settling the outstanding financial obligations of the factory with the supplying German companies. The German companies on the other hand could only negotiate with the National Bank since it was the only contractual partner they were in business with. During the meetings any doubt over the legitimacy of outstanding claims against the National Bank had been removed. The repeated calls from Gloye to show some moderation in demands in order not to endanger future German business with Persia were rejected. The participating companies were not convinced of the commercial viability or of an increase of future business opportunities for German companies dealing with the National Bank. These findings of the ministry of trade and industry foreshadowed the destructive side effects of the National Bank crisis for the future of German–Persian economic relations. The National Bank had been the largest single trade partner for German companies in Persia. Not only had German influence over the bank been effectively lost, but also the bank's potential as a future trade partner for German companies was put in doubt.[43]

The ministry of trade and industry instructed the Foreign Office to advise the German embassy in Tehran to support the negotiations between the concerned German companies and the National Bank. Likewise, the ministry recommended that the embassy should try to convey appropriately that it was of no advantage for the international relations of the National Bank of Persia if it appeared not to comply with the legitimate claims of its overseas trade partners. This statement is one of the few clear warnings issued by a German government agency against Persian authorities. However, it is doubtful that Blücher ever conveyed this message in its full strength to the responsible individuals. Blücher definitely did not want to exasperate further the situation for Lindenblatt and other German nationals employed in Persia.[44]

The Persian authorities' line of investigation against Germans had continued indiscriminately, targeting further German nationals employed by the National Bank. Heinrich Rust, the German director of the National Bank branch in Ahwaz, and former member of the executive of the National Bank in Tehran, was for example summoned to Tehran to give evidence in the court case against Lindenblatt. Blücher, who kept a watchful eye on Rust, was personally satisfied with the line of evidence presented by Rust, which established in essence that Lindenblatt had been, as the bank's director, fully in charge and responsible for all major activities of the bank. Nevertheless, the Persian judge reached a different conclusion and to Blücher's surprise had Rust arrested and in doing so set a bail of 15,000 toman for his release. Blücher immediately filed a complaint with the Persian foreign minister, criticising the fact that a 60-year-old man with an impeccable track record had been arrested under such questionable circumstances.[45]

A letter by H. S. Kazem Alavi made clear how respected and appreciated Rust actually was as the director of the Ahwaz branch of the National Bank:

> I can say that Banque National de Perse, Ahwaz, took a step towards progress only from the time you possessed the honourable art of management, and it was really the best and fairest root you considered for the merchants ... The merchants are all confidently sure that if you had stayed a longer period at Ahwaz, the banque would have got a very good situation, and no complaints would rise from any individual, and with the views that they have in favour of banque Nationale

> de Perse no one would have referred their business to the Imperial Bank of Persia ... The Khuzistan merchants in general and myself in special give you our best and purable salams and beg to remain.[46]

Blücher contacted director Walter Horschitz-Horst at the National Bank with the suggestion that he should try to persuade his colleagues jointly to come up with Rust's bail. Horschitz-Horst took over the initiative and managed to secure the support of all sixteen remaining German employees of the National Bank in Tehran and that of nine German branch managers. As a result the bail sum was raised and Rust was released from prison after four days. At this stage Blücher was still not convinced that a case could be brought against Rust and hoped that an out-of-court settlement could be reached. Yet the thought that Rust's arrest might have marked the beginning of a series of arrests of German nationals in Persia worried him. Nevertheless, for once the German staff of the National Bank demonstrated to the Persian authorities that in the event of indiscriminate arrests of German bank employees, the authorities would be faced not only with an individual but also, in solidarity, with all of them.[47] This should not, however, distract from the fact that the Persian authorities were frantically trying to tighten the circle of evidence against a number of Germans employed by the National Bank including Lindenblatt. Clearly a solution for the National Bank crisis was far from being reached. Nor was it apparent how a solution might constitute itself. After bargaining away the opportunity of an out-of-court settlement between Lindenblatt, Vogel and the board of directors of the National Bank, the only route left open to the Persian authorities was to formally press charges against Lindenblatt and his German colleagues.

Criminal Charges Brought against German Bank Employees

In one particularly perceptive report, Döcker, a German employee of the National Bank, presented his own account of the events that had taken place at the bank in conjunction with the allegations brought forward by the Persian authorities against the German employees of the National Bank, including Lindenblatt. Döcker provides a rare insight into the background of the events that took place behind the closed doors of the National Bank. His account of events reveals the motives behind the alleged fraudulent account manipulations and foreign exchange transactions at the bank, the individuals responsible, and the significance and scale of the alleged fraud in the context of the operations of the National Bank.

According to Döcker's accounts, from the time that the investigation of the National Bank had uncovered irregularities and improprieties committed by Lindenblatt and Vogel the main focus of all remaining German employees of the bank had been to prove to the outside world that a clear distinction had to be made between dishonest and honest employees of the National Bank, by readily assisting the Persian authorities with their investigative enquiries.[48]

Döcker recalled how the investigating judge, Chademann, had approached him personally with the request to assist with the inquiry into the National Bank. Döcker was made to believe that he was being questioned in his capacity as a witness, expert and banker. At no point was there a mention that his evidence might later be used against him as the accused. This modus operandi of the Persian authorities was similar to what Rust had experienced previously.

Döcker described the methods adopted by the judge during his inquiry and the process of his note-taking as questionable. Considering the recent events he felt helpless when faced with the anti-German attitude of the Persian courts, judges and their translators.[49] Following their interrogations the Persian authorities proceeded to formally charge Döcker and his colleagues Rust, Stephan, Scheiblich and Feubel.

Döcker had been employed by Lindenblatt as his personal secretary. His contract had clearly stated that he was directly responsible to Lindenblatt and that he was expected to follow his direct instructions. He recalled how strict and intolerant Lindenblatt had been. Whenever Döcker had tried to criticise something, Lindenblatt had replied, 'Keep out of this, I alone am responsible for this decision.' Döcker also recalled how a few days earlier at the manager's office of the National Bank the chairman of the board, Nawab, had described Lindenblatt as a person with the character of a dictator. Nawab had further stated that Lindenblatt did not even care to obey him, his superior. At the same occasion Nawab had also stated that were the five accused German employees of the bank to be prosecuted, then the whole board of the bank and the Persian government had also to be held responsible for entrusting a single individual with so much power in the first place. Döcker felt irritated by the fact that he and his colleagues, who had put enormous effort into developing the National Bank, were about to be punished for executing their superiors' orders.[50]

Döcker considered that the root of all problems lay in the Shah's request to the National Bank that it should implement a questionable reform of the foreign exchange law in order to stabilise the toman, the Persian national currency. This law reform had triggered a series of chain reactions that ultimately led to those irregularities on which the Persian authorities had based their charges against German employees of the National Bank. The new law possessed serious weaknesses that ultimately encouraged unwanted foreign exchange speculations by merchants and the emergence of black market trading. It did not take long for the National Bank to run out of foreign currency insofar as it could not even satisfy the demands of the government or of pilgrims travelling abroad. The National Bank had become the main victim of the reform. Döcker explained that the employees of the bank could not believe that the Persian government would entrust the responsibility for stabilising its currency to such a young (the National Bank was only one-and-a-half years old at the time) and inexperienced institution as the National Bank. However, the unthinkable had become true, and since the National Bank had lost tremendous amounts of money the German staff of the bank assumed that the financial losses had been approved through Lindenblatt by the Persian government or Taimurtash. They were certain that Lindenblatt would never have permitted such losses to accumulate.

In the absence of any genuine support by the Persian government for the bank's dire situation, Lindenblatt had decided to take matters in his own hands and introduced a system by which the bank would purchase durable goods in Persia for the sole purpose of exporting them abroad. His plan was that the foreign currency acquired through the sales of these goods would in turn be used to balance the prevailing foreign currency deficits of the National Bank. For this purpose, under the management of Rust, he created Secretariat B (Figure 6.1).[51]

In short, what followed was a series of account manipulations within the balance sheets of the bank to accommodate, from an accounting point of view, the new business of Secretariat B. The objective of this reorganisation was genuinely to combat further losses for the bank. According to Döcker, these movements were undoubtedly unorthodox but did not serve the benefit of any one member of staff. Hence those of the bank's staff who were aware of the changes felt quite confident that they had no cause for concern, since their operations were financially sound and approved by Lindenblatt. What they did not know was that Lindenblatt had not discussed or reported the reorganisation or account manipulations to the board of the National Bank. Döcker remained convinced that judgement over these proceedings was a matter of opinion. Regarding his own case, which was probably typical of the five accused German members of the National Bank's staff, he maintained that he had only followed Lindenblatt and Vogel's instructions and never intended to manipulate or hide anything.[52]

Considering his statement, it should be apparent that if Döcker's account was reasonably accurate, and if the Persian authorities' investigation

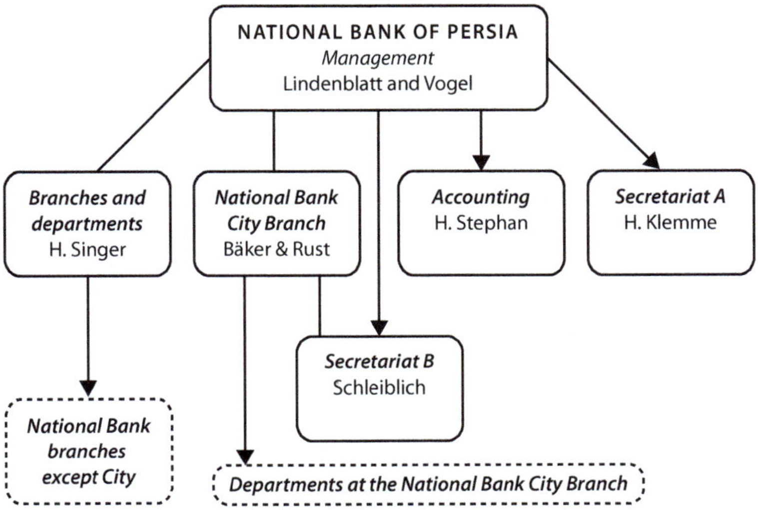

Figure 6.1 Management hierarchy at the National Bank of Persia as described by Döcker.

supported the evidence cited, the Persian courts would have had insufficient reason to justify seriously prosecuting the bank's accused German employees. That the situation for Lindenblatt, as the main person in charge, had to be different has also become evident. However, there remain too many gaps, open questions and uncertainties, not covered by the evidence available, to justify a conclusion. For example, it would have been interesting to find out what the objective of the Persian authorities' investigation was. Could it have been the actual explanation of the financial irregularities, or could political motives have played a role? An inquiry into the unfolding court cases against the German employees of the National Bank in Persia should provide more details about the actual motives behind the Lindenblatt and National Bank affair.

Lindenblatt's Prison Sentence and a New Opportunity for Germany

The subsequent unavoidable lawsuits against Lindenblatt and the other accused German employees of the National Bank took place from 1 to 13 October 1933. The court passed its judgement accordingly on 14 October 1933. Blücher reported that the Persian authorities, recognising the significance of what was the first major Persian court case brought against foreign nationals since Persia's abandonment of the capitulation rights, believed the case would attract much attention from the world media. Therefore the proceedings were conducted in an impeccable manner, leaving no room for criticism.

According to Blücher the court was made up of one presiding judge and two assessor judges, both of whom had lived for a long time in Berlin and spoke German. On the defence side, two Persian legal experts and his own attorney Hirschowitz from Berlin represented Lindenblatt. Rust was represented by one of the best-respected legal experts, influential lawyer, and Member of Parliament, Schariatzadeh. The other German nationals were represented by one Persian lawyer each. Blücher felt that thanks to Schariatzadeh's guidance all lawyers had agreed to pursue the same line of defence. Their main objective was to undermine jointly the prosecution's strongest claim by proving beyond doubt that there was no foundation on which the prosecution could base its accusation of deliberate forgery and deception regarding the National Bank's accounts. Success in proving this point in court would have eliminated one of the strongest allegations brought against Lindenblatt, and removed the only claim brought against Rust and the other accused Germans. Blücher explained that, as far as he could judge, the lawyers were pursuing their clients' cases in an outstanding manner, with profound sensitivity for the circumstances, and an excellent knowledge of the state of affairs.[53]

Surprisingly, the court case attracted less attention than Blücher had expected. Although the courtroom had been full to the last space during the first and final days of the trial, during the other days there were hardly any spectators. Moreover, almost no foreigners, Persian dignitary or members of the German expatriate community had attended the proceedings. Even the correspondent of the Times, resident in Tehran, had decided to stay away. Also the Shah appeared not to have interfered with the court proceedings. Blücher considered it fortunate that the Shah was away travelling throughout the trial. He also felt that the judges were performing their duties in a professional and unbiased manner.

During the court case, in reply to the defendants' lawyers, the public prosecutor clarified that the claims brought against a number of German nationals were in no way intended to represent Persia's verdict on Germany or its relations with German nationals. Blücher described how the public prosecutor had expressed his wish to be able to further contribute to the improvement of the current good relations between Persia and Germany.

The pronouncement of the judges' verdict followed on the thirteenth day of the trial. The court had reached its final verdict and declared Lindenblatt, and thereby also his other German colleagues, not guilty of the charge of forging the National Bank's balance sheets. Accordingly the judges pronounced Lindenblatt free of the main charge brought against him and completely dropped all charges against Rust and the other German nationals. Despite this, Lindenblatt was found guilty of the charge of breach of confidence and dishonest foreign exchange dealings. On those accounts, the law required Lindenblatt to be sentenced to three years imprisonment. However, taking into account Lindenblatt's track record and his services to the National Bank and thereby the Persian government, and in consideration of the circumstance that he was by nature not criminally inclined, the court decided to halve his sentence to eighteen months' imprisonment. In addition Lindenblatt was ordered to pay a cash fine of £7,000 as well as 46,000 rials.[54] Following the completion of his prison term Lindenblatt's release date was scheduled for 8 December 1934.[55]

As was then common in Persian courts, both the public prosecutor and Lindenblatt's lawyers planned to appeal against the court's sentence. Blücher was not very pleased with this plan because in the vast majority of cases the only result the appeal court had delivered was to verify the original sentence. Furthermore, Blücher was glad that this unhappy chapter of German history in Persia had finally ended. An appeal would have meant that the whole issue was raised again and would have unnecessarily extended the period of uncertainty for the other accused Germans. Blücher therefore planned to discreetly persuade the Persian authorities to refrain from revising the court's judgement and not to allow an escalation of the case to the court of appeal.[56]

The general impression left by the verdict was one of relief and satisfaction, ending several months of suspension in a legally faultless manner. Blücher held that Lindenblatt could not have received a milder sentence and that in reality a German court would probably have sentenced him more severely. Blücher was pleased that the remaining German employees of the National Bank were proven not guilty on all charges. This eliminated the basis for rumours that had alleged a conspiracy by all German employees to rob the National Bank. This also encouraged Blücher to believe that the court's verdict would contribute to an end of the negative state of affairs for German foreign policy and economic influence in Persia that had been fuelled by the National Bank crisis.

To minimise the after-effects of the court case he petitioned the Foreign Office to appeal to the German press to handle the Lindenblatt incident, which was highly embarrassing for Germany's status overseas, with utter sensitivity. He pointed out that the Persian press, although reporting on the Lindenblatt case on a daily basis, had voluntarily refrained from any kind of comments or criticism. Therefore Blücher felt it was necessary for the

German press also to refrain from criticising the Persian authorities' legal proceedings. Since two German nationals, Stratil-Sauer, and the former reporter for the publisher Ullstein Verlag, von Stwolinski, had frequented the court sessions, Blücher also had asked them to refrain from writing articles or publishing any photographs in conjunction with the Lindenblatt case in the German media. Nevertheless, Blücher reported to the Foreign Office that both men had been seen taking secretly notes during court sessions and therefore it was to be expected that they would try to publish sensationalist articles in German newspapers. He recommended that the Foreign Office should seek the assistance of the press department to prevent the publication of material connected to the Lindenblatt case in Germany.[57]

However, in a condemning report by an observer Blücher was criticised for not having tried to resolve the entire National Bank affair directly and discreetly behind closed doors and without publicity. Apparently, according to a senior member of the National Bank, Blücher was offered a resolution of the misappropriation case through repayment of the funds embezzled, similarly to an incident involving Italian nationals who had thereby resolved a comparable conflict. The accused Italian national was later prosecuted in Italy. In pursuit of resolving this incident the Italian ambassador had communicated directly with Mussolini. Hence Blücher was sharply criticised for having been in Berlin, and having even met with the Reichspräsident personally, and yet having taken no steps to discreetly settle the case of the National Bank. As described earlier, however, there is enough evidence to show that this strategy was not alien to Blücher, and that its execution might have been jeopardised by Vogel's escape.[58]

Further criticism condemned the incapabilities of the German embassy in Tehran, which had led to a tremendous loss of respect for German nationals in the eyes of the Persian population. Even other European nationals in Persia were furious with the Germans since they also had to suffer under the hostile anti-foreigner atmosphere thus created. The management of the National Bank and the German embassy were likewise considered to be fully responsible for the millions Germany had lost in business over the past years. Moreover, Lindenblatt's decision to appeal his court order, instead of forgetting the 'disgraceful' matter, had met with even more disapproval.[59]

Germany's lost ground in Persia becomes self-evident when looking at the trade figures for the year 1932, during which Persia exported goods worth 18.5 million marks to Germany. During the same period Germany exported goods worth only 5.5 million marks to Persia. In 1929 German exports to Persia had totalled 14 million marks but since then they had decreased constantly. Areas such as railway construction had suffered dramatically as well.

German companies had lost much business as a result of the Persian authorities distancing themselves from German suppliers. Otherwise it would be difficult to explain why, in the case of new sugar factories, they had placed an order for six plants with the Czechoslovakian company Skoda instead of as previously with German suppliers.[60]

During this period an initiative originating from the German embassy in Tehran, which proposed combating Germany's trade deficit with Persia by increasing German import duties on Persian goods, came under fire as being an easy solution for the embassy but likely to make Germans even more unpopular in Persia. In 1933 Persia was perceived as a rich country with almost no foreign debt, a reasonably safe currency, and a potentially large and regular income from the Anglo-Persian Oil Company's oil fields. Consequently, Persia was a country that was not only determined to invest in its development, but because of its ability to pay also remained a commercially attractive partner for economic ventures. Persia needed a wide range of heavy machinery for its factories. It also had to continue importing most of the material necessary for the construction of its ambitious railway project. Germany on the other hand remained a leading candidate for supplying the goods Persia required. Moreover, it was in the German interest to utilise income generated from its exports to balance its sizeable trade deficit with Persia. There was major criticism of the German embassy in Tehran for the failure to improve German trade with Persia. Moreover, it was accused of being completely out of touch with its nationals. The German embassy was further criticised for recommending increasing import duties on Persian goods instead of aiming to support German trade with Persia. In this context the resulting replacement of the senior embassy official, Meyer, with Zölch was considered as a first step in the right direction.[61]

The resources invested in the investigation of the National Bank by the Persian authorities and Nawab had paid off. The authorities were able to eliminate a degree of unorthodox activities within the bank. It was only unfortunate for the German authorities that the principal individuals accused of questionable activities were German nationals working for the National Bank. First the National Bank's director, Lindenblatt, came under fire, then its vice-director, Vogel, followed by five further German members of the bank's staff. It also transpired that the German ambassador in Tehran, Blücher, had been criticised for his inability to identify himself with his own nationals and help resolve the problems the accused faced in a discreet and diplomatic manner. Hence the negative publicity the case attracted greatly harmed the status of Germany and Germans in Persia. However, it can be regarded as constructive in that, except for Lindenblatt, the Persian courts cleared all the Germans who had been accused of any misconduct. This verdict came too late for Vogel, who, as a result of the Persian authorities' investigation, lost self-control and committed suicide.

It might therefore be regarded as only rational for the Persian government authorities to want simply to replace Lindenblatt by re-employing a German national, Horschitz-Horst, as the new director of the National Bank. The Persian authorities furthermore employed a German national, Acker, as director of the newly established agricultural bank in Tehran.[62]

These 'gestures' by the Persian government were suspiciously generous at first sight. They could have employed any expert from any other country they desired, but they remained true to Germany in spite of their recent negative experiences with the Lindenblatt affair and the consequent political and economic tensions between the two nations. One conclusion that might be drawn is that the Persian government, in view of its lack of significant trade partners, possibly saw its trade relations with Germany as indispensable. They might even have counted on encouraging the German government to repay the 'favour' by, for example, facilitating additional essential trade loans to Persia.

There are other conclusions that might be drawn from the facts presented here. However, since this examination focuses on German foreign policy and economic influence, and the National Bank of Persia, it is more significant to note that the existing situation called for a recovery and an improvement of relations between both countries.

Germany was well positioned to take advantage of the emerging business opportunities in Persia and had a vested interest in growing its trade to combat its sizeable trade deficit. Reassuringly, the Persian government eased the trade sanctions originally imposed on German imports, through its 1931 trade monopoly act. This measure was designed to encourage German companies to intensify their trade and boost the volume of German exports to Persia.

7

GERMANY'S POLITICAL RELATIONS ADVANCE ECONOMIC INFLUENCE IN PERSIA

A multitude of changes and joint efforts to improve economic relations between Germany and Persia marked the period immediately following the National Bank crisis. These ranged from changing Persia's name to Iran, to mutual trade agreements, and to the visit of Hjalmar Schacht, the minister of economics and president of the German Central Bank (Reichsbank) to Persia. It appeared that both countries were eager to improve the status quo. Whether or not the bilateral efforts of both governments could be genuinely successful in improving their economic relations depended on the degree of damage caused by the National Bank crisis and the Lindenblatt affair. For political and economic relations to improve it was critical that the German Foreign Office become more proactive, in contrast to its stance during the Leo Mattias crisis and the *Paykar* affair.

An Opportunity for Hitler's Germany to Win Back Lost Territory in Persia

The National Bank of Persia revealed a significant deficit for the financial year 1931. The bank's deficit had been estimated to amount to approximately 8 million rials. The new management of the National Bank later confirmed officially in a report to the Persian government a deficit of more than 8.7 million rials. This report held the former directors of the bank and their mismanagement responsible for the loss. This deficit exceeded the total value of the bank's issued shares and therefore was a major threat to the bank's existence. In a quest to prevent a breakdown of Persia's financial services industry, the Persian minister of finance agreed a rescue package with the National Bank. Accordingly, the Persian government covered the National Bank deficit in return for an annual repayment equivalent to 80 per cent of banks net profits.[1]

During the following accounting year, the National Bank made a gross profit of nearly 6 million rials, of which it used 2 million rials towards repaying its debt to the Persian government. By 1932 the bank had managed to further improve on the performance of its financial services. The report that highlighted this success praised the contribution of the German National Bank employee, Schneider, and his Persian colleague, Zand. Both had managed the National Bank during the difficult period between Lindenblatt's resignation and the appointment of the bank's new management, made up of Horschitz-Horst, Ala, and Farzin.

Blücher maintained that the main capital of the National Bank did not come from small shareholder assets but from the large assets that the Persian government had deposited. The National Bank's improved financial standing owed much to the bank's ability to agree an interest rate of only half a per cent for the Persian government's holdings at the bank. However, the government treasury was progressively pushing for an increase in interest rate. The National Bank's interests were represented by a German national and the treasury's interests by a Belgian national. Blücher felt that a solution to this challenge was not straightforward. More crucially, the Persian government appeared determined to support and protect its National Bank through financial and political commitments. Blücher considered the future of the National Bank to be closely linked to future political developments in Persia, and dependent on the time period during which foreign experts would still be tolerated at the bank.[2]

As already established, until just before the National Bank crisis German nationals were employed in high government positions important to trade and industry. German industrial products had benefited from a growing popularity in Persia, and even the Shah had built up rapport with a number of German nationals, including Lindenblatt. However, from the outset of the discoveries of irregularities at the National Bank, the tensions affecting Germans had increased so dramatically that for many it had become unbearable to remain in Persia. While tensions began to ease after the court proceedings, for many this change came too late. Smaller foreign companies, hitherto unknown to Persian trade, and similarly unfamiliar advisers, had replaced many of their German counterparts. By 1933, as mentioned, Czechoslovakian companies had secured contracts to set up sugar factories, the Danes had erected a cement plant, the British took over the construction of spinning mills, and a Swedish consortium had been appointed to manage the construction of the Trans-Iranian Railway. Therefore it must be re-emphasised that the breach of confidence between Lindenblatt, the Shah and the Persian public had not only caused considerable damage to Germany's prestige and image in Persia but had also resulted in vast economic losses for the German industry, amounting to millions of marks.[3]

A report compiled in Tehran for the German minister of propaganda, Joseph Göbbels, recommended that Germany should plan a political or diplomatic modus operandi, by which it would not only stop further damage to German prestige and economic influence in Persia but also devise a strategy to rejuvenate bilateral relations. The report expressed doubt about the German embassy's ability to take up such responsibility. It asked for a more high-profile approach by the German government that aimed at winning back the goodwill of the Shah. Moreover, it was suggested that the Shah's apparent admiration for Hitler's new government and Germany's declared fight against communism, which had already contributed to relaxing the situation for Germans in Persia, could be exploited to win back lost ground.[4] More appropriately, a political or diplomatic measure was required that would bring the Shah and the German government closer together. The stated purpose of this report was to inform Göbbels of the conditions Germany faced in Persia. Persia had already attracted considerable interest from other European countries looking for influence in the Middle East. Hence, in view of Persia's growing industrialisation, it was argued that it was inconceivable that a country such as Germany, with a leader such as Hitler, should want to relinquish its deserved presence in the Middle East to some small European nations.[5]

A further report also linked the dire situation for Germans in Persia to the breach of confidence between the Shah and Lindenblatt. In this report, Lindenblatt was singled out as being of Jewish decent. Based on his choice of words, it may be concluded that the report's author, Giese, was a strong advocate of the new German National Socialist movement. He stated, for example, that

> A man [Lindenblatt], particularly a European national, never had been given so much power under the Shah, and he chose to cheat; the Jewish, money-greedy blood had triumphed.[6]

This kind of language was new to German–Persian relations and foreshadowed a new turn in German foreign policy. Hitler had been elected to power on 30 January 1933 as Germany's new chancellor. Almost exactly a year later Giese had compiled his report and was using language much associated with Nazi Germany. In his detailed report about the National Bank affair, and its negative consequences for Germany, he stated that Vogel had jumped from a ship and had drowned near Beirut. Moreover, he added that many people in Persia were not convinced that Vogel's body had really been discovered. Giese further outlined how Blücher, relying on his own judgement, and persisting that Lindenblatt was innocent, had ignored all warnings and recommended Lindenblatt's return to Persia. Therefore, Lindenblatt, who was convinced that his friend Taimurtash would protect him, had returned to Persia, triggering a farrago of undesired events. To Lindenblatt's bad fortune, by the time he arrived, Taimurtash had already been arrested.[7]

The information revealed in Giese's report proves either that he was observing the state of affairs in Persia far closer than could be expected under normal circumstances, or that he at least had access to files such as those kept at the German embassy in Tehran. Unfortunately, the document does not identify Giese's background. However, his knowledge of Persia's railway construction was so comprehensive that he might well have been commissioned as a railway engineer.

Giese emphasised how much the Lindenblatt affair had harmed the perception of German honesty and correctness in the Shah's eyes and those of the Persian population. Giese alleged that it had formerly been easy to ask Germany's friends among Persian nationals to help to combat possible intrigues against Germany. But now no one dared to declare himself openly pro-German. Giese maintained that these Persian supporters of Germany, of whom there still were many, understood that the activities of a few 'moral pigs' did not represent the character of a whole nation. He believed that the first objective for Germany was to win back the Shah's sympathies, and then, when grass had grown over the Lindenblatt affair, Germany could begin to think about regaining its former privileged status in Persia.

Giese reported that although criticism against Germany had never been officially raised in the local media there had been times when German nationals had to be wary in order not to be physically attacked on the streets in Persia. Many Germans were made redundant, and all German nationals risked being deported. All this agony, Giese maintained, could have been prevented if the German authorities had reacted faster, and had paid more attention to the Lindenblatt affair, and if the Foreign Office had made more efforts to resolve the crisis through diplomatic channels. To allow Lindenblatt to return to Persia and present himself as an innocent man, instead of being severely prosecuted in Germany, was viewed by Giese as the biggest mistake made by the German embassy in Tehran and the German government. He was convinced that in a similar case the British would never have permitted such a scandal to unfold. In this context, he stated, 'well, what did the old red German government anyway know about [Germany's] prestige, particularly in relation to states overseas'. This statement is a further indicator of a new prestige-focused approach in German foreign policy toward Persia.[8]

In the context of the Lindenblatt affair, Giese also reflected on the unpopularity of Blücher with the German expatriate community, mainly for not dealing appropriately with the Lindenblatt affair. Beyond this, Blücher was criticised for being a man with a good heart but completely out of touch with reality, and hence lacking the necessary understanding for the needs of the German expatriate community. Blücher was described as externally unemotional and cold, displaying the stiff style of communication associated with the old diplomatic school. Giese pitied him for being unable to drop his protective shields and relate to his own people. Evidently Blücher had only a few friends among the Germans in Persia. Giese also condemned Blücher's apparent lack of awareness and understanding of the latest political changes in Germany. Moreover, he criticised Blücher for exhibiting the same lack of 'national socialist enlightenment' when dealing with the Shah and his cabinet ministers. Blücher's unpopularity was in sharp contrast to the popularity of his predecessor Schulenberg. Schulenberg had been well known for the good relations he had maintained with the Shah and a large number of Persian government officials. Giese concluded that to live in the Middle East and to be able to represent the interests of the *Vaterland* specific qualifications were essential, which Blücher had lacked.

In conjunction with the German construction and railway industry, Giese was convinced that Blücher had also failed to take the initiative in compliance with the new German government's ideology to develop a strategy aimed at improving economic relations with Persia. Giese recommended that a generous gesture by the German government, such as financial support for large German companies, enabling them to offer their services at more competitive price, would provide Germany with an opportunity to regain the sympathies of the Shah and the Persian public, as well as secure jobs for German nationals.[9] A copy of Giese's report was later forwarded to the German minister for foreign affairs, von Neurath, in Berlin.[10]

It is clear that the climate in Persia in early 1934 provided Germany with an opportunity to take its first steps towards regaining lost political and economic ground. One evident obstacle for Germany had been Lindenblatt.

But it was argued that the German ambassador Blücher had also become an obstacle, damaging Germany's standing in Persia. Considering this deduction, the removal of both would have opened the doors in Persia for a new phase of relations. The new German government had good reasons for reforming its Middle East policy. For one it had a bigger concern for its international status overseas. Furthermore, in line with its new National Socialist ideology it was determined to improve its trade and thereby increase employment. Giese's account placed the ball firmly in the hands of the German government. He made a case for the financial support of German companies with business interests in Persia and the replacement of the German ambassador in Persia, the objective being to secure Germany's presence in the Middle East.

Persia Reopens its Doors to Germany and Invites Trade

The Persian government declared in 1934 that it was prepared to draw a line under the past and encourage the recommencement of mutual and friendly relations with the German government. To demonstrate its commitment the Persian government communicated a number of requests through its Berlin embassy representative Daftari to Schmidt-Rolke at the Foreign Office in Berlin.[11]

For example, the Persian government asked the German authorities for assistance in identifying three experts for leading positions at the Persian department of industry and agriculture, a division of the Persian ministry of trade and economics in Tehran. It expected these German experts to administer Persia's industrial and agricultural development in close cooperation with the National Bank of Persia and the newly established, German-managed Persian bank for agriculture.

The Persian government also requested assistance with the recruitment of two German medical experts. One was earmarked to be the director of a newly erected hospital in Mashad, and the other would be responsible for the department of internal medicine at the same hospital. The Mashad hospital was a pet project of the Shah in which he took a particular interest. The Persian authorities explained that they were prepared to accept any experts the German government would recommend, the only condition being that they approve their remuneration packages.[12]

In this context, Daftari mentioned that the Persian government had received numerous applications from non-Aryan medical experts and scientists who had lost their positions in Germany. However, to avoid disagreements with Germany, the Persian authorities had refused to accommodate any of these applicants.

Daftari also emphasised that Persia intended to purchase machinery and railway material. He pointed out that the Persian authorities had been overwhelmed by offers from Czechoslovakian suppliers, profiting from their government's export incentives. He explained to Schmidt-Rolke that if the German government did support German exports to Persia the Persian government would be prepared to satisfy 90 per cent of all its industrial requirements from Germany and with immediate effect. He added weight to his pledge by mentioning the significant acquisitions plans of the Persian ministries of defence and transport, for which German companies had also been asked to submit bids.[13]

Zölch, a staff member of the German embassy in Tehran, explained in a letter to Schmidt-Rolke how pleased he was to hear this from his meeting with Daftari. Nevertheless, he alerted Schmidt-Rolke to the fact that Daftari's remark about Persia's enthusiasm to satisfy 90 per cent of its import requirements from Germany was more a Middle Eastern exaggeration than a factual statement. Zölch explained that, considering the strong international competition, commercial contracts with Persian authorities were predominantly secured through price competitiveness. Although Zölch was positive about the progress the embassy, the Foreign Office and German companies were making, he questioned the ability of German companies to underbid the majority of their competitors in Persia.[14]

In a further diplomatic move aimed at intensifying Persia's trade relations with Germany, the Persian government agreed to establish a new consulate in Hamburg. Hamburg's importance for Persia was based on the city's strategic and logistic significance for trade as well as its well-developed port facilities.[15] Although these developments suggest that the Persian authorities were looking at ways to create opportunities for the improvement of their economic and diplomatic relations with Germany, at the same time they had developed plans to reduce German influence over the National Bank of Persia.

Post-Lindenblatt Developments at the National Bank of Persia

After the crisis of 1934, the National Bank of Persia had only 27 German nationals left in its service. National Bank director Horschitz-Horst's agreement with the National Bank was also coming to an end. He was chiefly employed to reorganise the National Bank after the Lindenblatt affair.[16] This still left 14 German nationals in charge of major branches of the National Bank throughout Persia.[17]

A *Financial Times* article identified a number of reasons for Persia's financial problems, without referring to Lindenblatt. The author, Owen Tweedy, focused on the challenges Horschitz-Horst had faced, after Lindenblatt, while reorganising the bank:

> But there were other situations which in our post-war world were not peculiar to Persia, and which could not be so readily solved by mere forcefulness and narrow patriotism. Persia's two main problems are her currency and her trade balance. The currency, which is based on silver and not on gold, has fallen seriously with the depreciation of the metal. Although for a time Shah Reza vainly tried to 'peg' the exchange and to control the movements of foreign currency by legislation, he has now abandoned the attempt.
>
> Linked to this currency exchange policy was an arithmetically ingenious but otherwise quite unpractical effort to adjust Persia's trade balance. The essence of his import and export law that was passed in 1932 was that both imports and exports would be by licence only, and that import licences would be granted only to those who exported goods of equivalent value. The disastrous consequences of this legislation are at once apparent when it is realised on the one hand that Persia, apart from carpets and opium, has next to nothing to export (oil, incidentally, was excluded from the operation of the law); while on the other, the country as yet produces next to nothing of the modern essentials of modern life.'[18]

After one year in Persia Horschitz-Horst completed his special assignment at the National Bank and returned to Berlin.[19] His departure, which was widely reported in the German national press, signified also Germany's departure from the administration of the National Bank, an institution that had been managed and developed by Germans from its outset. After Horschitz-Horst the chances for a German national or indeed any foreign national to lead the National Bank of Persia were negligible. Already in April 1935, with the departure of the director of the National Bank branch in Esfahan, Erich Wiens, Zölch had reported to the Foreign Office that the number of Germans employed by the National Bank had further decreased, leaving just a few.[20]

In 1934, to maintain Germany's influence in banking, the German Orient Society had asked the German Dresdner Bank to examine the possibility of setting up a branch in Persia. In response, an official representative of the Dresdner Bank confirmed that the idea of establishing a branch of the bank in Persia had long been on the agenda of the banks management. However, since good and commercially successful relations were maintained with the National Bank of Persia there had been no urgency to establish a branch. He further explained that because of the high cost involved, projects such as this had to be postponed until Germany's financial and foreign currency situation improved.

Meanwhile, significant changes were taking place at the National Bank resulting from its transition from a foreign- to a Persian-administered organisation. A person with a major effect on the future development of the bank was its newly appointed administrator, Reza Gholi Khan Amir Khosravi. He reorganised the management structure of the bank with the objective of bringing the following departments under the direct control of the bank's head office in Tehran. The main accounting department came under the management of Stephan, the administration department was to be led by Zend, the bank's loan department came under Goldenberg, and the foreign exchange policy department was to be managed by Gold. Interestingly, the last two names mentioned appear to be of Jewish origin; their names had been highlighted on Blücher's original report, most likely by a Foreign Office civil servant. Moreover, in a world dominated by men, particularly in Persia, it is noteworthy to see that a woman, Goldenberg, had been employed by the National Bank to administer its loan department.[21]

Meanwhile, the German national Jedermann, who originally had been brought back to Tehran from the Shiraz branch of the bank as a main candidate for a director position at the National Bank, opted instead to manage the prestigious Bazaar branch. According to Blücher, he hoped that by doing so he would increase the chances of building a good rapport with the new directors of the National Bank. Jedermann's prospects to take up Ala's post as a director of the bank were minimal, since the alternative candidate, Khosravi, had been directly recommended by the Shah. This left three Persian nationals as joint directors of the National Bank. Ala and Farzin became joint presidents and Khosravi, who replaced Horschitz-Horst, was appointed administrator.

Although Blücher was not in a position to comment on the professional qualities of Khosravi, he noted that because he had been appointed by the Shah he would have a stronger leverage over the other directors compared to Horschitz-Horst. Blücher also reported that the remaining German National Bank employees seemed happy with the new management of the bank. Some employees had supposedly commented that the new management of the bank had proven to be far more prepared to consider their recommendations and ideas, and that in some cases these recommendations had been implemented. Also regarding remuneration, the banks new administrator appeared more sympathetic to the staff's concerns.[22]

Overall, the observations made by Blücher left the impression that the bank was well managed and that its staff appeared reasonably satisfied with the course of developments. This was a good omen for the bank, since if all went according to the Persian government's plans, an efficient and professionally managed National Bank would also provide a solid foundation for a subsequent increase in trade and commercial activities for Persia.

National Socialist German Attempts to Restore Relations with Persia

The new German government's initial attempts towards improving its foreign relations with Persia come across as tentative and more symbolic in nature. These included the proposal to invite the Shah as a guest of the government to Germany and the naming of a street in Berlin in honour of a Persian poet.

In 1934 Germany had officially hosted a larger number of foreign heads of states from exotic countries such as Liberia, Afghanistan, Iraq and Egypt; it therefore was not keen on inviting further high-standing foreign dignitaries. Nevertheless, the Foreign Office in Berlin made a special case for Persia to persuade the relevant German authorities to approve Blücher's suggestion to invite the Shah to Germany. States secretary Dieckhoff argued that even purely for economic reasons it was necessary to win back the Shah's faded sympathies for Germany. He cited two main justifications for his proposal. First, the Shah still appeared not to have overcome his rage over the leftist articles published against him in Germany, the Leo Mattias article, and the Vogel-Lindenblatt affair. Second, the Shah was above all the sole determining factor in Persia. Dieckhoff believed that if the Shah was invited and treated well in Germany, while also provided with the opportunity to visit major industrial companies such as Krupp, it would have a positive impact on German exports to Persia.[23]

Another initiative that aimed at improving German–Persian relations evolved around a plan of the Foreign Office. This plan recommended that the Berlin municipal authorities should name a street after the Persian poet Ferdosi in honour of his one-thousandth anniversary. The Berlin municipal authorities were essentially prepared to honour Persia by naming a street, but they had reservations over the suggested name 'Ferdosi'. Therefore they instead recommended naming a larger park in Berlin 'Persischer Platz'.[24]

On 28 November 1934 a number of events were organised in Berlin to honour the Persian poet Ferdosi. As a compromise, during the festivities in a ceremony a street in Berlin was named 'Persische Straße'. Other events of the day included a reception at the Persian embassy, lectures on Ferdosi and a choir performance.[25]

However, the legacy of the above plan did not last long, since unexpectedly the Persian government advised as early as January 1935 that all foreign missions should in future substitute Persia's name with the name 'Iran'. A further document released by the Persian authorities provided an insight into the background to this symbolic change of the country's name. According to this document, the initiative for the change of the country's name had originated from the Persian embassy in Berlin. What had attracted the Persian government to this idea was that, as officially stated, 'at a time when foreign nations were priding themselves for being of Aryan origin, the time had come for Persia to display through its name that it was the homeland of the Aryan race'. In this context, it is worth mentioning that the word Iran translates into 'of Aryan origin'.[26]

Blücher instantly responded to this directive by explaining to the Foreign Office that the Persian government's assertion about the Aryan race could not be historically correct. He added that the Aryan element in the Persian population had become diluted over centuries through the influence of Arabs and Mongols. Blücher feared that as a result of the Persian government's explanation for Persia's change of name the Persians would consider themselves the Aryan homeland and superior to Germany.[27] Nonetheless, from that date the country was named Iran. It is likely that German 'propaganda' had influenced the Persian embassy's proposal in Berlin. Moreover, even if Germany's role, if any, is discounted, it is certain that the Shah approved Persia's change of name to Iran. From a diplomatic point of view this is almost a guaranteed sign of the Shah's association with and approval of Persia's alliance with Germany, its people, and government. This hypothesis can be substantiated by looking at the developments following Persia's change of name, particularly regarding its relations with Germany. A reliable approach to evaluate such changes remains an analysis of the economic relations.

Opportunities for German Economic Influence

In a memorandum, the former National Bank employee Paul Martin had presented his personal views on how Germany could win back its lost markets in Persia. He maintained that since the unfortunate year of 1932 Germany had lost most of its business in Persia. However, the Shah was keen to advance Persia's industrialisation, the development of its cities and the improvement of its transport infrastructure. Martin maintained further that Persia needed to import many industrial goods available from the German market. He also presumed that since almost no other country had the sole capacity to absorb such a large percentage of Persia's exports this made Germany an ideal trade partner for Persia. In Martin's opinion it was nevertheless necessary to eliminate all bad memories of the tragic year of 1932 before any German progress in Persia could prove successful. To achieve this objective, he advised, it was essential for a number of preconditions to be met. His principal precondition was that Lindenblatt, the cause of Germany's disgrace in Persia, had to leave the country.[28]

In response Blücher reported to the Foreign Office his reservations over the accuracy of the information cited by Martin. Blücher felt that Martin had misrepresented the proportion of the failings associated with Lindenblatt. He confirmed that Lindenblatt, who had been freed from jail and was resident in Tehran, was only waiting for a technicality to be resolved before returning to Germany. He confirmed that the atmosphere in Persia had improved and that Germany indeed had the potential to absorb goods produced in Persia. He also pointed out that the number of German immigrants arriving in Persia had been on a steady increase, numbering seven to eight hundred.[29]

At the beginning of an extensive report on Persia's economic structure and the problems it faced, Alfred Tismer singled out as its greatest weakness the absence of reliable statistics. Therefore, when analysing German economic influence in Persia after 1935, as the case of Abbas Khan Alamir will show, reliance also on non-statistical data remains essential.[30]

Abbas Khan Alamir had been appointed head of the Iranian department of industry and agriculture in 1935. Alamir was well-known to the German authorities, since he had been the secretary of legation at the Persian embassy in Berlin. Moreover, Alamir had studied in Germany where he also had received his doctorate; he had a German spouse, and spoke perfect German. Alamir's appointment must have pleased the German government authorities, since he had become the head of the department from which the majority of the Iranian government contracts were awarded. This fact on its own is difficult to quantify in terms of an economic advantage for Germany.[31] Nor is it easy to qualify the effect of the unexpected replacement of the often criticised Blücher in March 1935 by one of his embassy staff, Zölch. However, Zölch's term of office did not last long. After four months a new German ambassador to Iran, Smend, replaced him.[32]

A further event that showed every sign of being advantageous to the German cause in Iran was the appointment in 1936 of Madjid Ahy as the new head of the Iranian ministry of transport. He benefited from the support of the Iranian minister of finance, Dawar. Ahy's sympathies towards Germany were transparent. He had proudly told Smend, the new German ambassador to Persia, that his brother had studied and practised medicine in Germany.

During a meeting, Smend explained to Ahy that German industry was keen to assist with the development of Iran's transport system. Ahy enthusiastically supported this proposal and added that in the past he had been pleased with his experiences with German companies and suppliers. In this context, he mentioned the big contract for the construction of the Tehran railway station that had been awarded to a German company. Ahy assured Smend that similar contracts would most likely follow, adding that the contract for building the Shah's royal train had already gone to a German company. Smend stressed that large German companies were interested in regaining their former standing in Iran, for example, by moving forward the construction of the Trans-Iranian Railway. For this purpose the German company Dyckerhoff & Widmann A.G. had already sent their representative Doering to Tehran to negotiate over the construction of a port facility in Bandar-Shapur. Ahy responded positively to Smend's suggestions, leaving him with the impression that he had found a further ally within the Iranian government who could help Germany to improve its economic relations with Iran.[33]

Arguably, these occurrences point to the fact that both the German and the Iranian governments appeared by this stage to be prepared finally to draw a line under their recent past and turn their focus to a positive future. However, although Germany's moves towards Iran in the past had usually been commercially motivated, indirect clues help to back up the argument that, for the first time, an export of German political ideology to Iran had also been taking place. These clues include the official use of phrases such as German prestige overseas, superiority of the Aryan race, and Hitler's national socialist ideology, in the context of Germany's foreign relations with Iran. This observation also features in the concluding words of an article published in the German newspaper *Bremer Nachrichten*. This article stated that, through appropriate efforts of the German government, it was possible not only to win back lost spheres of influence but also to develop trade relations serving the benefit of all involved. The article clearly reveals a distinct separation between what appears to be a primary political objective and a secondary economic objective.[34]

A Breakthrough for German–Iranian Trade

Persia's change of name to Iran can also be regarded as symbolic of the start of a new and promising era of German foreign policy and economic influence in Iran. German–Iranian relations during the post-1935 era were increasingly politically tainted, but at the outset they continued to be dominated by trade interests.

When considering the state of the Iranian economy in 1935, it can be argued that its trade relied on three distinct pillars. The first pillar represented Iran's general trade, based on export certificates and import licences. The second pillar was Iran's trade with Russia based on bilateral trade agreements. The third pillar relied on business generated by the Iranian government.[35]

Regarding the first pillar, it could be argued that if German companies could offer their goods at internationally competitive prices, Iranian merchants could import more from Germany, resulting in a potentially lucrative increase of German exports to Iran. The second pillar on which Iranian trade was based was confined to its trade agreements with Russia. Since Russia had the tendency to exhaust its agreed export limits, this left in reality no room for any German trade activities. Under the terms of its agreements with Iran, Russia had to export goods of the same value to its imports from Iran. However, the Russians regularly used a cunning practice to satisfy a demand for Iranian goods that exceeded the agreed quotas. They shipped a certain percentage of their Iranian imports from Iran to the port of Hamburg in Germany. These Iranian goods were then sold for Reichsmarks. With the Reichsmarks generated from the sale of the Iranian goods in Germany, the Russians then were in the position to buy, and indirectly import, an even greater volume of required Iranian goods. The German authorities did not welcome this Russian practice, nor did they like the fact that Russia was financing its exports to Iran through its re-exports to Hamburg. Since this practice was commercially damaging for Germany, the German authorities took formal steps to curb it.

The third pillar of Iranian trade developed around the requirements of the Iranian government. For several years Germany had been almost isolated from conducting direct business with the Iranian government. The generally large government contracts had the potential to provide the most attractive and profitable opportunities for German companies looking to trade with Iran.[36]

A further factor influencing the course of German–Iranian trade relations was that for several years the statistics on trade between Iran and Germany had been showing a significant negative balance of trade for Germany: Germany was importing more goods from Iran than Iran was importing from Germany. Consequently Germany's aim had to be to minimise its export deficit, which implied that fewer goods should be imported from Iran while simultaneously more German goods would be exported to Iran.

Because of the large import and export capacity of the German industry, Germany not only had the potential to import Iranian goods and natural resources such as oil but it could also export in exchange competitively priced goods of at least the same value to Iran, thereby balancing its trade deficit.[37]

By 1936 Iran appeared to be increasingly prepared to negotiate with and consider business from German companies. German companies had begun to seize the opportunity and had dispatched their representatives to Iran. One of these German company representatives was Leese, who had travelled to Iran on behalf of the German industrial manufacturer Forestall A.G. When in Iran, Leese had managed to achieve a significant breakthrough for his company by finalising a significant contract with the Iranian ministry of finance. This contract aimed at developing a framework that would support the development of Iran's industrialisation for the following four years. The Leese contract was valued at an estimated 20–80 million Reichsmarks. On his return to Germany Leese planned to set up a central office that could represent the interests of large German industrial companies in Iran. These companies included Krupp, Gute Hoffnungshütte, Vereinigte Stahlwerke, Otto Wolff and others. Leese's contract was possibly the first big milestone for German trade in Iran after the National Bank crisis.[38]

It was not long before the German company Siemens followed in the footsteps of Forestall A.G. by securing a further substantial contract with the Iranian government. Siemens had agreed to construct an automated telephone exchange with a capacity of 6000 connections, provide the required handsets and telephone line network for Tehran, equip the National Bank of Iran with telephones, clocks, fire alarms, and a security system. In the late 1860s Siemens had already constructed one of the first telegraph lines in Iran, which stretched over 2,000 kilometres. Later, in 1924, Siemens constructed the first telephone exchange in Tehran and had ever since remained a highly regarded company. This contract was a success for Siemens in Iran and a further triumph for German trade.[39]

To assist and promote German trade with Iran, as described in an article published in the German newspaper *Berliner Lokal-Anzeiger*, a German–Iranian chamber of commerce was inaugurated on 29 April 1936. The Iranian ambassador to Germany, Mohsen Rais, was invited to present an opening speech at the inaugural meeting of the chamber. In his speech, Rais emphasised primarily that from his point of view obstacles that could have obstructed German-Iranian trade had been removed. He added that Iran's natural resources were essential for Germany, and Iran in turn required German industrial products. Regarding the creation of the German–Iranian chamber of commerce, Rais expressed his gratitude to the German minister of economics and president of the German Central Bank, Hjalmar Schacht, for his personal support and encouragement. A further German government representative, Spitta, from the ministry of finance, also explained in a speech that preconditions for a successful trade relationship between both countries had been met. He added that during the past three years trade between both countries had increased and that all commercial differences had been resolved. The article in which both speeches were quoted was revealingly entitled 'Iran and Germany are natural partners'.[40] Other newspaper articles carried titles such as 'As economically growing countries, Germany and Iran can complement each other in many areas'.[41] Considering such robust foundations, the preliminary conclusion that may be drawn is that German–Iranian economic relations were heading towards a strong future.

Iran's economy was booming by 1935, compared to other countries in the region, and hence was driving the industrialisation of the country. To finance its projects the Iranian government was increasingly relying on the National Bank. To meet the projections of the government budget for the year 1935/36 it became necessary to take on large loans facilitated by the National Bank. The bank was also financing, with 150 million rials, the construction of the Trans-Iranian Railway. In 1934 the National Bank had accumulated 300 million rials capital and generated an operational profit of over 21 million rials. The bank itself contributed significantly to Iran's industrialisation. By 1934 Iran had already constructed more than 140 factories and industrial plants across the country. Two years later the government's approved budget exceeded 1 billion rials.[42]

Iran's emerging economy was becoming increasingly attractive to German trade. The country had almost no foreign debt and its income from taxes and custom duties was constantly rising. Also, its income from the Anglo-Iranian Oil Company had risen compared to the year before.[43]

With reference to trade, it is worth mentioning that in the years 1932/33 Germany, with about 93 million rials trade (imports and exports), had already regained fifth rank in Iran's trade statistics. The first four positions were held by Russia, with almost 318 million rials, Britain, with almost 144 million rials, the United States, with over 137 million rials, and British India, with more than 124 million rials trade value. Iran's imports during the period 21 March 1932 until 20 March 1933, totalled more than 611 million rials, while its exports excluding oil and fishery products from the Caspian Sea totalled over 522 million rials. Iran's total value of trade therefore amounted to over 1.13 billion rials.[44]

During the following statistical year 1933/34 Iran's imports amounted to just over 605 million rials, which was slightly reduced compared with the previous year. Iran's exports were also slightly down to just over 466 million rials. Overall the entire value of Iran's trade for the year 1933/34 amounted to 1.07 billion rials. During 1934 Germany moved down to eighth place in Iran's trade statistics. However, compared with the year before, Iran's imports from Germany had increased by 15 million rials, while Iran's exports to Germany had risen by about 23 million rials.[45]

During the statistical year 1934/35 Iran's total trade value grew to almost 1.12 billion rials. During the following year Iran's imports stayed almost constant but its exports rose from 466 to 514 million rials. Germany, with over 103 million rials trade, had regained position four in Iran's trade statistics ranking. It followed Russia with 385 million rials, the United States with over 125 million rials, and British India with 106 million rials trade value. Britain, with just over 102 million rials, moved to fifth place. Nevertheless, Germany's trade balance with Iran remained negative by about 15 million rials. In 1934/35 Germany imported goods to the value of just over 59 million rials from Iran but exported goods worth only just over 44 million rials. Again, these figures do not include Iran's oil exports or movements of valuable metals.[46]

Germany had to increase its exports to Iran to balance its trade deficit. The relevant Iranian government authorities had matured politically to a level that allowed them to facilitate Germany's stronger participation in the development of Iran's economy. They had also shown a keen interest in employing first-class German experts who could assist Iran to augment its productivity. Iran's demand for German goods and expertise was constantly increasing. Considering the comparatively healthy state of Iran's national budget and its key financial institutions, including the National Bank, the time had come for German trade to take a further step towards capitalising on the growing business opportunities in Iran.

Compared with 1935 German trade with Iran increased even more significantly in 1936. Germany's exports to Iran reached 30.4 million Reichsmarks, compared with 13.5 million Reichsmarks in 1935. This rise becomes even more significant if we consider that German exports in 1935 had already increased by almost 100 per cent in contrast to its export value of 7.5 million Reichsmarks in 1934. Thus Germany's exports to Iran had quadrupled in 1936 compared with its value in 1934. In 1936 the value of German exports to Iran thereby reached its highest ever level in the history of the two countries' economic relations. It had even almost doubled its record value of 17 million Reichsmarks in 1929.[47]

Table 7.1 Germany–Iran trade figures 1928–36

Year	*German imports from Iran*	*German exports to Iran*
1928	29.3	9.9
1929	30.6	17.0
1930	36.2	9.5
1931	35.3	6.0
1932	28.8	5.4
1933	20.6	6.6
1934	24.1	7.5
1935	15.3	13.5
1936	23.0	30.4

Likewise, the value of German imports from Iran in 1935 increased significantly compared with 1934, rising from 15.3 million Reichsmarks to 23 million Reichsmarks. The statistics for German-Iranian imports and exports presented in Table 7.1, in million Reichsmarks, are based on German trade data. These figures also reveal that during the National Bank crisis years 1932/33 German exports to Iran reached their lowest level. Except for 1935, 1933 marked the lowest level of German imports from Iran. The trade restrictions resulting from Iranian trade laws aimed at regulating the economy were the main cause for the exceptional low of 1935.[48]

A further important fact revealed in Table 7.1 is that in 1936 German exports to Iran exceeded its imports for the first time. Not only was this a success for the development of German trade with Iran but it allowed for German trade earnings of more than 7.5 million Reichsmarks. This is significant insofar as Germany had regularly been left with a trade deficit regarding its trade with Iran. In 1934 Germany's trade deficit had even reached 16.6 million Reichsmarks. What is more significant is that Germany had managed to achieve this surplus not by reducing its imports from Iran but by significantly increasing its exports to Iran.[49]

Table 7.2 shows the main German exports and imports to and from Iran for the year 1936. The remaining German exports to Iran were composed of motor vehicles, aircraft, chemical goods, steel pipes, copper wires, optical and precision mechanical goods, paper and paper products, and a further number of less significant categories. The remaining German imports from Iran consisted of a number of product categories with a low trade value.

Table 7.2 Commodity categories of Germany–Iran trade in 1936

German exports to Iran	*Value in million Reichsmark*
Metal products	3.9
Machinery for the textile and leather industry	3.1
Electrical equipment	2.5
Machinery for industry and agriculture	3.2
Textile products	2.3
Pharmacological products	0.9
German imports from Iran	*Value in million Reichsmark*
Fuel and petroleum	4.2
Selection of wool material	3.9
Animal skin (intestine)	3.2
Carpets and similar products	2.2
Leather	2.2
Fruits	1.9
Cotton	1.4

In this context a major contributor to Germany's growing trade with Iran was the German–Iranian clearing agreement signed on 30 October 1935. This clearing agreement produced good and fast results benefiting both countries. According to this agreement, payments derived from German–Iranian trade had to be cleared through a German clearing bank and the National Bank of Iran or special overseas accounts approved for foreigners for domestic payments. The subsequent success of the clearing agreement in 1936 promised also to increase the volume of trade in 1937. In Germany and Iran's case, the fact that their export goods complemented each other satisfied another major precondition for a healthy future growth in trade.[50]

A further positive short-term indication for the future growth of German trade with Iran was that because of Iran's rapid industrialisation the Iranian government had increased its quota for imports of machinery by 30 million rials. This meant that German companies could expect to continue to provide Iran's industry with machinery. Iran's planned and partly started road, railway and infrastructure construction projects had the potential to lead to additional contracts for German companies. The demand for German domestic and manufactured goods remained continuously high in

Iran. Despite the increasing competition from Russia, Britain, the United States and Japan, the cited figures and facts suggest that by 1937 Germany was heading for a leading position in Iran's trade statistics.[51] But how could Germany secure this trend for the future? That Iran's economy had a significant demand for goods and services that German companies could supply was not a strong enough guarantee for a sustainable future growth of German trade with Iran. A political solution would have been for Persia to grant Germany a preferred trading partner status. From a German perspective, the Foreign Office was aware that political steps had to be taken to strengthen the Shah's sympathies for Germany in order to foster and secure future long term economic relations with Iran.

The Visit to Iran by Hjalmar Schact, German Central Bank President and Finance Minister

In November 1936 the German Foreign Office elected to revive a recommendation of Germany's ex-ambassador to Iran, Blücher. Blücher had recommended facilitating an official state visit to Iran by a high-ranking German politician such as Hjalmar Schacht, the minister of economics and president of the Central Bank, with the objective of improving the political and economic relations of both countries. Consequently, a diplomatic dialogue was initiated to arrange the details of an official state visit by Schacht. However, just before the agreed date, Melchers, a German embassy official in Tehran, brought his concerns regarding the visit to the attention of the German Foreign Office. Melchers felt that, since Schacht's invitation to Iran had been issued by the Iranian director of the National Bank, this indicated either that the Iranian side failed to recognise Schacht's status, or that the Iranians had some political reservations regarding the visit. Moreover, Melchers feared that a recent visit of the Afghan defence minister to Iran would overshadow Schacht's visit. Melchers re-emphasised in a coded secret telegram to the foreign office that an invitation by the Iranian National Bank president could not warrant the required recognition for a visit by the German economics minister Schacht.[52]

On the same day, Ritter, from the German Foreign Office in Berlin, informed Melchers that he had created a difficult situation by suggesting that Schacht's visit to Iran should be reconsidered. On the one hand, since the invitation for the visit had come from the Iranian ministry of finance, and negotiations for the organisation of the event had begun, it would be embarrassing for Germany if the visit was cancelled. Moreover, for economic and political reasons the Foreign Office felt that it was crucial to maintain the appointment. On the other hand, the visit had to be of an appropriate format to reflect the status of Germany and the standing of Schacht. Ritter instructed Melchers to inform the Iranian president of the National Bank of the honour with which Schacht had been received when recently visiting Budapest, Belgrade, Sofia and Athens. The respect shown to Schacht was due not only to his role as president of the German Central Bank but also to his status as a cabinet minister of the German government. Hence heads of states, prime ministers and cabinet ministers of the countries visited had invited Schacht to meetings. Melchers was instructed to inform the president of the National Bank that in view of the excellent relations maintained between Germany and Iran it was desired that Schacht's visit to Iran should benefit from a similar format. Likewise, although Schacht felt honoured to be invited to Iran by the National Bank president, the Foreign Office insisted that the Iranian government should also invite him. In addition, it was expected that the Shah and the Iranian Prime Minister should meet with Schacht. Ritter also instructed Melchers to keep the entire matter secret from the press until a final agreement with Iran had been reached.[53]

On 16 November 1936 the German embassy in Tehran received a telegram from Kamphaevener at the German Foreign Office informing them that, during his visit to Turkey, Schacht had finally received an official invitation from the Iranian government. Therefore Schacht had decided to continue his voyage via Baghdad to Tehran. He was expected to stay in Tehran, accompanied by two officials from the ministry of finance, from 20 to 24 November 1936. The embassy was instructed to arrange landing permissions for the passengers, crew, and Schacht's aeroplane D-AKY.[54]

The protocol prepared by the Iranian Foreign Office for Schacht's visit arranged for him to be met on arrival at the airport in Tehran by Iran's minister of finance, Dawar, the president of the National Bank, General Amir Khosravi, and a member of the protocol department of the Iranian Foreign Office. During his stay Schacht was also scheduled to meet the Iranian prime minister, the president of parliament, the foreign minister and other high-ranking government officials. In addition, the Iranian minister of finance and the foreign minister had each arranged a dinner in Schacht's honour.[55]

During the discussions with Iranian officials in preparation for Schacht's visit on 17 November 1936, Melchers became more certain in his suspicion that the Iranians had political reservations concerning the visit. Although the Iranian authorities had assured Melchers that Schacht would meet the Shah, they had not determined when or where this meeting was to take place, nor did they know when the Shah was expected to be back in Tehran. On 18 November 1936 Melchers was informed that the Shah was not returning from Mazanderan to Tehran but that an audience at the Shah's residence in the north of the country could be arranged. The Iranian officials suggested that an aeroplane could fly Schacht in a few hours to Mazanderan where an airfield could be prepared at his meeting point with the Shah. Melchers became agitated over this suggestion and explained that this was against previously agreed arrangements. He emphasised to Ansari, director of the political department III, that an audience with the Shah was the most important event of Schacht's visit to Iran. Moreover, it was technically impracticable to expect a heavy aircraft to land on a temporary airfield. Hence a different solution had to be worked out.[56]

Melchers was incensed with Ansari when he suggested that he could arrange Schacht's transit by light military aircraft. Melchers explained that the German president of the Central Bank could not be expected to fly in an open-top aircraft over the 4,000-metre-high Elborz Mountain range. Finally it was agreed that at the end of his visit Schacht would be driven by motorcar to the five-hours distant town of Chalus. This would have inevitably required that Schacht stay a further day in Iran. Since this was not a practical suggestion and because of the significance of Schacht's meeting with the Shah an agreement was reached with the Iranian foreign minister and finance minister to cancel the planned dinner hosted by the National Bank president in favour of Schacht's audience with the Shah, on the third day of his stay in Iran. According to Melchers, as a goodwill gesture the Shah had ordered that Schacht should be accommodated during his visit in a designated section of his palace that previously had been reserved only for royal guests.[57]

Despite the challenges Schacht did finally visit Tehran as planned and succeeded in meeting with the Shah. In conjunction with Schacht's visit a German newspaper article reported that the audience he was granted by the Shah underlined the significance the Shah awarded to the presence of the German minister of economics and president of the Central Bank. Schacht's visit in turn not only was considered to reflect the commitment of the German government to its foreign and economic relations with Iran but also was anticipated to lead to stronger economic and cultural ties between the two countries.[58]

Schacht's Legacy in Iran and Nouri Esfandiari's Visit to Germany

German companies with economic interests in Iran saw in Schacht's visit a good opportunity to promote and expand their exports.[59] A German newspaper article confirmed that German trade with Iran had been growing annually since 1933, almost from month to month.[60] A further article stated that Iran had managed to emancipate itself of foreign influence as a result of the course of its foreign policy, throughout the years from 1927 to 1933. Schacht's visit to Tehran illustrated too that Iran was no longer the object of economic exploitation but had grown into an equal trade partner on the international scene.[61]

In 1937 the German authorities received intelligence about the Iranian parliament president Hassan Nouri Esfandiari's travel plans to Europe. According to this information Nouri, who had been asked to represent the Iranian government at the coronation ceremonies in London, had planned to interrupt his return trip in Berlin. Nouri's first overseas post, in about 1885, had been the Iranian embassy in Berlin. Back in Iran, he was appointed first foreign, then finance, and later education minister. During World War I he was supportive of Iran's pro-German stance. Nouri also had a distinguished relationship with the Shah, who held his opinion in high regard. Furthermore, one of Nouri's sons was a general in the Iranian armed forces, another, who had studied in Germany, was the Shah's personal physician, and a third was in charge of government protocol. In addition, one of the sons had married a daughter of the Shah.

In view of Nouri's significance, the German Foreign Office circulated ideas aiming at making the most of Nouri's visit to Berlin, to improve on the already excellent relations between both countries. Although Nouri's visit did not have an official character it was decided that he should be treated as an official guest of the German government. Through the mediation of the German ambassador in Tehran, the Iranian Foreign Office declared that by sending its president of parliament to visit Germany the Iranian government intended to underline its high regard for the friendly relations it maintained with Germany. Also Nouri's visit was in particular to symbolise the admiration of the Shah for the leader and chancellor of Germany, Adolf Hitler. As a result of such a positive approach, the German Foreign Office proposed to recommend an audience between Nouri and Hitler.[62]

In honour of Nouri's visit, Schacht forwarded him a personal invitation for a breakfast meeting through the German Foreign Office and the Iranian embassy.[63] On arrival in Berlin, before meeting with Schacht, Generaloberst Hermann Göring officially received Nouri. Göring, who had been assigned the responsibility for Germany's economy by Hitler, was Nouri's official host. At the ceremony hall of the German Central Bank Schacht warmly welcomed Nouri as his guest of honour. Other important guests who attended Schacht's breakfast reception included the Iranian ambassador Mohsen Rais, Ali Gharagozlou and other officials from the Iranian embassy. On the German side, government officials from the Foreign Office, the ministry of finance, and the executive of the Central bank were joined by a large number of leading German industrialists and banking experts. Both Schacht and Nouri used the opportunity provided by this occasion to express their mutual respect and admiration for their respective heads of state, and emphasised the good relations Germany and Iran maintained.[64] On the following day Hitler officially received Nouri as his guest, accompanied by Rais.[65]

When Nouri arrived back in Iran Smend invited him for dinner at the German embassy. Nouri expressed his gratitude for the warm reception he had received in Germany and asked Smend to convey his appreciation to the appropriate German authorities. Nouri told Smend that his experiences in Germany were evidence for the positive development of German–Iranian relations, which had possibly never been as sympathetic. Nouri also spoke highly of his reception with Hitler, as well as praising his official hosts Göring and Schacht for their hospitality and regard. Smend was convinced that German–Iranian foreign relations had been significantly enhanced as a result of Nouri's favourable experiences in Germany, on which he had in all probability reported in detail to the Shah.[66]

Soon after Schacht's visit to Iran, and before Nouri's return, Germany's strong political and economic relations with Iran resulted in a significant contract between the Iranian government and German suppliers of heavy industry. This contract included orders for the construction of two blast furnaces with a daily capacity of 150 tons, one rolling mill, one steelworks factory, one coking plant, and the required power station. These contracts, which had an estimated value of 27,000,000 Reichsmarks, were placed with the German companies DEMAG and Friedrich Krupp. Moreover, the Iranian government placed an order in Germany for 65 locomotives and 700 train carriages in a contract worth 20,000,000 Reichsmarks.[67] This was the first significant German supply contract for locomotives and railway carriages intended for the Trans-Iranian Railway. The German company Krupp was a major supplier for this contract as well.[68] A second smaller order for 20 locomotives and 200 railway carriages was later awarded to the German company Lincke-Hoffmann-Werke AG.[69] Another contract was for a large cement factory, with a daily production capacity of 300 tons, to be delivered and constructed by the German company Polysius Dessau. This factory was inaugurated by the Iranian crown prince in a suburb of Tehran.[70] In addition, the production level of matches in Iran rose from 56 million boxes in 1933 to 113 million boxes in 1938. During the same period production of sugar increased from 1,200 tons to over 14,000 tons.[71] German newspapers not only increasingly reported on the booming trade between Germany and Iran; they also reported on record turnovers.[72]

During a meeting between the members of the political department of the German company I. G. Farbenindustrie with representatives of the German ministry of finance, both parties forecast that the import of Iranian goods to Germany for the year 1937 could be increased by a further 28–30 million Reichsmarks. This assessment was mainly based on the data made available to the German ministry of finance by trade monitoring agencies and relied on projections of future growth potential of imports of carpets, skins and fruits, and so forth, from Iran. By June 1937 Germany had already imported goods worth more than 40 million Reichsmarks from Iran. The German ministry of finance expected German exports to Iran in 1937 to reach 50–60 million Reichsmarks, leaving a positive trade balance of approximately 10–20 million Reichsmarks for Germany.[73]

Considering the above we may draw three conclusions. First, compared to the years preceding the National Bank crisis, and based on clearer political strategies, significantly more attempts were made by the German and Iranian government authorities to improve bilateral foreign relations and economic ties. Second, although the Lindenblatt affair had resulted in political and economic damage for Germany in Iran, compared to the earlier controversy surrounding Leo Matthias and the leftist newspaper campaigns opposing the Shah, both countries overcame the challenges associated with the banking crisis in a significantly shorter time and much more effectively. Third, it can be concluded that by 1938 the Foreign Office had learned valuable lessons from its experiences in Iran, partly owing to political and economic changes on the German domestic scene, and partly owing to favourable international developments. The Foreign Office's proactive approach brought about a significant improvement of German political relations with Iran which in turn resulted in opportunities that allowed Germany to significantly and effectively expand its economic influence in the country.

One of the few losses suffered by Germany during this period was its forfeiting of influence over the National Bank of Persia, which nevertheless still remained a key financial institution for facilitating German trade with Iran. Ultimately, it has been shown that when economic relations between both countries improved political relations followed suit. The newly established political relations became the motor for the advance of economic influence. Moreover, it has been proven that after World War I, while facing multiple challenges, Germany managed to firmly establish its standing in Iran, turning it into one of the country's leading trade partners. The promising expansion of German political relations and economic influence in Iran came to an abrupt end through the unexpected British–Russian invasion of Iran in 1941.

8

CONCLUSION

The development of German foreign policy towards Iran during the first half of the twentieth century can be divided into three distinct phases. The first phase, which was initiated before World War I, collapsed as a consequence of the war and the Versailles Treaty, achieving little success. The second, more significant phase began around 1924, and was marked by the appointment of the German national Lindenblatt as director of the National Bank of Persia, the appointment of his compatriot Schniewind as financial adviser to the Persian government, the granting of contracts to German companies and consortiums for the construction of the Trans-Iranian Railway, the re-establishment of trade relations between Germany and Iran, and the granting by the Iranian government of wide-ranging flight concessions to the German company Junkers. The third phase of Germany's involvement in Iran resulted from the achievements that followed the trade agreement of 1935. This phase saw Germany become Iran's leading trade partner and lasted until the British–Russian invasion of Iran in 1941.

The French publication *L'Économiste français* perceived the German economic success in Iran after 1935 as so overwhelming that it stated:

> If we are to learn from history we should try not to forget one painful lesson [from Germany's success in Iran]. It is wrong to believe that Iran is a faraway country in which one does not need to show interest. As a result of the tremendous developments brought about by the country's monarch, Iran has not only become a significant factor for Near and Middle Eastern politics, but, aided by the arrival of modern transportation, it has moved on to the threshold of the Mediterranean sea.[1]

German Foreign Policy Towards Iran Before World War II

It is hardly an exaggeration to state that German foreign policy towards Iran came a long way during the period under investigation. Before the outbreak of World War II, from a political point of view both countries appeared to maintain sympathetic relations based on mutual respect and trust. In 1938 Germany's ambassador in Tehran, Smend, highlighted two politically tainted reasons for this positive development. First, Germany was an agreeable partner for Iran, to whom it felt related by common history and culture. The second was Reza Shah's admiration for the policies of Hitler, in whose actions he saw a model for the tasks he faced in Iran and its society. The emphatically friendly way in which German dignitaries, such as Schacht, were received in Iran was undeniable evidence of the good relations between the two countries. From an economic point of view, by 1938 Germany had moved in just a few years from fifth to second rank in Iran's international trade statistics. At that time Smend was convinced that Germany could within a few years take over Russia's position as Iran's largest trade partner. Smend felt that Germany's future strategy in Iran should be to seek a peaceful, trust-based, and goal-oriented economic policy, to further the cultural bonds, to preserve friendly relations, and remain politically neutral.[2]

The start of World War II in 1939 had inescapable consequences for Germany's relations with Iran. Public opinion in Iran displayed a certain degree of admiration for the post-1938 direction of German foreign policy. Moreover, almost immediately after Germany's invasion of Czechoslovakia on 15 March 1939 the Iranian foreign minister, Alam, spontaneously congratulated Smend, and remarked that at last an intolerable state of affairs had been resolved, allowing order to return to central Europe. These developments also impressed the Shah, who during a cabinet meeting stated his admiration for Hitler's re-unification of Austria and Germany.[3]

On another occasion, Smend was congratulated and overwhelmed by Iranian dignitaries, including the prime minister, who expressed their sympathies for Germany's new political achievements. The reasons for Iran's positive embrace of events in Germany are manifold. For one, there appeared to have been a genuine admiration for Nazi Germany and Hitler. Then there was a regard for traits implicit within National Socialist policy such as order, national honour, and *Führerprinzip*. In addition there was a natural admiration in Iranian society for large-scale and ambitious military and political operations, particularly when power was regained by what was perceived as a suppressed nation through its own strength. The Iranian esteem for Germany's fast rise was all the more genuine because it was believed that it did not have a negative effect on Germany's relations with Iran. Moreover, the Iranians found satisfaction in the political desolation inflicted upon their long disliked adversaries, Britain and even more so Russia. This was displayed through ridiculing what Smend labelled as events led by the heads of state of the most brutal imperialist countries. However, the admiration Iran displayed for Germany was in strong contrast to the disapproval from the rest of the diplomatic corps in Iran, except for the representatives of Japan and Italy.[4]

By 1939, tensions had built up so high that, for example, the British embassy refused to communicate its acknowledgement to the crew of a German airliner for the brave rescue of British citizens, including guests of the British embassy, from the flames of an Iranian aeroplane that had crashed in a tragic air accident.[5]

However, it is not hard to see why Reza Shah, who wanted to keep Iran free from foreign influence, felt that any involvement in Germany's war efforts could only result in harm for his country.[6] On 6 September 1939, faced with having to make a decision in view of the escalating conflict, he formally declared Iran to be a neutral country.[7]

Germany's Contribution to Iran's Pre-war Achievements

The National Bank of Persia had been established in keeping with the nationalistic element of the Shah's reform and development policies. Considering that in 1939 Iran became the fourth largest oil-producing country in the world,[8] it can be concluded that the National Bank's successful development allowed a modest start to Iran's industrialisation, by providing the first experience of a modern economy outside the British-controlled oil sector. Central to the initial success of the bank, as has been shown, were German nationals.

Before World War I Iranian banking had been in the hands of foreign powers. The gradual nationalisation of the Iranian banking system took place shortly after Reza Shah's coronation. The foundational action was a law passed in May 1927, which regulated the framework for setting up a national bank for Persia. The National Bank of Persia underwent steady growth from its inauguration until today, when it continues to exist under the name Bank Melli Iran. Under German management, the bank set up its headquarters in Tehran, from where it controlled its operations centrally. By 1932 its role as a leading financial institution was secured through money-printing rights and other banking privileges, which were acquired from the British controlled Imperial Bank of Persia. The starting capital of the National Bank, which had been organised as a joint-stock company with special rights, was around 20 million rials. In July 1935 this figure had increased to 300 million rials. The initial founding capital of the National

Map 8.1 Map of Iran (1941) illustrating branches and agencies maintained by major banks operating out of Tehran. These include branches of the National Bank of Persia, marked by squares, with a dot in the centre. Approximately 1941, map. Bundesarchiv Dahlwitz-Hoppegarten, files of the IG Farbenindustrie AG, 80 IGF/A4053.

Bank originated from the sale of crown jewels and government estates. The bank's increase in capital was later facilitated by the Iranian government's decision to transfer its gold reserves to the Bank. At the same time the Iranian government remained the sole shareholder of the National Bank. Along with its day-to-day business as a financial institution, the bank was actively involved in Iran's industrialisation, and financed and managed major projects. The National Bank also provided a large share of the capital required for the development of Iranian industry, trade and transport.

German companies were from the outset increasingly involved in the industrialisation and development of Iran. Initially they acted as partners with the National Bank and were able to deliver on a great number of factories, power plants, infrastructure projects and trade initiatives. Moreover, in accordance with the Shah's reform plans, and backed by German loans

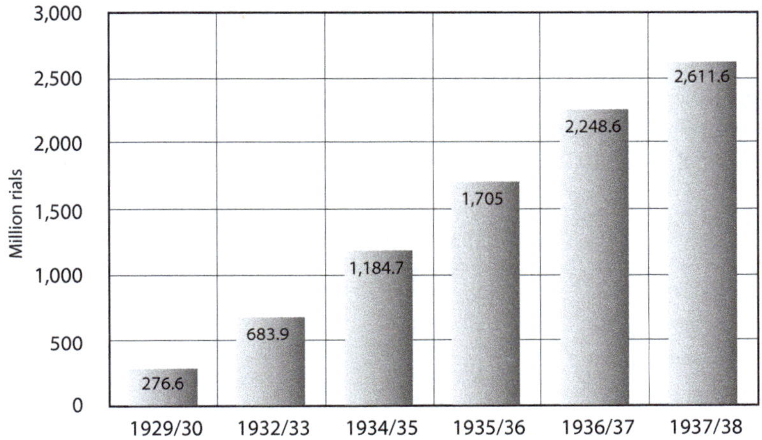

Figure 8.1 National Bank of Persia: growth in balances 1929–38

and government guarantees, German companies managed to finance and implement many commercial projects which contributed substantially to the industrialisation that supported Iran's development into a modern and independent country.

By the end of 1939, the National Bank held branches at 47 locations throughout Iran (Map 8.1), and the number of its staff had risen to over 1800 employees. Moreover, by this time the National Bank depended to a lesser degree on its German staff and was almost exclusively managed and run by Iranian nationals. Accordingly, the bank's balance had grown from 276 million rials in 1929/30 to over 2.6 billion rials in 1937/38 (Figure 8.1).[9]

The second prominent achievement of Iran during the inter-war period was the Trans-Iranian Railway project. Owing largely to the persistent efforts of German companies, the massive construction project of the Trans-Iranian Railway came to its conclusion just after over ten years of construction, on 27 August 1938. The inauguration ceremony took place in the central Iranian town of Arak, the location where the final set of rails connected the southern with the northern sections of the Trans-Iranian Railway. This project, truly grand for its time and for a developing country such as Iran, resulted in a railway network measuring a total length of 1394 kilometres. For this project 224 tunnels, covering an accumulated distance of 83 kilometres, and 90 railway stations were constructed. Fifty-two locomotives and 8,300 railway carriages had been delivered, and the arrival of more rolling-stock from Germany was anticipated. The total cost for the construction of the Trans-Iranian Railway (1927–38) amounted to almost 2.2 billion rials, which was equivalent to 375 million Reichsmarks.[10]

The prosperity of trade relations between Iran and Germany highlights the third major success for Iran. In 1939/40, Iran for the first time during the inter-war period, exported significantly more than it imported (Figure 8.2). In 1938/39 Iran's imports amounted to 562 million rials and

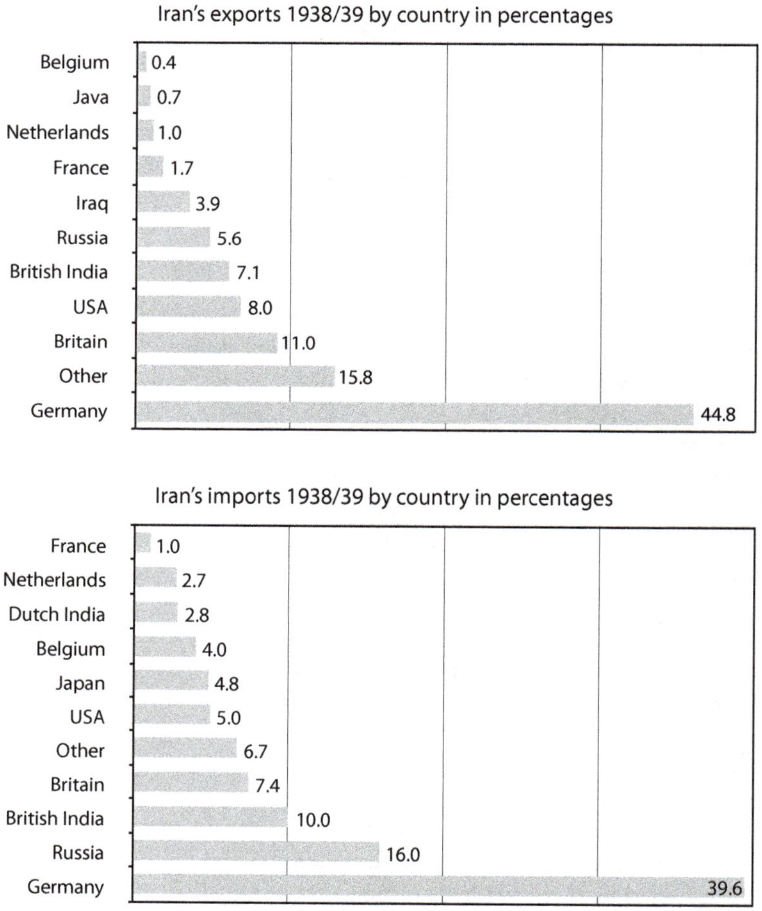

Figure 8.2 Iran's imports and exports in 1938/39. Charts are based on data provided by report from Militär Archive Freiburg. Report detailing the economic and political situation of Iran, particularly with respect to German interest, approximately 1940. Bundesarchiv, Militär Archiv Freiburg, Wi II A.6/8

its exports to 464 million rials, leaving a trade deficit of 98 million rials. However, in 1939/40 Iran's imports amounted to 612 million rials, whereas its exports amounted to 803 million rials, leaving a trade surplus of over 191 million rials for Iran. The biggest beneficiary of Iran's increase in trade was Germany. By 1938/39 Germany had become the country with the largest volume of exports to Iran (Figure 8.2). Germany satisfied with its exports nearly 40 per cent of Iran's total demand. Russia at this stage had slipped to second place with 16 per cent, and Britain to third place with about 10 per cent. Moreover, Germany had also become the largest importer of Iranian goods. Germany imported almost 45 per cent of all Iranian exports during this period, followed by Britain with about 11 per cent.[11]

Hence Germany had succeeded in securing the majority of the Iranian export market. In 1939/40 Germany went on to import 50 per cent of all Iranian exports. Compared to 1938/39, when German imports from Iran reached nearly 206 million rials, in 1939/40 this figure almost doubled, exceeding the amount of 393 million rials. During the same period Germany's exports to Iran increased by almost a third. In 1938/39 German exports to Iran reached a value of almost 160 million rials, while in 1939/40 German exports to Iran rose to about 214 million rials.[12]

By 1940, therefore, Germany had become by far the largest and most important trade partner of Iran. Much credit for this achievement can also be given to the Iranian admiration for Germany's industrial, scientific, and organisational achievements, as well as to the sympathies of the Iranian public for German culture. Yet it was the National Bank of Persia and the successful completion of the Trans-Iranian Railway project that contributed most to the sustainable growth of economic ties, facilitating Germany's subsequent political dialogue with Iran. This provided the basis for Germany's exceptionally good foreign political relations with Iran and also its economic influence, allowing Germany as a trade partner to become the leading contributor to the Shah's modernisation and reform plans before World War II.

Conclusion

Within the context of German foreign policy towards Iran before World War II we have analysed the characteristics of the political and economic developments, their underlying causes, the consequences of Germany's relations and influence with and in Iran, and the role of the National Bank of Persia. Before we continue with summarising the findings, it is noteworthy that the investigation has revealed that individuals played a key role in the early formation of German foreign and economic policy towards Iran, either in the person of entrepreneurs or civil servants.

It was the German entrepreneur Thomas Brown who in the early 1920s initiated the first vital phases of German–Iranian relations. Brown's motivation was clearly a commercial one, but through his negotiations with Iranian authorities he simultaneously opened Iran's doors to Germany. A further result of Brown's activities, which had aimed at establishing and maintaining economic relations between the two countries, was that when Reza Shah decided to create a National Bank for Iran his government appointed a German national, Lindenblatt, as the Bank's director. As a German-managed project the bank soon turned into a valuable vehicle for German economic influence in Iran. The resulting emergence of a low level of trade between Germany and Iran, and the appointment of a small number of German experts by the Iranian government, could be regarded as successes for Germany's foreign relations with Iran. This is particularly so considering the dominance of British influence in the south, and Russian influence in the north of Iran, which left little scope for a third power to create its own sphere of influence.

The dominant German role during the initial phases of the creation of the National Bank presented a good opportunity for the promotion of German trade and economic influence in Iran. There were no other Iranian institutions that would have served the German national interest, albeit indirectly, as well as the National Bank. Moreover, if Germany had not succeeded in gaining a degree of economic influence in the country it is conceivable that it would have found it difficult to establish any foreign political relations with Iran during the critical inter-war period.

However, it was not all plain sailing for Germany. Britain and Russia did not just stand back and watch Germany enter their spheres of interest and consequently threaten their status quo. Their political and economic opposition, and Reza Shah's misgivings regarding German trustworthiness, began to have serious implications for German foreign policy towards Iran. As a result Germany's Iran initiative was frustrated. Moreover, German government authorities such as the Foreign Office initially showed little interest in what was perceived as a faraway, developing country dominated by the influence of the two most powerful empires. German economic influence in Iran during the late 1920s was still insignificant compared to Iran's other trade partners. To make matters worse, the less than diplomatic approach of the German Foreign Office regarding the maintenance of relations with Iran caused probably the most serious political crises between both countries before World War II. The German authorities' indecisive response to communist threats against Reza Shah and Iran from Iranian opposition groups based in Germany suggested the German government did not perceive its national interests in Iran as important enough to justify immediate and concerted action or any other type of effective diplomatic solutions.

The consequences for Germany's status in Iran were manifold. Commercially, it caused the loss of key contracts for German companies and a sharp downturn in bilateral trade. It also resulted in what Reza Shah perceived as his public defamation by exiled communist forces based in Germany. The impression left in Iran was that German authorities were happy to stand by while a number of activists attacked Iran and its monarch from its territory. Commercially, although the National Bank of Persia continued to be managed by German nationals, their powers were strongly curtailed. Moreover, Iran's industrial projects, which had been managed by the National Bank to the great benefit of German companies, were unexpectedly made the responsibility of other government agencies, such as the Iranian department of industry. Not even Taimurtash, Reza Shah's longtime right-hand man and an advocate of Germany, could remedy the situation. Moreover, his enemies exploited Germany's misfortune in Iran as part of a propaganda campaign that destroyed him.

Germany's fate in Iran and Taimurtash's removal from power were both factors that contributed to a new era in Iranian history. This era was marked by the rise of nationalism and Reza Shah's increased desire for power. In 1933, these factors forced the renegotiation of the contract between the Iranian government and the British-controlled Anglo-Persian Oil Company, which generated the highest earnings of any oil company of its time. As a result, the royalties of the oil company to the Iranian government were increased, providing the country with a stronger financial standing. In Germany this period was marked by the rise of the National Socialist party, which gradually affected German foreign policy, consequently resulting in a shift of German national interests in Iran.

At a time when Germany's status in Iran was already damaged, particularly in the eyes of Reza Shah, and trade had decreased, German relations with Iran experienced a further setback. While less critical than the communist propaganda affair preceding it, nonetheless it had a damaging effect on the relations of both countries. To the surprise of all involved, this setback revolved around the institution that had been at the centre of German economic influence in Persia, the National Bank. The ill-starred escalation of a corruption case brought against the National Bank's German director, Lindenblatt, and his vice-director, Vogel, led to a dramatic chain of events that ended in Lindenblatt's prosecution and Vogel's suicide. This time, however, the German government authorities tried harder to influence developments positively, though to little effect. Fortunately for them, the Iranian courts found that Lindenblatt and Vogel were the only Germans employed by the National Bank who could be held responsible for the alleged embezzlement and creative accounting, which saved Germany's standing to a degree in Iran. Claims brought against other Germans employed by the National Bank were dismissed by the court. As a result of these two crises, Germany had to react quickly and decisively if it wanted to retain any political relations with Iran and secure economic influence by means of increasing its trade. In contrast to the 1920s it was unlikely for charismatic individuals single-handedly to exert positive influence over Germany's relations with Iran. At this juncture the German government authorities were faced by a political challenge: they must either become proactive and show initiative, or lose Iran altogether as an ally and trade partner.

By the mid-1930s Iran had evolved into an attractive emerging market for international trade. Goods imported into Germany from Iran were in high demand, and vice versa. Newspaper articles in Germany highlighted the good trade relations between the two countries, pointing out that German and Iranian exports complemented each other in an ideal way. It could be argued that having recognised the significance of the economic opportunities in Iran, the German government for the first time had become politically proactive, advancing the evolution of its foreign relations with Iran. Germany's political initiative, strongly backed by its economic accomplishments, helped to win back lost territory in Iran. In addition, Reza Shah's reported admiration for Hitler and Germany's National Socialist attacks against communism worked in favour of Germany.

By this time, the National Bank of Persia had matured into an indispensable financial institution and the Central Bank of the Iranian government. However, from a German point of view, a significant shift had taken place. Towards the end of the 1930s the National Bank had lost irrevocably its significance for German economic activities in Iran. As a firmly established Iranian institution, Iranian nationals replaced gradually most foreign employees of the bank, including its German fiscal experts. This development was in line with Reza Shah's desire to minimise the control of foreigners over the bank.

Nevertheless, the improvement in foreign political relations and diplomacy appears to have more than compensated Germany for its loss of influence over the bank. Germany had managed to secure its position as a leading trade partner of Iran. By 1939 trade between Germany and Iran reached its highest level in the history of the countries' economic relations. These developments highlight that the role of the National Bank of Persia as a vehicle for German economic influence in Iran had become marginal.

From a German perspective, after 1933 foreign policy and diplomacy began to replace the influence of the National Bank as the prime vehicle for Germany's economic influence in Iran. From the mid-1930s, intergovernmental negotiations, rapprochement, agreements, and appraisements marked the new proactive German foreign political approach. To underline its political determination for better relations with Iran, the German government approved state visits of high government officials. An example for this was the visit of Schacht, the German minister of economics and Central Bank president, to Iran. The German government also facilitated high-level meetings with Iranian dignitaries in Berlin, for example with the German foreign minister or the German Reichspresident von Hindenburg.

Germany's foreign policy towards Iran had achieved its central objective by concentrating on developing bilaterally beneficial economic relations. Germany's foreign political success towards the end of the inter-war period resulted in an expansion of its economic relations, which elevated Germany from a country with almost no trade relations with Iran to its largest trading partner.

After the outbreak of World War II in 1939, Iran officially declared its neutrality. Nonetheless, Germany continued to maintain its unusually strong economic relations with Iran. Moreover, the sympathies of the Shah for Hitler and his war efforts made the allied powers suspicious of Iran's impartiality. Furthermore, the British suspected widespread and well-organised combatant activities of German nationals and agents in Iran. Hence, it feared that Germany's relations with Iran, as they stood, could sabotage possible allied operations in the region.

Even the desperate efforts of the alerted Shah in 1940 to rid himself of his pro-German image by taking action against German influence in Iran did not result in any actual change in perceptions. The fact that the number of German nationals in Iran was far fewer and their influence far less than British propaganda had stated made no difference either. As Churchill stated, German prestige stood high among Iranians.

Germany contributed to its own fate in Iran as a consequence of its invasion of Russia, which forced Stalin to enter an alliance with Britain. Russia's defence of its territory against the German invaders depended on arms supplies from Britain and the United States. The strategic defence plan of the allied powers included a strong defence-wall widely known as the 'Orient front', which stretched from the east to the west and could resist Hitler's invasion of the region and the strategically important oilfields of Baku.

This strategy relied on a logistical solution that utilised the Persian Gulf as the waterway for the transportation of allied war shipments to the southern coasts of Iran. From there the Trans-Iranian Railway network would be used to carry the allied war shipments across Iran to Russia. The access to oil and the British infrastructure in the south of Iran was regarded as an added advantage, maximising the effectiveness of this strategy. However, Reza Shah when presented with this allied strategy rejected it, insisting on Iran's neutrality. Consequently, he refused to allow the transit of any war shipments through his country.

When the United States joined the war efforts against Germany, provoked by the Japanese attack on Pearl Harbour in 1941, it increased the pressure on the allied powers to find a rapid solution to their Iranian problem. Inevitably, any German interference in Iran had to be countered and the country had to be completely won over for the overall strategic goals of the allied front against Hitler.

As a result, in August 1941 Britain and Russia invaded Iran. On 25 August 1941, the Shah ordered his troops to resist the allied invasion, but only a few days later there was a change of cabinet, followed by a declaration of capitulation. The Shah was presented with an ultimatum in a deal offered by the allied powers. According to this deal, the Shah was asked to leave his country in a quest to ensure that his 21-year-old son would become his successor. On 17 September 1941 his son Mohammad Reza became the last king of Iran. Reza Shah was sent abroad into exile, where he died a few years later in Johannesburg in 1944.

Not only did these events signal an end to the Reza Shah period but they also opened the doors to the Allied powers who, in the absence of any real authority from the new Shah, now had in actuality taken control of Iran. As a result all Iranian ties to Germany were broken off. The German embassy in Tehran was forced to close its gates in September 1941 and thereby conclude all its political and economic links with Iran. The majority of German citizens in Iran were instructed to leave the country and a number were detained. The end of Reza Shah's period therefore also marked the end of German involvement in Iran for years to come.

The inescapable conclusion is that Germany's status in Iran during the late 1920s and early 1930s relied almost solely on the efforts of a small number of German entrepreneurs who did not work for or formally represent Germany or its foreign policy in Iran.

These individuals, who went to Iran for their own motives, tried to negotiate commercial deals which ultimately forced a German government, almost oblivious of its political relations with Iran, to show a degree of support for the overseas business interests of German companies. The German government was not prepared and had little incentive or will to accommodate Iran in its newly evolving post World War I foreign political strategy. Only when faced with an ultimatum, or when under external and international pressure did the government take action, by granting loans, proposing experts, or preventing leftist activities and attacks against Iran and its monarch originating in Germany.

However, when Iran's emerging markets became increasingly attractive for German business, encouraged by Hitler and his National Socialist foreign political objectives, the interest of the German government in Iran became stronger and thereby proved instrumental to the success of bilateral foreign and economic relations. This resulted in a shift of the economic and political driving force from individual entrepreneurs to the government, as established in the case of the National Bank of Persia. This evolution in German foreign policy resulted in a number of government-initiated agreements with Iran and the exchange of major political figures, contributing to amicable political relations and significant economic influence for Germany in Iran. The positive evolution of German–Iranian relations towards the end of the inter-war period ended abruptly with the British Russian invasion of Iran in 1941, which effectively left the country under the control of the allied powers, whose war strategy inherently included clearing Iran of German influence.

The evidence exposed in this investigation in pursuit of its core hypothesis supports the fact that in practice Germany did not have a structured and consistent foreign policy towards Iran in the years before World War II. Instead, it was the economic interests of entrepreneurs that facilitated German foreign policy in Iran. These interests were defined and implemented by the activities of German entrepreneurs through their commercial ambitions in Iran. Although Germany initially had a reactive foreign policy, it was in fact the economic ambitions of individual German entrepreneurs, aided by early German utilisation of the National Bank of Persia, which initiated the development of a consistent proactive German foreign policy, and consequently resulted in the unexpectedly successful establishment of German economic influence in Iran before World War II.

NOTES

Chapter 1

1 See Sykes, Percy. *A History of Persia* (London: Macmillan, 1951), vol. 2, pp. 244–6. The will of Tsar Peter the Great provides a degree of insight into Russian foreign political motives towards the Middle East.

2 Nayyeri, Mostafa. *Das Bankwesen im Iran und seine Entwicklung* (Köln: Dissertation, 1964), p. 11. Jones, Geoffrey. *Banking and Empire in Iran* (Cambridge: Cambridge University Press, 1986), vol. 1, p. 87.

3 Jones. *Banking and Empire in Iran*, vol. 1, pp. 83–5.

4 Kazemzadeh, Firuz. *Russia and Britain in Persia 1864–1914* (New Haven, London: Yale University Press, 1968), p. 324.

5 Ibid., p. 325.

6 Ibid., p. 325.

7 Nayyeri. *Das Bankwesen im Iran*, pp. 12–13. Kazemzadeh. *Russia and Britain*, p. 384.

8 Kazemzadeh. *Russia and Britain*, p. 326.

9 Nayyeri. *Das Bankwesen im Iran*, pp. 12–13. Kazemzadeh. *Russia and Britain*, pp. 365–78.

10 Jones. *Banking and Empire in Iran*, vol. 1, p. 89.

11 Ibid., pp. 89–91.

12 Martin, Bradford. *German-Persian Relations 1873–1912* (The Hague: Mouton & Co. s'Gravenhage, 1959), pp. 107–120.

13 From a British or Russian perspective a German bank implied the loss of power to British and Russian banks.

14 Schöllgen, Gregor. *Imperialismus und Gleichgewicht* (Munich: R. Oldenbourg Verlag, 1984), p. 227.

15 The German school in Tehran, established in 1907, is an example of this. One aspect leading to its founding, from a political point of view, was that of a German 'good-will investment' with regard to further relations with Persia, particularly after the rejection of the banking concession by Germany.

16 See Martin. *German-Persian Relations*, chs. 3 and 4. For further reading on the Weimarer Republik see Fischer, Fritz. *Griff nach der Weltmacht* (Düsseldorf: Droste Verlag, 1961), pp. 136–7.

17 Fischer. *Griff nach der Weltmacht*, p. 17.
18 Schöllgen. *Imperialismus und Gleichgewicht*, p. 435.
19 Ibid., p. 453.
20 Barth, Boris. *Die deutsche Hochfinanz und die Imperialismen. Banken und Außenpolitik vor 1914* (Stuttgart: Franz Steiner, 1995), p. 121. Fn. 1 provides an extensive literature list on the Baghdad Railway Project.
21 Schaefer, C. A. *Die Entwicklung der Bagdadbahnpolitik* (Weimar 1916), p. 17.
22 Barth. *Die Deutsche Hochfinanz*, p. 123.
23 Gross, Nachum T. 'Die Deutsche Palästina-Bank 1897–1914', *Zeitschrift für Unternehmensgeschichte*, 33. Jahrgang (Heft 3/1988), p. 150.
24 Ibid., p. 155.
25 Ibid., p. 174.
26 Kazemzadeh. *Russia and Britain*, pp. 596–8.
27 Ibid. See for a detailed account of Persia, imperialism and foreign powers from 1864 to 1914.
28 Griffith, William E. 'Iran's Foreign Policy in the Pahlavi Era', in George Lenczowski, ed., *Iran under the Pahlavis* (Stanford: The Hoover Institution Press, 1978), p. 367.
29 Platt, D. C. M. *Finance, Trade, and Politics in British Foreign Policy 1815–1914* (Oxford: Clarendon Press, 1968), p. 236.
30 Ibid., p. 238.
31 Report entitled *Die Aufschließung Persien*. August 1921, 9-page report, PAAA, Department III–Economy, R92527, pp. 1–2.
32 William Knox D'Arcy had obtained an oil concession for £200,000 from Muzaffar ad-Din Shah (1896–1907) in 1901.
33 Platt. *Finance, Trade, and Politics in British Foreign Policy*, pp. 239–42.
34 Strobaugh, Robert B. 'The evolution of Iranian oil policy, 1925–1975', in George Lenczowski, ed., *Iran under the Pahlavis* (Stanford: The Hoover Institution Press, 1978), p. 201.
35 Hirschfeld, Yair P. *Dutschland und Iran im Spielfeld der Mächte internationale Beziehungen unter Reza Schah, 1921-1941* (Düsseldorf: Droste, 1980), p. 31.
36 Report entitled *Die Aufschließung Persiens*. August 1921, 9-page report. PAAA, Department III–Economy, R92527, p. 1.
37 See also Olsen, W. J. *Anglo-Iranian Relations during World War I* (London: Frank Cass, 1984). Gehrke, Ulrich. *Persien in der Deutschen Orientpolitik während des Ersten Weltkrieges* (Stuttgart: W. Kohlhammer GmbH, 1961). Keddie, Nikki. *Roots of Revolution: An Interpretive History of Modern Iran* (New Haven and London: Yale University Press, 1981), p. 78.
38 Amanat, Mehrdad and Keddie, Nikki. 'Iran under the later Qajars, 1848–1922', in Peter Avery, Gavin Hambly, and Charles Melville, eds, *The Cambridge History of Iran*, vol. 7, *From Nadir Shah to the Islamic Republic* (Cambridge: Cambridge University Press, 1991), p. 208.
39 Keddie. *Roots of Revolution*, pp. 79–80.
40 Schöllgen. *Imperialismus und Gleichgewicht*, p. 429.
41 Ibid., p. 430.
42 Fischer. *Griff nach der Weltmacht*, pp. 143–8.
43 Gehrke. *Persien in der Deutschen Orientpolitik*, p. 87.
44 Ibid., p. 88.

45 Ibid., p. 89.
46 Ibid., p. 86.
47 Ibid., p. 323.
48 Ibid., p. 60.
49 Ibid., p. 61.
50 Ibid., pp. 318–19.
51 Ibid., p. 319.
52 Ibid., p. 64.
53 Ibid., p. 65.
54 Ibid., p. 66.
55 Ibid., p. 321.
56 Among the many things Wassmuss protested against were the arrest of German individuals by the British, such as Dr Landers, and the confiscation of his own expedition property, on transit through southern Persia to India.
57 Gehrke. *Persien in der Deutschen Orientpolitik,* p. 81.
58 Ibid., p. 325.
59 The Germans could not accept this justification particularly as the Ottomans were a Sunni and the Persians a Shiite state.
60 Gehrke. *Persien in der Deutschen Orientpolitik,* p. 326.
61 Ibid., p. 327.
62 Ibid., pp. 309–10.
63 Ibid., p. 312.
64 Ibid., p. 313.
65 Ibid., p. 315.
66 Ibid., p. 316.
67 Miron, Rezun. *The Soviet Union and Iran* (Geneva: Institut Universitaire de Etudes Internationales, 1981), pp. 12–14.
68 Report entitled *Die Aufschließung Persiens*. August 1921, 9-page report. PAAA, Department III–Economy, R92527, p. 7.
69 Ibid., pp. 7–8.
70 From German embassy in Tehran to Russian foreign minister Tschitscherin in Moscow. 20 October 1921, letter. PAAA, Department III–Economy, R92527.
71 Ibid.
72 From Joseph Addicon in Berlin to Minister of Foreign Affairs Dr. Wirth. 29 November 1921, letter. PAAA, Department III-Politics, R78105. Number 1369, pp. L014916-L014917.
73 Ibid.
74 German embassy in Moscow to German Foreign Office in Berlin. 25 December 1921, report. PAAA, Department III–Economy, R92527. Number 38.
75 Report from Schulenberg in Berlin. 4 September 1922, report. PAAA, Department III–Economy, R92363.
76 Zürrer, Werner. *Persien zwischen England und Rußland 1918–1925* (Bern: Verlag Peter Lang AG, 1978), p. 302.
77 Tapper, Richard. *The Conflict of Tribe and State in Iran and Afghanistan* (London, Canberra: Croom Helm, 1983), pp. 386–9.
78 Report from Schulenberg in Berlin. 4 September 1922, report. PAAA, Department III–Economy, R92363.
79 Ibid.

80 From Radowitz in Moscow to German Foreign Office in Berlin. 17 October 1922, telegram. PAAA, Department III–Economy, R92362. No. 574.
81 Report entitled *Die Aufschließung Persiens*. August 1921, 9-page report. PAAA, Department III–Economy, R92527, p. 9.
82 Keddie, *Roots of Revolution*, p. 81.
83 Lord Curzon was at the same time Chairman of the eastern Committee.
84 Sabahi, Houshang. *British Policy in Persia 1918–1925* (Exeter: BPCC Wheatons Ltd, 1990), p. 3.
85 Olsen. *Anglo-Iranian Relations during World War I*, pp. 234–236. See for text of Persian proposal for an agreement with Britain.
86 Katouzian, Homa. *The Political Economy of Modern Iran* (London: Macmillan Press Ltd, 1981), Chapter V.
87 Zürrer. *Persien zwischen England und Rußland*, p. 481.
88 Olsen. *Anglo-Iranian Relations during World War I*, pp. 247–9.
89 Ibid., pp. 224–49. For further discussion of 1919 agreement.
90 Report entitled *Die Aufschließung Persiens*. August 1921, 9-page report. PAAA, Department III–Economy, R92527, p. 6.
91 Ibid., p. 8.
92 Ramazani, Rouhollah K. *The United States and Iran* (New York: Praeger Publishers, 1982), pp. 5–6.
93 Zürrer. *Persien zwischen England und Rußland*, p. 400.
94 Yeselson, Abraham. *United States–Persian Diplomatic Relations 1883–1921* (New Jersey: Rutgers University Press, 1956), pp. 131–55.
95 Ibid., p. 148.
96 Ibid., p. 149.
97 Ibid., p. 162.
98 Ibid., pp. 149–51.
99 Sabahi. *British Policy in Persia*, ch. 6.
100 Zürrer. *Persien zwischen England und Rußland*, p. 302.
101 Sabahi, *British Policy in Persia*, ch. 6.
102 From German embassy in Tehran. 30 August 1923, report. PAAA, Department III–Economy, R92478. No. 374.
103 Zürrer. *Persien zwischen England und Rußland*, p. 312.
104 From German embassy in Tehran. 30 August 1923, report. PAAA, Department III–Economy, R92478. No. 374.
105 Zürrer. *Persien zwischen England und Rußland*, p. 319.
106 From Schulenburg at the German embassy in Tehran to the German Foreign Office in Berlin. 2 January 1924, report. PAAA, Department III–Economy, R92478. No. 1.
107 Sabahi, *British Policy in Persia*, ch. 6.
108 Ibid., p. 151.
109 Miron, *The Soviet Union and Iran*, p. 17.
110 Elwell-Sutton, L. P. 'Reza Shah the Great: Founder of the Pahlavi Dynasty', in George Lenczowski, ed., *Iran under the Pahlavis* (Stanford: The Hoover Institution Press, 1978), p. 4.
111 Amanat and Keddie, 'Iran under the later Qajars', pp. 174 ff.
112 Elwell-Sutton, 'Reza Shah the Great', p. 13.
113 He was later to be known as Sardar As'ad

114 Sabahi, *British Policy in Persia*, pp. 157–9.
115 Wilber, Donald. *Riza Shah Pahlavi: The Resurrection and Reconstruction of Iran* (New York and Hicksville: Exposition Press, 1975), p. 43.
116 Katouzian, *The Political Economy of Modern Iran*, pp. 79–80.
117 Avery, Peter. *Modern Iran* (London: Praeger, 1965), pp. 229–31.
118 Abrahamian, Evand. *Iran Between Two Revolutions* (Princeton: Princeton University Press, 1982), p. 118.
119 See Benab, Younes. *The Soviet Union and Britain in Iran, 1917–1927: A Case Study of the Domestic Impact of East-West Rivalry* (Washington D.C.: unpublished Doctor of Philosophy thesis, The Catholic University of America, 1974), pp. 239–41.
120 See also Sabahi, *British Policy in Persia*, pp. 180–93.
121 See Banani, Amin. *The Modernization of Iran: 1921–1941* (Stanford: Stanford University Press, 1961), p. 43. Earlier, on 31 October 1925, the Majlis had passed the following Act:

'Majlis-e Showra-ye Melli, in the name of the welfare of the nation, declares the end of the Qajar Monarchy and bestows the provisional government, with the bounds of the Constitution and the laws of the land, to Reza Khan Pahlavi. The final form of the government shall be decided by a Constituent Assembly which shall convene for revision of Articles 36, 37, 38, and 40 of the Supplement to the Constitution.'

122 See Banani, *The Modernization of Iran: 1921–1941,* p. 43. 'In December 1925 the Constituent Assembly, elected under the watchful eye of the government, met in Tehran and revised article 36 of the Supplement to the Constitution to read as follows: The Constitutional Monarchy of Iran is vested by the Constituent Assembly, on behalf of the nation, in the person of His Majesty, The Shahanshah Reza Shah Pahlavi, and shall remain in his male progeny generation after generation.'
123 See Banani, *The Modernization of Iran*: *1921–1941*, p. 13. The Shah presented a speech on this day that encompasses and foreshadows much of his ambitions for the country:

'On this occasion, as I perform the ceremonies of my coronation, I wish to bring to the attention of the whole people my views regarding the carrying out of fundamental reforms in our country. The expression of these views may serve both as a comprehensive instruction to my governments and a guide to the people. Firstly, my particular attention has been and always will be directed to the preservation of the principles and foundations of religion, for in my opinion one of the most effective means of ensuring national unity and strengthening the spirit of the community of the Iranians is the fortifying of the bases of religious faith.

'My imperial governments must therefore remember without fail that the duty of carrying out the fundamental reform of the country – the establishment of security, the spread of education, proper attention to public health, the improvement of the economic situation, the increase of national wealth, the completion of communications, the welfare of agriculture and commerce, and urgent reform of the judicial system – leave no time for contemplation and laxity. Government officials must provide an example of industry, high morality, and firmness of purpose, and strive for the health, strength, education, and wealth of the people, so that well-being and prosperity may be available to all in accordance with my expectations.'

124 Hambly, Gavin R. G., 'The Pahlavi autocracy: Riza Shah, 1921–1941', in Peter Avery, Gavin Hambly and Charles Melville, ed., *The Cambridge History of Iran*, vol. 7, *From Nadir Shah to the Islamic Republic* (Cambridge: Cambridge University Press, 1991), pp. 223 ff.

125 Hirschfeld, *Deutschland und Iran im Spielfeld der Mächte*, p. 41.

Chapter 2

1 From an article on Persia's industrialisation in the publication for German engineers, *VDI-Nachrichten*, 1927. PAAA, Department III–Economy, R92430.

2 German newspaper article, 'The Industrialisation of Persia', 23 January 1927. PAAA, Department III–Economy, R92430.

3 Letter from German Foreign Office in Berlin to the editor of the *Kölnischen Zeitung* Dr W. Croll, with regard to article on 'Germany and Persia' in issue number 292 (21 April 1927), 1927. PAAA, Department III–Economy, R92360.

4 Reply of German Foreign Office in Berlin to an inquiry by the company Bergman and Simons GmbH in Köln-Mühlheim, 11 May 1927. PAAA, Department III–Economy, R92360.

5 Ibid.

6 Letter from German Foreign Office in Berlin to the chamber of commerce, Halle, 27 March 1927. PAAA, Department III–Economy, R92360.

7 Letter from German embassy in Tehran to German Foreign Office in Berlin, 7 May 1927. PAAA, German legation files-Iran, PKT 74/XB 6. Vol. 1, telecom.

8 Letter (7pp) from Schulenberg to German Foreign Office in Berlin, 15 May 1927. PAAA, Department III–Economy, R92395.

9 Letter (6pp) from Schulenberg in Tehran to German Foreign Office in Berlin, 18 June 1927. PAAA, Department III-Politics, R78114.

10 Ibid.

11 Account of *Izvestia* article, from Hey in Moscow to German Foreign Office in Berlin, 10 June 1927, telegram. PAAA, Department III-Politics, R78151.

12 Letter (6pp) from Schulenberg in Tehran to German Foreign Office in Berlin, 18 June 1927. PAAA, Department III-Politics, R78114.

13 Ibid.

14 Millspaugh, A. C. *The American Task in Persia* (New York and London: The Century Company, 1925).

15 From an article on Persia's industrialisation in the publication for German engineers, *VDI-Nachrichten*, 1927. PAAA, Department III–Economy, R92430.

16 Letter from Schulenberg in Tehran to German Foreign Office in Berlin, 12 May 1927. PAAA, Department III–Economy, R92310. Number 129.

17 Letter from Schulenberg to German Foreign Office in Berlin, 31 July 1927. PAAA, Department III–Economy, R92310. Number 239.

18 Dr Ziemke, letter from German Foreign Office in Berlin to the German ministry of finance Berlin. 16 August 1927. Bundesarchiv Potsdam, ministry of trade and industry, 31.01/19096. LB 953027, p. 3.

19 Letter from Schulenberg in Tehran to German Foreign Office in Berlin, 31 July 1927. PAAA, Department III–Economy, R92320. Number 241.

20 Ibid.

21 Ibid.
22 Article in Capital City News Association, Washington DC, 8 September 1927. PAAA, Department III–Economy, R92320. CCNA Number 1. (Exclusive).
23 Article in Capital City News Association, Washington DC, 17 September 1927. PAAA, Department III–Economy, R92320. CCNA Number 9.
24 Letter by Dr Ziemke from the German Foreign Office in Berlin to German ministry of finance in Berlin, 16 August 1927. Bundesarchiv Potsdam, ministry of trade and industry, 31.01/19093. LB 953027, p. 3.
25 Letter (8pp) from Thomas Brown to German ministry of finance in Berlin, 28 September 1927. Bundesarchiv Potsdam, ministry of trade and industry, 31.01/19093, p. 21.
26 Ibid., p. 22.
27 Letter from Thomas Brown to German ministry of finance in Berlin, 12 April 1928. Bundesarchiv Potsdam, ministry of trade and industry, 31.01/19093, p. 87.
28 Letter (8pp) from Thomas Brown to German ministry of finance in Berlin, 28 September 1927. Bundesarchiv Potsdam, ministry of trade and industry, 31.01/19093, p. 23.
29 Ibid., p. 23.
30 Ibid., p. 24.
31 Ibid., p. 25.
32 Letter from Schulenberg to German Foreign Office in Berlin, 31 July 1927. PAAA, De partment III-Politics, R92310. Number 239.
33 Letter (8pp) from Thomas Brown to German ministry of finance in Berlin, 28 September 1927. Bundesarchiv Potsdam, ministry of trade and industry, 31.01/19093, p. 25.
34 Telegram from Schulenberg to German Foreign Office in Berlin, 10 August 1927. PAAA, Department III-Politics, R92310.
35 Letter from Ministerialrat Ruelberg, German ministry of finance, Berlin, to Reichsbahndirector Dr Baumann, 19 August 1927. Bundesarchiv Potsdam, ministry of trade and industry. 31.01/2669/2, p. 59.
36 Letter (8pp) from Thomas Brown to German ministry of finance in Berlin, 28 September 1927. Bundesarchiv Potsdam, ministry of trade and industry, 31.01/19093, p. 26.
37 Telegram from Schulenberg to German Foreign Office in Berlin, 4 September 1927. PAAA, Department III–Economy, R92320. Nr. 93.
38 Report by German Foreign Office in Berlin, 24 October 1927. PAAA, Department III–Economy, R92320.
39 Letter (8pp) from Thomas Brown to German ministry of finance in Berlin, 28 September 1927. Bundesarchiv Potsdam, ministry of trade and industry, 31.01/19093, p. 27.
40 Ibid., p. 26.
41 Letter from Dr Ziemke, German Foreign Office in Berlin, to the German ministry of finance Berlin, 16 August 1927. Bundesarchiv Potsdam, ministry of trade and industry, 31.01/19096. LB 953027, p. 4.
42 Letter (8pp) from Thomas Brown to German ministry of finance in Berlin, 28 September 1927. Bundesarchiv Potsdam, ministry of trade and industry, 31.01/19093, p. 28.

43 Minutes of a meeting between Ministerial Director Schäffer, Ministerial Rat Dr Heintze, Ministerial Rat Flach, Dr Daniel, Thomas Brown and representatives of Krupp and Siemens-Bauunion at the German ministry of finance Berlin, 17 November 1927. Bundesarchiv Potsdam, ministry of trade and industry, 31.01/19093. 1B11821 27, p. 32.
44 Ibid., p. 32.
45 Letter (8pp) from Thomas Brown to German ministry of finance in Berlin, 28 September 1927. Bundesarchiv Potsdam, ministry of trade and industry, 31.01/19093, p. 26.
46 1 toman = 10 gheran; £1 = 50 gheran.
47 Statistic department of the Reichsbank in Berlin. 31 October 1927, report. PAAA, Department III–Economy, R92320, pp. 2–3.
48 Letter from German embassy in Tehran to German Foreign Office in Berlin. 7 July 1927. PAAA, German legation files-Iran, National Bank of Persia, PKT 73/IX A 11a. See also official announcement of the National Bank's inauguration. PAAA, Department III–Economy, R92341.
49 Report of statistics department of the Reichsbank in Berlin, 31 October 1927. PAAA, Department III–Economy, R92320, p. 4.
50 Note by Dr Grobba, head of Orient-department, at the German Foreign Office in Berlin, 7 December 1927. PAAA, Department III–Economy, R92320.
51 Ibid.
52 Telegram from Dehaas at the German Foreign Office in Berlin to Sofia, 7 December 1927. PAAA, Department III–Economy, R92320. Number 91.
53 Report on Dr Kurt Lindenblatt, 1 March 1928. PAAA, Department III–Economy, R92321.
54 Ibid.
55 Briefing notes for German foreign minister Dr Stresemann, 12 April 1928. PAAA, Department III-Politics, R78105. L014971.
56 Newspaper article published in *Frankfurter Zeitung*, 27 April 1928. Bundesarchiv Potsdam, Deutsche Reichsbank, 25.01/5289. Number 315. See also newspaper article in *Berliner Lokal-Anzeiger*, 26 April 1928. Bundesarchiv Potsdam, Deutsche Reichsbank, 25.01/5389. Number 188.
57 Letter from German embassy in Tehran to German Foreign Office in Berlin, 7 July 1927. PAAA, German legation files-Iran, National Bank of Persia, PKT 73/IX A 11a. An almost identical statement with reference to the German Foreign Office in Berlin can be found (four months later) in a report of the statistical department of the Reichsbank in Berlin, 31 October 1927. PAAA, Department III–Economy, R92320, p. 4.
58 Article in *Capital City News Association*, Washington DC, 8 September 1927. PAAA, Department III–Economy, R92320. CCNA Number 1. (Exclusive).
59 Letter from German embassy in Tehran to German Foreign Office in Berlin, 7 July 1927. PAAA, German legation files-Iran, National Bank of Persia, PKT73/IXA11a

Chapter 3

1 Report compiled by Dr Fritz Hesse, chairman of the German–Persian Association (Deutsch-Persische Gesellschaft), most probably for German Foreign Office in Berlin, approximately 1930. PAAA, Department III–Economy, R92360, p. 1.

2 Ibid., p. 2.
3 Ibid., p. 3. For further information on Persian trade see also document from statistical department of the Reichsbank, 20 August 1930, report. Bundesarchiv Potsdam, Deutsche Reichsbank, 25.01, 6594/1. And article by Fritz Hesse. 'Deutsche Waren in Persien', *Berliner Tageblatt*, 19 September 1930, 443.
4 Report compiled by Dr Fritz Hesse, chairman of the German–Persian Association (Deutsch-Persische Gesellschaft), most probably for German Foreign Office in Berlin, approximately 1930. PAAA, Department III–Economy, R92360, p. 4.
5 Ibid., p. 6.
6 Ibid., p. 9.
7 Ibid., p. 11.
8 For details on the Trans-Iranian Railway project see letter from Brown to Heintze at the ministry of trade and industry, 12 April 1928. Bundesarchiv Potsdam, ministry of trade and industry, 31.01/19093.
9 Report compiled by Dr Fritz Hesse, chairman of the German–Persian Association (Deutsch-Persische Gesellschaft), most probably for German Foreign Office in Berlin, approximately 1930. PAAA, Department III–Economy, R92360, p. 13.
10 Ibid., p. 14.
11 Article entitled 'Persien' published in *Industrie- und Handelszeitung*, 89, 15 April 1928. Bundesarchiv Potsdam, Deutsche Reichsbank, 25.01/5289.
12 Briefing (6-page) prepared by the Foreign Office for the breakfast meeting of German foreign minister with Persian foreign minister in Berlin, 29 March 1928. PAAA, Department III-Politics, R78166, p. 1.
13 Ibid., pp. 2–3.
14 Ibid., pp. 3–4.
15 This was a direct result of Brown's negotiations with the Persian government, as shown in the previous chapters.
16 Briefing (6-page) prepared by the Foreign Office for the breakfast meeting of German foreign minister with Persian foreign minister in Berlin, 29 March 1928. PAAA, Department III-Politics, R78166, pp. 4–5.
17 Ibid., pp. 5–6.
18 Foreign office record of suggested topics of discussion for Stresemann for a breakfast meeting on 13 April 1928 at the Persian embassy, 12 April 1928, briefing. PAAA, Department III-Politics, R78105. L014968-L014971, p. 1.
19 Ibid., p. 2.
20 Ibid., pp. 2–3.
21 Ibid., pp. 3–4.
22 Letter from German Foreign Office in Berlin to Brown, 12 July 1928. PAAA, Department III–Economy, R92321.
23 Taimurtash had previously visited Germany in 192.
24 Letter from Ministerialdirektor de Haas to Staatssekretär von Schubert over reception of Taimurtash in Berlin, 27 July 1928. PAAA, Department III-Politics, R78166, p. 1.
25 Ibid., pp. 1–2.
26 The guest list as recommended included Taimurtash, Farzin, Azodi, de Haas, Gaus, Ritter, von Richthofen, Martius, Köster, Eisenlohr, Terdenge, Grobba,

Siemens, Bücher, Bötzkes, Schniewind, Junkers, Bamberger, Brown and von Cramon.

27 Letter from Ministerialdirektor de Haas to Staatssekretär von Schubert over reception of Taimurtash in Berlin, 27 July 1928. PAAA, Department III-Politics, R78166, p. 3.

28 Foreign office document entitled: Topics for the visit of the Persian Hofminister Taimurtash, 10 September 1928, 6-page briefing. PAAA, Department III-Politics, R78166, p. 1.

29 Ibid., p. 3.

30 Diplomatic telegram from de Haas to Tehran. 11 September 1928. PAAA, Department III-Politics, R78166.

31 Foreign office document entitled: Topics for the visit of the Persian Hofminister Taimurtash, 10 September 1928, 6-page briefing. PAAA, Department III-Politics, R78166, pp. 4–6.

32 Telegram from de Haas from Berlin to German delegation in Geneva, 5 September 1928. PAAA, Department III-Politics, R78166.

33 Five-page letter, probably from de Haas to Schulenberg, 18 September 1928. PAAA, Political department III, R78166. See also diplomatic telegram from de Haas to Tehran, 11 September 1928. PAAA, Department III-Politics, R78166.

34 Five-page letter, probably from de Haas to Schulenberg, 18 September 1928. PAAA, Department III-Politics, R78166.

35 Ibid.

36 Letter from Lindenblatt to Schulenberg. 30 August 1928. PAAA, German legation files-Iran, PKT 73/IX A 11a.

37 Ibid. See also letter from Lindenblatt to Schulenberg, 24 November 1928. PAAA, German legation files-Iran, PKT 73/IX A 11a. And confidential letter from Lindenblatt to Schulenberg, 17 December 1929. PAAA, German legation files-Iran, PKT 73/IX A 11a.

38 Coded telegram from Schulenberg to German Foreign Office in Berlin, 18 November 1928. PAAA, Department III–Economy, R92321.

39 Letter from Lindenblatt to Schulenberg. 24 November 1928. German legation files, PAAA, German legation files-Iran, PKT 73/IX A 11a. See also official legal document (French and Persian) of the National Bank of Persia, 14 February 1929. German legation files, PAAA, German legation files-Iran, PKT 73/IX A 11a.

40 Ibid. And confidential letter from Lindenblatt to Schulenberg, 17 December 1929. German legation files, PAAA, German legation files-Iran, PKT 73/IX A 11a.

41 Official legal document (French and Persian) of the National Bank of Persia, 14 February 1929. German legation files, PAAA, German legation files-Iran, PKT 73/IX A 11a.

42 Confidential letter from Lindenblatt to Schulenberg, 17 December 1929. German legation files, PAAA, German legation files-Iran, PKT 73/IX A 11a.

43 Letter from de Haas from German Foreign Office in Berlin to the Prussian ministry of trade and industry, 13 August 1928. PAAA, Department III–Economy, R92321.

44 Confidential 8-page letter from Schulenberg to German Foreign Office in Berlin, 1 February 1930. PAAA, Department III–Economy, R92322.

45 Ibid.

46 Ibid.
47 Ibid.
48 Telegram from Schulenberg to German Foreign Office in Berlin, 26 February 1930. PAAA, Department III–Economy, R92322.
49 Financial analysis of Persian situation enclosed with a report (number 194) of German embassy in Tehran for German Foreign Office in Berlin, 17 May 1930, 18-page report. PAAA, Department III–Economy, R92322.
50 Financial analysis of Persian situation enclosed with a report (number 194) of German embassy in Tehran for German Foreign Office in Berlin, 17 May 1930, 18-page report. PAAA, Department III–Economy, R92322.
51 Ibid.
52 Ibid.
53 Ibid.
54 Ibid.
55 Ibid.
56 Letter from Schulenberg to German Foreign Office in Berlin, 30 May 1930. PAAA, Department III-Politics, R78147. Number 208.
57 Ibid.
58 Letter from Schulenberg in Tehran to Grobba at the German Foreign Office in Berlin, 23 May 1930. PAAA, Department III-Politics, R78107. See also letter from Schulenberg in Tehran to German Foreign Office in Berlin, 30 May 1930. PAAA, Department III-Politics, R78151.
59 Ibid.
60 Ibid.
61 Article entitled 'Aus Persiens Wirtschaftsleben', in *Deutsche Tageszeitung*, 433, 14 September 1930. Bundesarchiv Potsdam, Arbeitswissenschaftliches Institut, 62DAF3/35688.
62 Ibid. See also article by Ernst Victor Meyer, entitled 'Persiens Währungsreform', in *Berliner Bareness-Courier*, 481, 16 September 1930. Bundesarchiv Potsdam, Arbeitswissenschaftliches Institut, 62DAF3/35688.
63 Letter from Meyer from Tehran to German Foreign Office in Berlin, 23 February 1931. Bundesarchiv Potsdam, ministry of trade and industry, 31.01/20225. Number 71. See also article by Ernst Victor Meyer, entitled 'Persiens Währungsreform', in *Berliner Bareness-Courier*, 481, 16 September 1930. Bundesarchiv Potsdam, Arbeitswissenschaftliches Institut, 62DAF3/35688.
64 Letter from Schulenberg in Tehran to Grobba at the German Foreign Office in Berlin, 23 May 1930. PAAA, Department III-Politics, R78107.
65 Letter from Schulenberg to German Foreign Office in Berlin, 5 December 1930. PAAA, Department III–Economy, R92322.
66 Schniewind's evaluation report on his task as financial adviser to the Persian government, 1930/1931. PAAA, Department III–Economy, R92322.
67 Ibid.
68 Letter from Lindenblatt to Ritscher, director of the Reichs-Kredit-Gesellschaft in Berlin, 6 December 1930. Bundesarchiv Potsdam, Reichskreditgesellschaft, 80 Re2/2080.
69 Letter from Grobba at the German Foreign Office in Berlin to the Deutsche Revisions-und Treuhand Aktiengesellschaft in Berlin, 25 August 1930. Bundesarchiv Potsdam, ministry of trade and industry, 31.01/19094.

70 Letter from Schulenberg to German Foreign Office in Berlin, 6 December 1930. PAAA, Department III-Politics, R78147.
71 Ibid.
72 Article by Leo Matthias, entitled 'Deutsche Arbeit in Persien', in *Berliner Tageblatt*, 311, 4 July 1930. Bundesarchiv Potsdam, Deutsche Reichsbank, 25.01/5289.

Chapter 4

1 Letter from German Foreign Office in Berlin, 18 April 1928. PAAA, Department III–Economy, R92307.
2 Letter from Schulenberg to German Foreign Office in Berlin, 25 January 1930. PAAA, Department III–Economy, R92431. Number 34.
3 Letter from Mayer from the German embassy in Tehran to German Foreign Office in Berlin, 21 March 1931. PAAA, Department III-Politics, R78107.
4 Translated copy of *Paykar*, issue number 16, from 15 September 1931; translation of leaflet, 30 October 1931. PAAA, Department III-Politics, R78109.
5 Letter from Mayer from the German embassy in Tehran to German Foreign Office in Berlin, 21 March 1931. PAAA, Department III-Politics, R78107.
6 Letter from Grobba from German Foreign Office in Berlin to the Prussian minister of the interior Severing, 28 August 1931. PAAA, Department III-Politics, R78108.
7 Ibid.
8 Ibid.
9 Telegram from Blücher to German Foreign Office in Berlin, 19 October 1931. PAAA, Department III-Politics, R78108.
10 Ibid.
11 Ibid.
12 Report (14 page) entitled 'Die Vorgeschichte des deutsch-persischen Konflikts' compiled by Grobba at the German Foreign Office in Berlin, 27 October 1931. PAAA, Department III-Politics, R78109.
13 Ibid.
14 Ibid.
15 Ibid.
16 Ibid.
17 Internal communiqué of the German Foreign Office in Berlin, 24 June 1931, letter. PAAA, Department III-Politics, R78166.
18 Letter from Schulenberg to German Foreign Office in Berlin. 1 September 1931. PAAA, Department III-Politics, R78162.
19 The order for the return of the Persian embassy staff to Tehran was issued on 18 October 1931. The Italian embassy in Berlin was asked to represent Persian interests in Germany.
20 Telegram from Blücher to German Foreign Office in Berlin, 20 October 1931. PAAA, Department III-Politics, R78108.
21 Ibid.
22 *Münchener Neueste Nachrichten* to German Foreign Office in Berlin. 23 October 1931, letter. PAAA, Department III-Politics, R78108. See also 14-page report entitled 'Die Vorgeschichte des deutsch-persischen Konflikts' compiled by Grobba at the German Foreign Office in Berlin, 27 October 1931. PAAA, Department III-Politics, R78109.

23 Exposé by Sebastian Beck. Late 1931, report. PAAA, Department III-Politics, R78109.
24 Report (14-page) entitled 'Die Vorgeschichte des deutsch-persischen Konflikts' compiled by Grobba at the German Foreign Office in Berlin, 27 October 1931. PAAA, Department III-Politics, R78109.
25 Letter from Grobba to the Persian embassy in Berlin, 27 October 1931. PAAA, Department III-Politics, R78109.
26 Report (14-page) entitled 'Die Vorgeschichte des deutsch-persischen Konflikts' compiled by Grobba at the German Foreign Office in Berlin, 27 October 1931. PAAA, Department III-Politics, R78109.
27 Telegram from Blücher to German Foreign Office in Berlin, 25 October 1931. PAAA, Department III-Politics, R78109.
28 *Narodnoe Khozeistvo Zakavkasia*. Published in April 1931, number 6/7.
29 Letter from German embassy in Tiflis to German Foreign Office in Berlin, 21 July 1931. PAAA, Department III–Economy, R92513.
30 Letter from Schulenberg to German Foreign Office in Berlin, 2 September 1931. PAAA, German legation files-Iran, PKT 73/IX A 11a. Vol. 3, National Bank.

Chapter 5

1 Translation of article published in the government newspaper *Iran*, 19 October 1931. PAAA, Department III-Politics, R78111.
2 Ibid.
3 Letter from Blücher to German Foreign Office in Berlin, 5 January 1932. PAAA, German legation files-Iran, IX A 11a. Vol. 3, National Bank. Number 42.
4 Ibid.
5 Note by unknown Persian author, early 1932. PAAA, Department III-Politics, R78111.
6 Letter from Blücher to German Foreign Office in Berlin, 29 April 1932. PAAA, Department III-Politics, R78179. Number 1456.
7 Ibid.
8 Letter from Blücher to German Foreign Office in Berlin, 9 June 1932. PAAA, Department III-Politics, R78111. Number 1868.
9 German embassy in Stockholm to German Foreign Office in Berlin, 17 February 1932, report. PAAA, Department III–Economy, R92309. Number 90. See also document regardingr consortium for the construction of railways in Persia, 2 March 1932, memorandum. PAAA, German legation files-Iran, VI C4. Vol. 11, railway.
10 Letter from German embassy in Tehran to German Foreign Office in Berlin, 12 March 1932. PAAA, German legation files-Iran, VI C4. Vol. 11, railway.
11 Letter from Blücher to German Foreign Office in Berlin, 14 April 1932. PAAA, Department III–Economy, R92518. Number 1259.
12 Ibid.
13 Letter from Blücher to Grobba at the German Foreign Office in Berlin, 8 February 1932. PAAA, German legation files-Iran, IX A 11a. Vol. 3, National Bank.
14 Ibid.

15 Letter from Robert Wönckhaus & Co. in Tehran, presumably, to Reichskreditgesellschaft in Berlin, 13 May 1932. Bundesarchiv Potsdam, Reichskreditgesellschaft, 80 Re 2/2080.
16 Letter from Blücher to Grobba at the German Foreign Office in Berlin, 8 February 1932. PAAA, German legation files-Iran, IX A 11a. Vol. 3, National Bank.
17 Document entitled 'The political reasons for driving German influence out of Persia'. Document is marked 'Only for information, not to be published'. Date has been inserted in handwriting and may not be the precise date of publication. 6 April 1932, report. PAAA, Department III-Politics, R78112.
18 Letter from Blücher to German Foreign Office in Berlin, 9 June 1932. PAAA, Department III-Politics, R78111. Number 1868.
19 Letter from Weil from Junkers bureau in Berlin to Blücher at the German embassy in Tehran, 25 April 1932. PAAA, German legation files-Iran, VI C7. Vol. 8, Junkers.
20 Document entitled 'The political reasons for driving German influence out of Persia', 6 April 1932, report. PAAA, Department III-Politics, R78112.
21 Ibid.
22 Ibid.
23 Report from Brown in Berlin to consul Kalisch at German Foreign Office in Berlin, 12 July 1932. PAAA, Department III-Politics, R78111.
24 Document entitled 'The political reasons for driving German influence out of Persia', 6 April 1932, report. PAAA, Department III-Politics, R78112.
25 Ibid.
26 Telegram from Blücher to German Foreign Office in Berlin, 9 June 1932. PAAA, Department III-Politics, R78111.
27 Report by Brown in Berlin to consul Kalisch at German Foreign Office in Berlin, 12 July 1932. PAAA, Department III-Politics, R78111.
28 Document entitled 'The political reasons for driving German influence out of Persia', 6 April 1932, report. PAAA, Department III-Politics, R78112.
29 Ibid.
30 Report by Brown in Berlin to consul Kalisch at German Foreign Office in Berlin, 12 July 1932. PAAA, Department III-Politics, R78111.
31 Ibid.
32 Report by Blücher to German Foreign Office in Berlin, 12 August 1932. PAAA, Department III–Economy, R92341. Number A 266.
33 Ibid.
34 Ibid.
35 Ibid.
36 Ibid.
37 Ibid.
38 Ibid.
39 Ibid.
40 Report by Blücher to German Foreign Office in Berlin, 30 April 1932. PAAA, Department III-Politics, R78162. Also copies at, PAAA, Department III-Politics, R78179, and, PAAA, Department III–Economy, R92510. Number A 157.
41 Document marked secret and forwarded by von Dirkse in Moscow, possibly, to the German Foreign Office in Berlin, 6 January 1933, report. PAAA, Department II-Economy, secret files 1920–1936, R30617.

42 Text delivered by Taqizadeh to Anglo-Persian Oil Company in Tehran as published in British article entitled 'Anglo-Persian oil, origin of the dispute', early 1933. PAAA, Department III–Economy, R92524.
43 Report on the British-Persian oil conflict compiled by Prüfer at the German Foreign Office in Berlin, for the German embassies and consulates in London, Paris, Rome, Moscow, Tokyo, Ankara, Tehran, Baghdad, Bucharest, Cairo, Trifles, Calcutta, Jerusalem, New York, Beirut and Geneva, 20 December 1932. PAAA, Department III–Economy, R92524.
44 Ibid.
45 Article entitled 'Der Britische Oelkonflikt', in *Auslandsbriefe*, number 141, early December 1932. PAAA, Department III–Economy, R92524.
46 Report by Blücher to German Foreign Office in Berlin, 17 December 1932. PAAA, Department III–Economy, R92524. Number 3963.
47 Ibid.
48 Ibid.
49 Report by Blücher to German Foreign Office in Berlin, 3 February 1933. PAAA, Department III–Economy, R92525. Number 374.
50 Document marked secret and forwarded by von Dirkse in Moscow, possibly, to the German Foreign Office in Berlin, 6 January 1933. PAAA, Department II-Economy, secret files 1920–1936, R30617.
51 Report by Blücher to German Foreign Office in Berlin, 28 January 1933. PAAA, Department III–Economy, R92525. Number A 27.
52 Telegram from Blücher to German Foreign Office in Berlin, 27 December 1932. PAAA, Department III-Politics, R78151.
53 Report by Blücher to German Foreign Office in Berlin, 3 February 1933. PAAA, Department III–Economy, R92525. Number 374.
54 Report by Blücher to German Foreign Office in Berlin, 31 December 1932. PAAA, Department III-Politics, R78166.
55 Ibid.
56 Report by Blücher to German Foreign Office in Berlin, 24 December 1932. PAAA, Department III-Politics, R78166.
57 Report by Blücher to German Foreign Office in Berlin, 31 December 1932. PAAA, Department III-Politics, R78166.
58 Report by Blücher to German Foreign Office in Berlin, 6 January 1933. PAAA, Department III-Politics, R78147.
59 Ibid.
60 Report by Blücher to German Foreign Office in Berlin, 24 February 1933. PAAA, Department III-Politics, R78147. See also identical document at PAAA, Department III–Economy, R92525.
61 Ibid.
62 Ibid. In Chapter 6, we examine more closely the role of Lindenblatt, and the National Bank of Persia, in the Taimurtash affaire.
63 Report by Blücher to German Foreign Office in Berlin, 4 March 1933. PAAA, Department III-Politics, R78147. Number A 58.
64 Report by Blücher to German Foreign Office in Berlin, 11 March 1933. PAAA, Department III-Politics, R78112. Number A 69.
65 Report by Blücher to German Foreign Office in Berlin, 7 October 1933. PAAA, Department III-Politics, R78167. Number A 351.

Chapter 6

1 Document entitled '*Politische und wirtschafliche Beziehungen zu Persien*', 1932/33, report. PAAA, Department III-Politics, R78156.
2 Report by Blücher to German Foreign Office in Berlin about the crisis surrounding the National Bank, 17 June 1932. PAAA, Department III–Economy, R92341. Number 1972.
3 Ibid.
4 Ibid.
5 Ibid.
6 Report marked secret from German Foreign Office in Berlin to Prussian ministry of Justice, 25 June 1932. PAAA, Department III-Politics, R78111.
7 Report by Schering-Kahlbaum A.G. in Berlin to German Foreign Office in Berlin over economic relations with Persia, 7 July 1932. PAAA, Department III-Politics, R78111.
8 Ibid.
9 Secret coded telegram from Blücher to German Foreign Office in Berlin, 27 July 1932. PAAA, Department III–Economy, R92341. See also identical report at PAAA, German legation files-Iran, IX A 11a. Vol. 3, National Bank.
10 Secret coded telegram from Blücher to German Foreign Office in Berlin, August 1932. PAAA, Department III–Economy, R92341.
11 Secret coded telegram from Blücher to German Foreign Office in Berlin, 5 September 1932. PAAA, Department III–Economy, R92341. See also identical report at PAAA, German legation files-Iran, IX A 11a. Vol. 3, National Bank.
12 Ibid.
13 Secret coded telegram from Blücher to director Dieckhoff at German Foreign Office in Berlin, 9 September 1932. PAAA, Department III–Economy, R92341.
14 Ibid.
15 Secret coded telegram from Blücher to director Dieckhoff at German Foreign Office in Berlin, 11 September 1932. PAAA, Department III–Economy, R92341.
16 Ibid.
17 The German national, and bank director, Nadolny had already been short-listed for the directorship of the National Bank of Persia.
18 From Schmidt-Ralke at the German Foreign Office in Berlin to the German League of Nations office, 14 September 1932, notes prepared for meeting with the Persian foreign minister Forughi in Geneva. PAAA, Department III–Economy, R92341.
19 Secret coded telegram from Blücher to German Foreign Office in Berlin. 20 September 1932. PAAA, Department III–Economy, R92341.
20 Ibid.
21 Secret coded telegram from Ziemke from Beirut to German Foreign Office in Berlin, 22 September 1932. PAAA, Department III–Economy, R92341.
22 Secret coded telegram from Blücher to director Dieckhoff at German Foreign Office in Berlin, 11 September 1932. PAAA, Department III–Economy, R92341.
23 Secret coded telegram from Blücher to German Foreign Office in Berlin, 26 September 1932. PAAA, Department III–Economy, R92341.

24 Report from Ziemke from Beirut to German Foreign Office in Berlin, 30 September 1932. PAAA, Department III–Economy, R92341. See also identical report at PAAA, German legation files-Iran, IX A 11a. Vol. 4, National Bank.
25 Ibid.
26 Director Vogel's suicide note from Beirut, 25 September 1932, letter. PAAA, Department III–Economy, R92341.
27 Director Vogel's confession note from Beirut, 25 September 1932, report. PAAA, Department III–Economy, R92341. See also secret coded telegram from Dieckhoff at the German Foreign Office in Berlin to Blücher in Tehran, 12 October 1932. PAAA, German legation files-Iran, IX A 11a. Volume 3, National Bank.
28 Ibid.
29 Director Vogel's letter to his wife, 23 September 1932. PAAA, Department III–Economy, R92341.
30 Director Vogel's letter to Lindenblatt, 23 September 1932. PAAA, Department III–Economy, R92341.
31 Ibid.
32 Ibid.
33 Ibid.
34 Secret coded telegram from Dieckhoff at the German Foreign Office in Berlin to Blücher in Tehran, 12 October 1932. PAAA, German legation files-Iran, IXA 11a. Vol. 3, National Bank.
35 Letter by Altenburg from Borudjerd to German embassy in Tehran, 13 November 1932. PAAA, German legation files-Iran, PKT 25/III 10. Vol. 2, bank.
36 Transcript of interview with Foroughi by the Turkish publication W. T. B., forwarded by its representative, Dr Schmidt-Dumont, to Aschmann from the German embassy in Ankara, for the German Foreign Office in Berlin, 16 November 1932, letter. PAAA, Department III-Politics, R78111.
37 Ibid.
38 Ibid.
39 Letter from Lindenblatt to German embassy in Tehran, 14 April 1933. PAAA, Department III–Economy, R92342.
40 Ibid.
41 Ibid.
42 Ibid.
43 Letter from Koehler at the German ministry of trade and industry in Berlin to, among others, the German Foreign Office in Berlin, 2 June 1933. Bundesarchiv Potsdam, ministry of trade and industry, 31.01/19094.
44 Ibid.
45 Letter from Blücher to German Foreign Office in Berlin, 10 June 1933. PAAA, Department III–Economy, R92342.
46 Letter from H. S. Kazem Alavi in Ahwaz to Heinrich Rust in Tehran, 16 July 1933. PAAA, German legation files-Iran, IX A 11a. Volume 4, National Bank.
47 Letter from Blücher to German Foreign Office in Berlin, 10 June 1933. PAAA, Department III–Economy, R92342.
48 Draft of 13-page report by Döcker on allegations brought against the National Bank, second half of 1933, report marked highly confidential. PAAA, Department III–Economy, R92342.

49 Ibid.
50 Ibid.
51 Ibid.
52 Ibid.
53 Report from Blücher to German Foreign Office in Berlin, 20 October 1933. PAAA, Department III–Economy, R92342. Number 3195.
54 Ibid.
55 Letter from German Foreign Office in Berlin to Lindenblatt's legal representative, Hirschowitz, in Berlin, 11 January 1935. PAAA, Department III–Economy, R92342.
56 Report from Blücher to German Foreign Office in Berlin, 20 October 1933. PAAA, Department III–Economy, R92342. Number 3195.
57 Ibid.
58 Copy of report from Shiraz, criticising the German embassy in Tehran for its approach, when faced with the National Bank affair, 2 November 1933. PAAA, Department III-Politics, R78112.
59 Ibid.
60 Copy of report from Shiraz, entitled 'Trade relations between Germany and Persia', 4 November 1933. PAAA, Department III-Politics, R78112.
61 Ibid.
62 Document entitled '*Politische und wirtschafliche Beziehungen zu Persien*', 1932/33, report. PAAA, Department III-Politics, R78156.

Chapter 7

1 Report from Blücher to the German Foreign Office in Berlin, 2 November 1933. PAAA, Department III–Economy, R92340.
2 Ibid.
3 Report from Tehran to German minister for propaganda, Dr Joseph Göbbels, in Berlin, 17 December 1933. PAAA, Department III-Politics, R78112.
4 Hitler's *Drittes Reich* (Third Reich) had been established in 1933 on the basis of a brutal terror against everybody not concordant with the Nazi dogmas, extreme nationalism combined with contempt for everything not matching the ideal of 'Aryan' culture, propagation of a pure 'Aryan' *Herrenrasse* (master race) of fair-haired, blue-eyed people, an uncompromising racism culminating in persecution, misappropriation and destruction of its large Jewish communities, and the claim to expand into territory lost after World War I or at some time ruled by Germans (Austria, Czechoslovakia, Poland, Rheinland, Saarland). The inaccurate Persian identification of propagated 'Aryan' roots also reinforced its leaning towards Hitler's Germany.
5 Report from Tehran to German minister for Propaganda, Dr Joseph Göbbels, in Berlin, 17 December 1933. PAAA, Department III-Politics, R78112.
6 Report (18 page) on the progress of the Trans-Iranian Railway and the German standing in Persia, compiled by M. Giese in Tehran for Hosbach in Germany, 20 January 1934. PAAA, Department III-Politics, R78112.
7 Report (18 page) on the progress of the Trans Iranian Railway and the German standing in Persia. Compiled by M. Giese in Tehran for Hosbach in Germany. 20 January 1934, report. PAAA, Department III-Politics, R78112.
8 Ibid.

9 Ibid.
10 Ludwig Hossbach, retired construction engineer in Berlin, to foreign minister von Neurath at the German Foreign Office in Berlin. PAAA, Department III-Politics, R78112.
11 Report by Schmidt-Rolke in Berlin, on a meeting with Daftari, 27 January 1934. PAAA, German legation files-Iran, PKT 40/VI A1. Vol. 5, trade.
12 Ibid.
13 Ibid.
14 Letter from Zölch at the German embassy in Tehran to Schmidt-Rolke at the German Foreign Office in Berlin, 17 February 1934. PAAA, Department III–Economy, R92534.
15 Article entitled 'Persiens Wirtschaft und Finanzlage-Ein Land fast ohne Schulden', in *Volkswirtschaftliche Correspondenz,* 26 June 1934. Bundesarchiv Potsdam, Reichslandbund, Presse Archiv, 61 Re 1/8153.
16 Article entitled 'Persische National bank', in *Berliner Börsen Zeitung,* 9 March 1934. Bundesarchiv Potsdam, Deutsche Reichsbank, 25.01/5289.
17 Telegram from Blücher to German Foreign Office in Berlin, 12 February 1934. PAAA, Department III–Economy, R92340.
18 Article by Owen Tweedy, entitled 'Persia's unfortunate trade legislation', in *The Financial Times,* 15 February 1934. Bundesarchiv Potsdam, Deutsche Reichsbank, 25.01/5289.
19 Article entitled 'Persische Nationalbank', in *Frankfurter Zeitung,* 12 March 1934. Bundesarchiv Potsdam, Deutsche Reichsbank, 25.01/5289.
20 Letter from Zölch at the German embassy in Tehran to German Foreign Office in Berlin, 16 April 1935. PAAA, Department III–Economy, R92340.
21 Report from Blücher to German Foreign Office in Berlin, 7 April 1934. PAAA, Department III–Economy, R92340.
22 Ibid.
23 Letter from Dieckhoff at the German Foreign Office in Berlin to unidentified German government department, 21 March 1934. PAAA, Department III-Politics, R78112.
24 Letter from Pilger from German Foreign Office in Berlin to German embassy in Tehran, 3 October 1934. PAAA, Department III-Politics, R78112.
25 Letter from Prüfer at the German Foreign Office in Berlin to Persian embassy in Tehran, 8 December 1934. PAAA, Department III-Politics, R78112.
26 Letter from Blücher to German Foreign Office in Berlin, 22 January 1935. Bundesarchiv Potsdam, German legation files-Iran, PKT 1/IA 2. Vol. 7, Persia.
27 Ibid.
28 Memorandum by Dr Paul Martin entitled 'Denkschrift betreffend die Rückgewinnung des Persischen Absatzmarktes', 31 August 1934. PAAA, Department III–Economy, R92513.
29 Report from Blücher to German Foreign Office in Berlin, 26 October 1934. PAAA, Department III–Economy, R92513.
30 Report (63-page) by Dr Alfred Tismer entitled 'Aufbau- und Krisenprobleme der iranischen Wirtschaft', approximately 1936. Bundesarchiv Dahlwitz-Hoppegarten, files of IG Farbenindustrie AG, 80 IGF/A3818.
31 Letter from Blücher to German Foreign Office in Berlin, 14 January 1935. PAAA, Department III-Politics, R78151. Number 94.

32 Mina Zahirnezhad Ershadi. *Selected Documents Relations between Iran and Germany* (Tehran: Publishing division of the Iranian Ministry for foreign affairs, 1998), p. 176.
33 Report from Smend to German Foreign Office in Berlin, 8 February 1936. PAAA, Department III-Politics, R78167. Number A 51.
34 Article by J. P. W.(sic) entitled 'Persien und seine Bedeutung für den Deutschen Außenhandel', in *Bremer Nachrichten*, 18 April 1935. Bundesarchiv Potsdam, Deutsche Reichsbank, 25.01/5290.
35 Report entitled '*Deutsch-Iranische Handelsbeziehungen*', approximately 1935. PAAA, Department III–Economy, R92369.
36 Ibid.
37 Ibid.
38 Report from Tehran entitled 'Iran. Lagebericht', 22 April 1936, report marked confidential. PAAA, Department III-Politics, R78112.
39 Article by Eicke entitled 'Neue Siemens Aufträge im Iran', in *Siemens Mitteilungen*, no. 174, June 1936. Bundesarchiv Potsdam, Arbeitswissenschaftliches Institut, 62 DAF 3/35717. See also Mina Zahirnezhad Ershadi. *Selected documents relations between Iran and Germany* (Tehran: Publishing division of the Iranian Ministry for foreign affairs, 1998), p. 312.
40 Article entitled 'Iran und Deutschland sind die gegebenen Partner', in *Berliner Lokal-Anzeiger*, 22 July 1936. Bundesarchiv Potsdam, Deutsche Reichsbank, 25.01/5290. See also for same article, Bundesarchiv Potsdam, Arbeitswissenschaftliches Institut, 62 DAF 3/35684.
41 Article by H. Bassewitz entitled 'Ein Land im Wirtschaftsaufstieg, Deutschland und Iran können sich in vielem ergänzen', in *Berliner Nachtausgabe*, no. 380, 1936. Bundesarchiv Potsdam, Deutsche Reichsbank, 25.01/5290.
42 Article by Massih Samiy entitled 'Die Wirtschaftliche Entwicklung Irans', in *Berliner Börsen-Zeitung*, 22 July 1936. Bundesarchiv Potsdam, Deutsche Reichsbank, 25.01/5290.
43 Report entitled 'Günstige Entwicklung der iranischen Wirtschaft im Jahre 1935/36', 25 August 1936. Bundesarchiv Potsdam, Deutsche Reichsbank, 25.01/5290, p. 24.
44 Article in Turkish magazine entitled 'Persien-Der Aussenhandel', 20 June 1934. PAAA, Department III–Economy, R92355.
45 Article entitled 'Der Aussenhandel von Iran', in *Pressedienst Hansa, Wirtschaft und Verkehr*, 11 June 1935. Bundesarchiv Potsdam, Deutsche Reichsbank, 25.01/5290.
46 Report entitled 'Günstige Entwicklung der iranischen Wirtschaft im Jahre 1935/36', 25 October 1936. Bundesarchiv Potsdam, Deutsche Reichsbank, 25.01/5290, pp. 24–32.
47 Article entitled 'Starker Aufschwung des deutschen Handelsverkehrs mit Iran', in *Pressedienst Hansa, Wirtschaft und Verkehr*, 25 March 1937. Bundesarchiv Potsdam, Deutsche Reichsbank, 25.01/5290.
48 Ibid.
49 Ibid.
50 Ibid.
51 Ibid.

52 Secret coded telegram from Melchers from German embassy in Tehran to German Foreign Office in Berlin, 12 November 1936. PAAA, German legation files-Iran, PKT 28/III 11 d. Vol. 2, Schacht.
53 Coded telegram from Ritter at the German Foreign Office in Berlin to German embassy in Tehran, 12 November 1936. PAAA, German legation files-Iran, PKT 28/III 11 d. Vol. 2, Schacht.
54 Telegram from Kamphaevener at the German Foreign Office in Berlin to German embassy in Tehran, 16 November 1936. PAAA, German legation files-Iran, PKT 28/III 11 d. Vol. 2, Schacht.
55 Programme for the reception of Schacht in Iran, November 1936, report. PAAA, German legation files-Iran, PKT 28/III 11 d. Vol. 2, Schacht.
56 Report from Melchers at the German embassy in Tehran to the German Foreign Office in Berlin, 19 November 1936. PAAA, German legation files-Iran, PKT 28/III 11 d. Vol. 2, Schacht.
57 Ibid.
58 Article entitled 'Iran strebt vorwärts', in *Berliner Lokal Anzeiger*, 27 November 1936. Bundesarchiv Potsdam, Reichslandbund, Presse Archiv, 61 Re 1/8153.
59 Report by the German 'Iran consortium', 1937. PAAA, German legation files-Iran, PKT 41/VI A2. Vol. 1, economy.
60 Article entitled 'Deutschlands Handelsbeziehungen zu Iran', in *Die Deutsche Volkswirtschaft*, no. 31, 1937. Bundesarchiv Potsdam, Deutsche Reichsbank, 25.01/5290.
61 Article entitled 'Iran's "regulierte" Wirtschaft', in *Neue Zürcher Zeitung*, 21 January 1937. Bundesarchiv Potsdam, Deutsche Reichsbank, 25.01/5290.
62 Protocol meeting of German authorities in Berlin regarding Nouri's visit to Germany, 4 May 1937, protocol. PAAA, Department VII-Politics, R104782.
63 Letter from Schacht's office to German Foreign Office in Berlin, 13 May 1937. PAAA, Department VII-Politics, R104782.
64 Article entitled 'Der iranische Parlamentspräsident bei Generaloberst Göring und Dr. Schacht', in *Völkischer Beobachter*, 17 June 1937. Bundesarchiv Potsdam, Arbeitswissenschaftliches Institut, 62 DAF 3/35684.
65 Article entitled 'Der Führer empfing den iranischen Parlamentspräsidenten', in *Deutsche Allgemeine Zeitung*, 17 June 1937. Bundesarchiv Potsdam, Deutsche Reichsbank, 25.01/5290.
66 Report from Smend from the German embassy in Tehran to German Foreign Office in Berlin, 24 July 1937. PAAA, Department VII-Politics, R104782.
67 Report by Erwin Spiegel in Tehran, 23 May 1937. Bundesarchiv Dahlwitz-Hoppegarten, files of the IG Farbenindustrie AG, 80 IGF/B 2857.
68 Article entitled 'Iranian contract for Germany', in *The Times*, 15 May 1937. Bundesarchiv Potsdam, Deutsche Reichsbank, 25.01/5290.
69 Article entitled 'Iran- Waggonauftrag für die deutsche Industrie', in *Nachrichten für Außenhandel*, 19 January 1940. Bundesarchiv Potsdam, Deutsche Reichsbank, 25.01/5291.
70 Article entitled 'Einweihung eines großen iranischen Zementwerkes', in *Berliner Börsen-Zeitung*, 20 May 1937. Bundesarchiv Potsdam, Deutsche Reichsbank, 25.01/5290. See also article entitled 'Einweihung eines großen iranischen Zementwerkes', in *Deutscher Handelsdienst*, no. 20, 19 May 1937. Bundesarchiv Potsdam, Deutsche Reichsbank, 25.01/5290.

71 Article entitled 'Fortschritte der Industrialisierung in Iran', in *Pressedienst-Hansa*, 22 January 1940. Bundesarchiv Potsdam, Deutsche Reichsbank, 25.01/5291.
72 Article entitled 'Deutschland und Iran, Rekordumsätze', in *Bremer Nachrichten*, 15 June 1937. Bundesarchiv Potsdam, Deutsche Reichsbank, 25.01/5290.
73 Report from economic policy department of IG Farben in Berlin to IG Farben director Voigt in Frankfurt, 20 July 1937. Bundesarchiv Dahlwitz-Hoppegarten, files of the IG Farbenindustrie AG, 80 IGF/B 2857.

Chapter 8

1 Article by B. Nikitine entitled 'Germany's penetration into Iran', in *L'Économiste français*, no. 31, 31 July 1937. Bundesarchiv Potsdam, Deutsche Reichsbank, 25.01/5290.
2 Political report on the state of affairs in Iran for German Foreign Office in Berlin, compiled by Smend at the German embassy in Tehran, 22 January 1938, 15-page report. PAAA, Department VII-Politics, R104782.
3 Report from Smend from German embassy in Tehran to German Foreign Office in Berlin, 25 March 1939. PAAA, Department VII-Politics, R104782.
4 Ibid.
5 Ibid.
6 Report marked confidential by a German agent based in Iran looking at Iran on the verge of World War II, October 1939. Bundesarchiv, Militär Archiv Freiburg, RW 5 V. 583.
7 Article entitled 'Amtliche iranische Neutralitätserklärung', in *Deutsche Allgemeine Zeitung*, 7 September 1939. Bundesarchiv Potsdam, Deutsche Reichsbank, 25.01/5291. See also article entitled 'Amtliche Neutralitätserklärung von Iran', in *Deutsches Nachrichtenbüro*, 6 September 1939. Bundesarchiv Potsdam, Deutsche Reichsbank, 25.01/5291.
8 Article entitled 'Piping the oil from Iran's deserts to the tankers', *Daily Telegraph*, 27 January 1940. Bundesarchiv Potsdam, Deutsche Reichsbank, 25.01/5291.
9 Special report on Iran, approximately 1940/41. Bundesarchiv Dahlwitz-Hoppegarten, files of the IG Farbenindustrie AG, 80 IGF/B 954.
10 Report marked *Sonderdienst vertraulich*, and entitled 'Iran- Zur Eröffnung der Transiranischen Bahn', 19 September 1938. Bundesarchiv Potsdam, Deutsche Reichsbank, 5290/25.01.
11 Report detailing the economic and political situation in Iran, particularly with reference to German interest, approximately 1940. Bundesarchiv, Militär Archiv Freiburg, Wi II A.6/8.
12 Statistical data published by Hamburgisches Welt-Wirtschafts-Institut E. V., in *Welt-Kartei der Wirtschaftspresse*, 22 February 1940, report. Bundesarchiv Potsdam, Arbeitswissenschaftliches Institut, 62 DAF 3/35717. This report also highlights the effect of Iran's continuous development during the period 1931–39 by stating that 2,050 companies with a total capital of over 1 billion rials had been registered in Iran. During the same period 537 companies were removed again from the register, leaving 1,513 companies with a total capital of almost 1.7 billion rials in March 1939.

BIBLIOGRAPHY

Abrahamian, Evand. *Iran Between Two Revolutions* (Princeton: Princeton University Press, 1982).

Amanat, Mehrdad and Keddie, Nikki. 'Iran under the later Qajars, 1848–1922', in Peter Avery, Gavin Hambly, and Charles Melville, eds, *The Cambridge History of Iran*, vol. 7, *From Nadir Shah to the Islamic Republic* (Cambridge: Cambridge University Press, 1991).

Avery, Peter. *Modern Iran* (London: Praeger, 1965).

Banani, Amin. *The Modernization of Iran: 1921–1941* (Stanford: Stanford University Press, 1961).

Barth, Boris. *Die Deutsche Hochfinanz und die Imperialismen: Banken und Außenpolitik vor 1914* (Stuttgart: Franz Steiner, 1995).

Benab, Younes. *The Soviet Union and Britain in Iran, 1917–1927: A Case Study of the Domestic Impact of East–West Rivalry* (Washington, D.C.: unpublished PhD thesis, The Catholic University of America, 1974).

Elwell-Sutton, L. P. 'Reza Shah the Great: founder of the Pahlavi dynasty', in George Lenczowski, ed., *Iran under the Pahlavis* (Stanford, Cal.: The Hoover Institution Press, 1978).

Fischer, Fritz. *Griff nach der Weltmacht* (Düsseldorf: Droste Verlag, 1961).

Gehrke, Ulrich. *Persien in der Deutschen Orientpolitik während des Ersten Weltkrieges* (Stuttgart: W. Kohlhammer GmbH, 1961).

Griffith, William E. 'Iran's foreign policy in the Pahlavi era', in George Lenczowski, ed., *Iran under the Pahlavis* (Stanford, Cal.: The Hoover Institution Press, 1978)

Gross, Nachum T. 'Die Deutsche Palästina-Bank 1897–1914', *Zeitschrift für Unternehmensgeschichte*, 33. Jahrgang (Heft 3/1988).

Hambly, Gavin R. G. 'The Pahlavi autocracy: Riza Shah, 1921–1941', in Peter Avery, Gavin Hambly and Charles Melville, ed., *The Cambridge History of Iran*, vol. 7, *From Nadir Shah to the Islamic Republic* (Cambridge: Cambridge University Press, 1991).

Hirschfeld, Yair P. *Deutschland und Iran im Spielfeld der Mächte: Internationale Beziehungen unter Reza Schah, 1921–1941* (Düsseldorf: Droste, 1980).

Jones, Geoffrey. *Banking and Empire in Iran* (Cambridge: Cambridge University Press, 1986).

Katouzian, Homa. *The Political Economy of Modern Iran* (London: Macmillan Press Ltd, 1981).

Kazemzadeh, Firuz. *Russia and Britain in Persia 1864–1914* (New Haven, Conn. and London: Yale University Press, 1968).

Keddie, Nikki. *Roots of Revolution: An Interpretive History of Modern Iran* (New Haven, Conn. and London: Yale University Press, 1981).

Martin, Bradford. *German-Persian Relations 1873–1912* (The Hague: Mouton & Co. s'Gravenhage, 1959).

Millspaugh, A. C. *The American Task in Persia* (New York and London: The Century Company, 1925).

Miron, Rezun. *The Soviet Union and Iran* (Geneva: Institut Universitaire de Etudes Internationales, 1981).

Nayyeri, Mostafa. *Das Bankwesen im Iran und seine Entwicklung* (Köln: Dissertation, 1964).

Olsen, W. J. *Anglo-Iranian Relations during World War I* (London: Frank Cass, 1984).

Platt, D. C. M. *Finance, Trade, and Politics in British Foreign Policy 1815–1914* (Oxford: Clarendon Press, 1968).

Ramazani, Rouhollah K. *The United States and Iran* (New York: Praeger Publishers, 1982).

Sabahi, Houshang. *British Policy in Persia 1918–1925* (Exeter: BPCC Wheatons Ltd, 1990).

Schaefer, C. A. *Die Entwicklung der Bagdadbahnpolitik* (Weimar 1916).

Schöllgen, Gregor. *Imperialismus und Gleichgewicht* (Munich: R. Oldenbourg Verlag, 1984).

Strobaugh, Robert B. 'The evolution of Iranian oil policy, 1925–1975', in George Lenczowski, ed., *Iran under the Pahlavis* (Stanford, Cal.: The Hoover Institution Press, 1978).

Sykes, Percy. *A History of Persia.* (London: Macmillan, 1951).

Tapper, Richard. *The Conflict of Tribe and State in Iran and Afghanistan* (London, Canberra: Croom Helm, 1983).

Wilber, Donald. *Riza Shah Pahlavi: The Resurrection and Reconstruction of Iran* (New York and Hicksville: Exposition Press, 1975).

Yeselson, Abraham. *United States–Persian Diplomatic Relations 1883–1921* (New Jersey: Rutgers University Press, 1956).

Zürrer, Werner. *Persien zwischen England und Rußland 1918–1925* (Bern: Verlag Peter Lang AG, 1978).

Zahirnezhad Ershadi, Mina. *Selected Documents Relations between Iran and Germany* (Tehran: Publishing division of the Iranian Ministry for foreign affairs, 1998).

INDEX

www.ingramcontent.com/pod-product-compliance
Lightning Source LLC
Chambersburg PA
CBHW071251180926
51613CB00001B/4
9781848853249